VIRTUAL
CITIES

VIRTUAL
CITIES

AN ATLAS & EXPLORATION OF
VIDEO GAME CITIES

Konstantinos Dimopoulos

MAPS AND ILLUSTRATIONS BY MARIA KALLIKAKI
Additional maps by Vivi Papanastasiou

THE COUNTRYMAN PRESS
A Division of W. W. Norton & Company
Independent Publishers Since 1923

Text copyright © 2020 by Konstantinos Dimopoulos
Illustrations copyright © 2020 by Maria Kallikaki
Special thanks to Vivi Papanastasiou for her work on the map illustrations

For information about permission to reproduce selections from this book, write to
Permissions, The Countryman Press, 500 Fifth Avenue, New York, NY 10110

For information about special discounts for bulk purchases, please contact
W. W. Norton Special Sales at specialsales@wwnorton.com or 800-233-4830

Manufacturing through RR Donnelley Asia Printing Solutions Limited
Book design by Faceout Studio, Paul Nielsen
Production manager: Devon Zahn

The Countryman Press
www.countrymanpress.com

A division of W. W. Norton & Company, Inc.
500 Fifth Avenue, New York, NY 10110
www.wwnorton.com

978-1-68268-609-6

10 9 8 7 6 5 4 3 2 1

CONTENTS

INTRODUCTION

An incorporeal thread connects the ominous spires of Anor Londo with the bustling streets of cyberpunk Hong Kong, the ancient black-and-white edifices of Antescher with the futuristic three-dimensional wards of the Citadel space station. Separated by eons and light-years, these spires, streets, edifices, and wards all exist exclusively in gaming's virtual cities, in the ambitious civic nodes of the video gaming universe. They were imagined, designed, and created to be interactively experienced and explored.

Virtual cities are places of often-fractured geographies, impossible physics, outrageous assumptions, and almost untamed imaginations given their freedom from the constraints of reality. This book, the first atlas of its kind, aims to explore, map, study, and celebrate them. To imagine what they would be like in reality. To paint a lasting picture of their domes, arches, and walls.

This work combines my love of video gaming and urbanism. It has slowly been building in my mind for years. In its pages, you will find childhood dreams of working on games, two decades of studying and researching cities, and a continuous attempt at fusing spatial sciences with game design. Here, wide-eyed me watching an older cousin play Berzerk on the Atari 2600 seems to have finally met game-urbanist me, and then spent two years of hard, but fulfilling work making *Virtual Cities* happen.

Through my own professional experience of planning and engineering, the maps I am familiar with have always been more concerned with clarity than aesthetics. And as screenshots are often too restrictive (or even dull) to conjure the essence of gaming's cities, the work of visual artist Maria Kallikaki was important to the creation of the atlas. She somehow turned my crude sketches and vague descriptions into beautiful, ink-colored illustrations, and captured the sense of wonder far-off places used to evoke before the advent of photography. These illustrations, Maria's interpretation of these game worlds, allow for a sense of immersion that neither text nor map can convey. They are illustrations meant to guide the imagination and not confine it. Besides, it was Maria who also took most of my sketches and concepts of maps, finalized their shapes, and imbued them with color and beauty. Additionally, the crucial map-making and editing skills of my wife Vivi Papanastasiou (handily also a spatially focused engineer) are what allowed many of the cities to finally express themselves in a sensible cartographic manner.

Ever since the very first atlas was published, our collective desire for exploration has been fueled by strange pictures, evocative words, and mysterious maps. It seems human beings have always loved reading about exotic locations, organizing imaginary expeditions, and trying to interpret magical places through the eyes of artists. Of course, no matter how exhaustive a description is, it can never be all-encompassing nor satisfy all of our senses, and thus atlases often inspire a lust for first-hand experiences. Evoking this lust is a main aspiration of *Virtual Cities*. I want to awake curiosity and longing for unknown or vaguely remembered digital cities. To create a yearning for savoring the delights that virtual urbanism has to offer, and to lure explorers into artfully constructed, elegantly abstracted, and wistfully reconstructed civic realities of a young and growing artistic medium; of a medium that truly shines when it comes to building immersive settings.

Virtual Cities showcases some of the finest cities of video gaming, and invites you to get to know, and perhaps even grow to love, these places that uniquely exist somewhere between art, engineering, urban planning, literature, game design, and architecture.

Each of the forty-five cities contained within this atlas is presented from an in-universe point-of-view. These cities, you see, have been reimagined not simply as game spaces, but like actual urban formations that can be visited, and can sensibly exist within the confines and rules of their respective settings. Nobody in Midgar would ever reference New York, and only survivors could attempt to describe the madness of Silent Hill. I have chosen to avoid employing omniscient narrations, and chose instead to imagine in-universe characters describing each city—a geographer perhaps, a chronicler, or someone writing a tourist guide. Similarly, the maps accompanying each entry were never meant to replicate game spaces, but to cartographically describe settlements plausibly existing in fantastical worlds. These are meant to fill in gaps, and to tie disparate locations into cohesive cities; cartographic artefacts of the described realities. After all, many game cities are heavily stylized, and thoroughly abstracted, and what I felt I had to do was to critically reimagine them in ways that would look familiar in the eyes of a fictional local surveyor.

So, every *Virtual Cities* entry comes with an in-world description of the city, a map, Maria's atmospheric illustrations, and a shorter text attempting to provide readers with design insights on its creation. The latter is a short, almost technical text mainly meant for world-builders, game designers, writers, artists, and level-builders, but also for the curious people who want to further appreciate the craft that went into their favorite games. In a select few cases, I let the creators responsible for the cities provide us with a behind-the-scenes look at their construction, allowing them to highlight the points worth noting.

As for the selection of the included virtual cities, I have to admit it was a taxing process. Many excellent creations had to be left out, but I did strive to include some of the most historically important, beautiful, and representative ones. These forty-five entries cover much ground, and span as many literary and gaming genres and types as possible, while also presenting thirty-five years of gaming history. From 1983's *Ant Attack*, and the black-and-white, isometric city of Antescher on the ZX Spectrum, to 2018 cities like Neketaka or New Bretagne;

and from the 3D open world of *Assassin's Creed*'s London to the text-based vastness of Fallen London, I tried to represent most of game urbanism. Obviously, achieving a perfect balance was impossible, but I do believe I assembled a characteristic selection featuring some of the most fascinating virtual cities ever built.

I sincerely hope you enjoy *Virtual Cities*. I hope the love and work poured into it will inspire you, and that you will take the time to explore the cities presented in its pages. As a games urbanist myself, I hope to help bring an extra bit of appreciation to the often-hidden art of crafting immersive, imaginative, and stunning virtual cities.

—**Konstantinos Dimopoulos**, Athens, April 2020

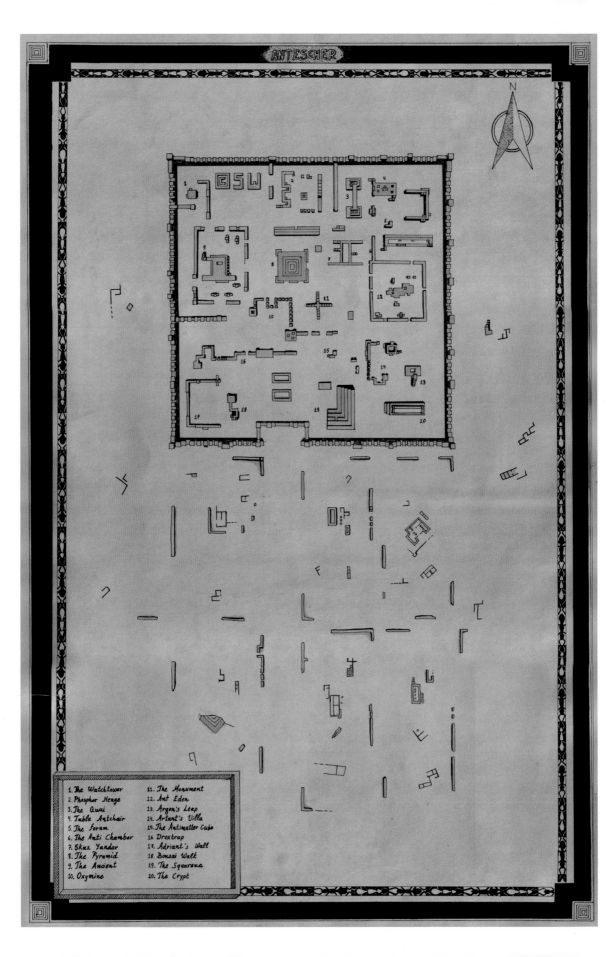

ANTESCHER

1. The Watchtower
2. Phosphor Henge
3. The Quai
4. Table Antchair
5. The Forum
6. The Anti Chamber
7. Skuz Yandor
8. The Pyramid
9. The Ancient
10. Oxymine
11. The Monument
12. Ant Eden
13. Argon's Leap
14. Ariant's Villa
15. The Antimatter Cube
16. Droxtrap
17. Adriant's Wall
18. Bonsai Walk
19. The Squareua
20. The Crypt

ANTESCHER
Ant Attack

GENERAL INFORMATION /////////////////////

City: Antescher

Game: *Ant Attack*

Developer: Sandy White, Angela Sutherland

Publisher: Quicksilva

Release Date: 1983

Genre: Arcade

Platforms: Commodore 64, ZX Spectrum

Dreaming of glories long forgotten, the acropolis of Antescher has rested undisturbed in the midst of the Great Desert for a thousand, thousand years. Hiding behind cyclopean fortifications, the ancient city was but a fading fable for centuries, and its windswept streets were solely travelled by gigantic ants. Its solid, unmoving, eternal mass bears the signature of a long-forgotten race many don't dare imagine, and its discovery has proven a challenge to our notions of life and civilization. Even after countless scientific expeditions, Antescher remains a dangerous, awe-inspiring place filled with enigmas and arcane wisdom. The sounds of surveying boots are often all one can hear through the unchanging streets.

The dangerous ruins of Skaz Yandor

To explore the eerie ruins, without at least a motion scanner to warn of the sudden appearance of the gigantic ants, is still considered suicidal. The ancient, unique breed of insects infesting Antescher has mutated to achieve sizes biology hasn't encountered since the early Permian period, and is aggressive and brisk enough to be a real threat. These ants seemingly kill carrying out biological imperatives. Their paralyzing poisonous bites render victims defenseless for powerful mandibles to dismember, while their spindly legs allow for quick, silent, and jerky yet precise movement.

Ignoring the deadly fauna reveals a vast, majestic city consisting of roughly cuboid, tomb-like structures begging to be scaled and explored. Time has sadly erased most of the urban fabric's details, and has obscured the functions of most buildings; some are almost recognizable—a select few make obvious sense—but most remain as abstract and alien in their purpose as the day they were discovered. Those imposing structures are teeming with secrets. Despite decades of research and informed speculation, they stay as silent and inexplicable as the sands that have piled up on the walls, burying most of what we presume must have been the original metropolis, yet almost magically never encroaching upon the central city.

This walled, and apparently monumental, core of the city has survived untold eons, and, as it doesn't seem to include any residences, the assumption that it must have been a ceremonial, administrative center sounds reasonable. The equivalent of a palace wouldn't feel out of place here, either.

A single south-facing gate, the only opening in the perfect square of the walls, hints at the fact that greater Antescher extended southward of the discovered formation along a north–south axis. These outer districts must have been where most of the city's elusive residents lived, toiled, and, presumably, died; where the majority of activities and functions we associate with the vibrancy of urban life must have taken place. Of course, scholars could have completely misunderstood those ancient configurations, and the suspiciously sparse remains outside the walls may have been either misdated or their roles completely misunderstood. Bizarre as it might sound, the notion that this large, rectangular civic center was exclusively used as an elaborate, uninhabited religious center simply cannot be fully disproven.

Then again, provided our scientific methods are even vaguely applicable, and that our estimates regarding the few finds outside the walls hold some truth, a nebulous yet rather sensible picture of what must have been the main residential area of Antescher can be painted. Organized in mostly symmetrical, seemingly self-sufficient walled subdistricts, this must have been a rigorously planned urban area with strong geomantic influences. The occasional complex structures, implied by elaborate remains, seem aligned to ancient celestial phenomena, whereas all surviving underground networks face Earth's geodetic north.

Crossing the gate into the walled city itself, explorers will encounter the Bonzai Walk to their west, and the theater of Squarena to their east. Passing the impossibly sleek Antimatter Cube, they will eventually reach the still-incomprehensible monument at Antescher's geometric center; this is flanked by the colossal stepped pyramid, and the Skaz Yandor complex that many assume could have served as a palace or similar official residence. Merely alluding to the former glory of the city, and to

Monstrous ants have been the sole users of the halls of the Ancient for centuries untold

the center's south, lies the Oxymine, whereas to the north, what has become popularly known as the Phosphor Henge can be admired in its blinding whiteness.

After pausing to appreciate the barely visible bas-reliefs of Skaz Yandor, one can explore the parts of what must have once been the town's forum to the east, or climb the imposing and miraculously still standing northwestern Watchtower. Reaching its top will offer a panoramic view of the entire site all the way to the partly unexplored crypt, Artant's Villa, the gardens, and the obviously mislabeled Argon's Leap astronomical observatory. Just to the south of the Watchtower lies the so-called Ancient: a walled, elaborate compound of possible ritual value where archaeologists have been focusing their attempts to look for the remains of the city's lost inhabitants. Nothing

The Great Pyramid of Antescher is strongly reminiscent of Aztec and early Egyptian architecture

has been unearthed yet, but a graveyard in what must have been a religiously significant place is a possibility worth exploring.

Scholars are always advised to keep an open mind though. Assumptions regarding unknowable societies and their urban embodiments are, after all, profoundly and unavoidably influenced by our knowledge of human history and evolution. We may perceive a structure as a forum or an amphi-theater. We can imagine what the function of a pyramid might have been. We think in terms of tombs and ceremonial centers, but we do not really know. We merely presume. The Rosetta Stone that will unlock Antescher's mysteries has yet to be discovered, and although this added layer of mystique does enhance the local ambience, it's something beyond atmosphere that makes this a place capable of shattering minds.

In fact, several field scientists have been committed to asylums over the years. The utterly alien cityscape is so thoroughly challenging to our preconceptions, and its geometries so impos-ingly odd, that, especially when combined with tiny doses of ant poison and the scorching heat, devastating tricks on the psyche can be played. Such tricks are surely evident in the naming of certain surviving buildings. Although toponyms such as Skaz Yandor and names such as Argon or Adriant have been preserved through impossibly old myth and legend, locales named Table Antchair or Ant Eden are certainly the byproduct of incredibly fertile imaginations coupled with Antescher's overbearing eeriness, toxic ants, and often unsettling architecture.

Washed clean by the sun's rays, and stylized through the millennia of erosion, the city's volumes are both unique and strangely evocative. Buildings look like sculptures that can fleetingly conjure terrifying images in dehydrated minds, while majestic constructs and intricate passages suggest advanced engineering, even if a single scrap of metal has yet to be found in the wider region. What has been found in abundance, though, are undeniable archetypes of human architectural styles, from the Egyptian and the Minoan to the Aztec and Roman, leading the more daring to speculate this was a point of origin of some sort.

Fueled by the sheer possibility of groundbreaking discoveries, research has recently intensified, and there's hope that surveying the dark, still unreachable catacombs and unlocking the mathematical secrets of the Pyramid might provide us with invaluable insights, and some semblance of understanding. Investigating the biology of the giant ants might also be enlightening, even if science alone doesn't seem capable of ever explaining the unshakable feeling of an eldritch presence looming over Antescher's buildings, whispering to all, felt by all.

DESIGN INSIGHTS

Ant Attack was a game of many firsts. Many have been convinced by the argument that it kickstarted the survival horror genre—and it surely was the very first game to let players choose between a male or female protagonist, at least on an 8-bit microcomputer. Even more impressively, Antescher, the game's arthropod-infested setting, is fondly remembered for being the very first three-dimensional game city many gamers ever explored in an era of simple arcade offerings. Sandy White's innovative 3D Softsolid technique and groundbreaking isometric graphics allowed for a scrolling open world nobody really believed was technically feasible.

Antescher felt like a real, fully formed, if abandoned, place, uniquely allowing players to visit anything they could see. Being fully explorable and rotatable helped massively, although being groundbreaking wasn't what made it immersive. The city was constructed in order to be believable, and was treated as a gameplay feature itself. It used landmark structures, recognizable districts, clear paths, and the edges of its square walls to help guide players through space. Gameplay was, after all, almost entirely about exploring, avoiding the deadly ants, and efficiently navigating the city. Making it easy for players to construct a mental map must have been a major consideration, along with, naturally, the need for some evocative architecture.

The inspiration from actual historical structures provided memorable buildings such as the stepped pyramid and the theater, and helped cement the place's believability. Furthermore, the influences from Sandy White's native city of Edinburgh—itself replete with imposing stone buildings ancient and new, along with a handful of viaducts, graveyards, and stone staircases—are evident. Avoiding garish colors, opting for ghostly, elegant black-and-white graphics, and infesting the place with hard-to-kill ants added another layer of atmosphere to the proceedings.

The city's effect on players was further amplified by the well-written backstory the tape insert provided, and the incredibly evocative cover art showing a gigantic ant looming over two tiny humans. Inserts and covers were an integral part of the gaming experience during the eighties, at least in Europe, but they also serve to show that game cities and their feel are about more than neatly arranged buildings. They often have to rely on words, cryptic hints, and successful artwork to conjure a more immersive illusion. Admittedly, a then-unprecedented virtual place made of isometric cubes combined into weird and wonderful shapes never needed too much help to stand out.

DUN DARACH
Dun Darach

GENERAL INFORMATION //////////////////////

City: Dun Darach

Game: *Dun Darach*

Developer: Gargoyle Games

Publisher: Gargoyle Games

Release Date: 1985

Genre: Adventure

Platforms: Amstrad CPC, ZX Spectrum

Lightning split the long night asunder, and thunder tore the Voice of Darkness, bringing forth the oak whose roots would bind together the fabric of the earth. The canopy of the sky rested on the branches of the oak. The hill of the oak, Dun Darach, was where the secret and sacred grove was hidden, its location entrusted only to the chosen of the Druidhan. But the Druidhan had human needs and mortal fears, and decided to build the great castle of Dun Darach to surround the oak, hide it from prying eyes, and protect and safeguard its divine secrets. And as the ways of history dictate, around the castle grew the great city of Dun Darach, where knowledge of the sacred oak filled the minds of men with longing and strange tales.

The tales traveled far, and the longing was ignited in all mortals, and thus conquerors, invaders, and brigands were all gathered around the mighty walls. In desperation, the great conclave of the Druidhan summoned the cold white mist to settle on the hill of the oak and shroud the city. Dun Darach was both freed from invaders and the bounds of the mortal world, and set to drift across the tides of time until it once again came to rest on treacherous mortal shores. Still covered in eternal mists, its black towers and streets of perpetual twilight welcome back all men willing to make the long, perilous journey toward its mythical gates.

Timeless Dun Darach has now risen as a vast melting pot of civilizations and ideas, and only partially succumbed to the base allure of wealth. Iridi, literally rainbows, have become the common currency of the growing city. They still haven't fully displaced barter economy, but these small, vibrantly colored, minted gold sequins are what the Thieves' Guild is after, and what most citizens are paid in. Iridi can be gambled with at the gaming houses, magically sold at a profit, or safely deposited in a vault, as the corruption of banks is spreading and encompassing all. The ancient Druidhan never dared imagine dangers such as bribes or muggings; instead, they tailored their defenses against monsters and wizards—not greed.

Aspects of life may have been corrupted, but thankfully the soul of the city still stands strong, pure of heart, and proud. In the north-west, the great castle of Dun Darach overlooks all, dominates

The old Druidhan castle overlooking peasant settlements

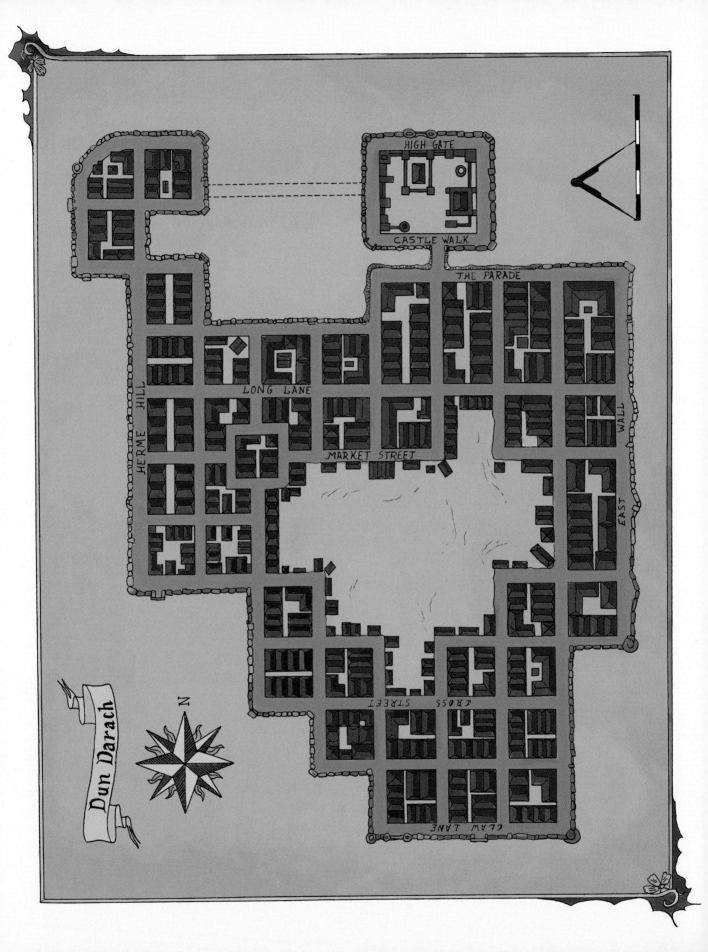

the skyline, and forever protects the sacred oak within its cyclopean fortifications. To its east, and directly accessible only via a secret passage, is the Old Quarter, which is the smallest and most ancient of the quarters, proud of its famed Wall streets. Directly south of the Old Quarter lies Argot, named after the massive bank of Argot, notorious for its loan sharks, money lenders, assayers, and, appropriately, the Thieves' Guild. This district of gold, rainbows, and money often gathers around Mead Square, and is crossed by the Long Lane: the equator of Dun Darach, and the spacious avenue leading west to Graymarket. The latter is the largest of the city's districts, and its roads are filled with salters, barbers, grocers, armourers, skinners, and all sorts of merchants making their business among the homes of artisans, workers, and farmers. To the south of Graymarket and Argot, one can find Iomain, the pleasure quarter, and the pious streets of Ratha-De, and, finally, traveling past Lady Q's infamous establishment, ancient antiquarians, gamblers, and shrines—past even Cross Street, one will encounter the dispossessed of the Soke.

Mercifully, the lost souls of the Soke can also be close to the sacred oak any time they wish, as all city quarters—rich and poor—are connected to one another via magical portals allowing for instantaneous travel. Magic also seems to be what simultaneously lights the torches of the city when night falls and what hides many of its primordial doors. It is the mysterious galleries though—shrines dotted around the city that require the strangest of offerings—that are Dun Darach's most fascinating secret. If the legends are true, when Cuchulainn the Great entered the city—years before departing for Tir Na Nog and the Lands of the Young—it was these very galleries he sought to tame in his battle against the mighty sorceress Skar for the freedom of Lóeg the charioteer.

DESIGN INSIGHTS

Inspired by Celtic myth, *Dun Darach* (essentially "Hill of the Oak" in Celtic) built its story around an evocative original name. Dun Darach was—and sounded like—a mysterious, intriguing place, effortlessly recreating the feel of arriving at an alien city with outlandish customs and confusing geography. Aptly, this was a pioneering, urban, open world that, although slightly confusing, managed to fit a whole, continuously mapped fantasy town in 48 kilobytes of RAM. Constantly reusing elements such as street corners or door frames was required, as was a high degree of modularity, and a quasi-3D environment that could only be rotated in 90-degree increments and scrolled in 2D.

This seemingly vast, three-dimensional city also broke ground by feeling complete, alive, and begging to be explored. Dun Darach itself was the central character and puzzle of the game; mapping it was crucial, and thankfully helped by the town's realistic structure. It featured specialized districts of distinct character, sensible land-use patterns, an economy, and details such as lit torches to signify night-time, while its layout attempted to simulate the complexity of a real city. A quarter could be focused on entertainment and another on finance, but crucially, each one was designed and color-coded to look recognizable. Seeing artisans and shops would mean the player was in Graymarket, whereas a cluster of banks on a yellow background would have to be Argot. Each quarter was subdivided into districts with named streets, and all doors were handily numbered and opened into proper interiors. Using a modified grid for the layout of the city made it (presumably) easier to design, and eventually to navigate.

Among the portals, temples, and gambling dens, Dun Darach also allowed a modest, civic life to flourish. Large, individually named, fully animated characters wandered in believable patterns, while shopkeepers stuck to their tasks and locations. The passing of time, rat infestation, citizens reacting to player actions or going about their daily chores, and shops opening according to their schedule, further allowed *Dun Darach*—despite monstrous technical constraints—to behave like a dynamic, abstract but convincing simulation of a functioning city.

3

WOODTICK
Monkey Island 2: LeChuck's Revenge

GENERAL INFORMATION /////////////////////

City: Woodtick

Game: *Monkey Island 2: LeChuck's Revenge*

Developer: LucasArts

Publisher: LucasArts

Release Date: 1991

Genre: Adventure

Platforms: Amiga, FM Towns, Macintosh, MS-DOS

Deep in the Caribbean, hidden below materials not yet imagined, haunting the dreams of every self-respecting pirate, rests the fabled treasure of Big Whoop. Legend has it the map leading to its fabulous riches has been inconveniently torn in four pieces and scattered across Phatt, Booty, and Scabb Islands. Of these three though, only Scabb, originally settled to serve as a quarantine station for skin diseases, is a true haven for pirates and buccaneers. There is no governor here, no authority to stop a pirate from being, well, a pirate, and no place on the island able to aesthetically please a free spirit more than its major (and only) town: Woodtick.

Lawless, and located at the northern shore of Scabb, Woodtick is the perfect starting place for any Big Whoop hunter, even if famously, and according to the aging sign located at its very entrance, the town is considered a "No trezerhuntin zone." Crossing the bridge at the Woodtick city limits or, to be pedantic, at the downtown's limits, one can truly smell the freedom. Also, the pirates.

Thankfully, local bully Largo LaGrande has finally been kicked out and the highly irritating Largo Embargo is now over. That obnoxious man of poor taste, a henchman of the Ghost Pirate LeChuck, undermined the place's freedom, took advantage of the expected lack of a constabulary, preyed upon traditionally piratic metaphysical anxieties (i.e., being murdered by the undead), and usurped power. For too long a period, he became the island's only authority, imposing enormous taxes on anyone entering or leaving it. Few possessed the large sums of gold required to roam the sea, and thus all citizens were only too happy when (allegedly) mighty pirate Guybrush Threepwood disposed of the tiny tyrant—possibly with the help of a voodoo doll. Or was it LeChuck himself who summoned his minion away?

Admittedly, nobody really cares. Beautiful, rickety Woodtick is able to breathe the fresh sea air of anomie once again. This wonderful web of jetties, piers, and platforms made of assorted bits of wood, flotsam, and distinct ship parts revels in being a free town once more, and, of course, remains a rather literal ship town, too. Woodtick was constructed by salvaging and modifying

Wally B. Feed, widely known as Wally the Cartographer, in his hut

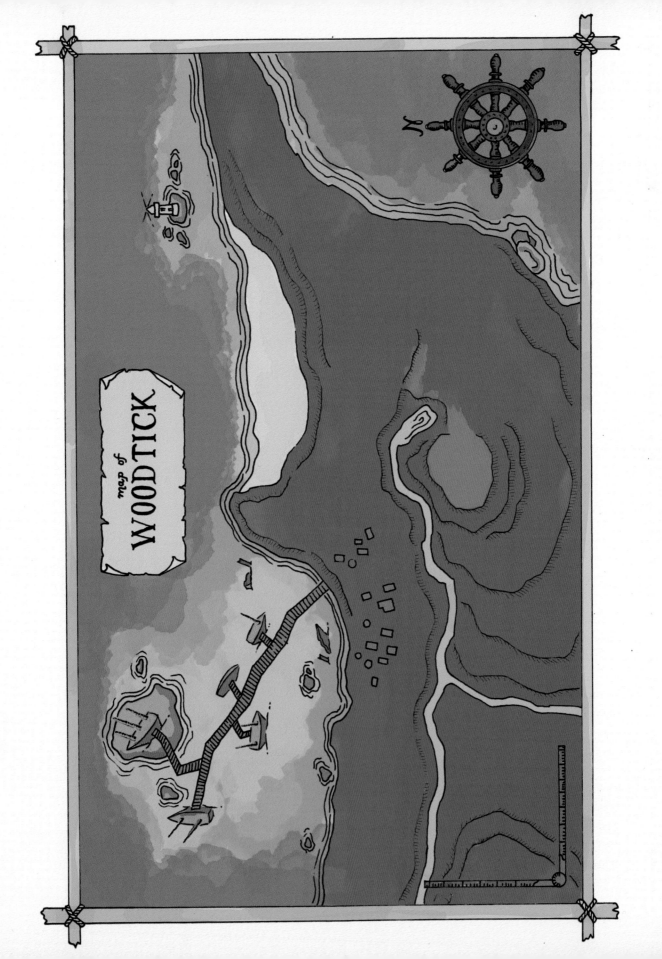

overturned, wrecked, and occasionally floating ships, you see. Shipwrecks are strewn around it, tiny islands serving as the final resting places of converted sloops and galleons, while an assortment of crow's nests, masts, bowsprits, and rudders have all been absorbed in the floating urban tissue.

Half-sunken ships, rickety pathways, and calm waters give downtown Woodtick its unique ambience

This, a most unexpected town of surprises, is filled with glorious anachronisms and rather odd activities and characters. In the Cartographer's Hut, one can find the monocled Wally B. Feed, a hero of the anti-Largo movement and a connoisseur of all things Big Whoop. Woody the Wood-smith's Woodtick Woodshop, on the other hand, may seem unremarkable even if it is *the* place to discover that a woodchuck could chuck no amount of wood since a woodchuck can't chuck wood. Alternatively, visitors can drop down the hatch to the Bloody Lip Bar and Grill for a selection of grogs and gazpacho soups, or walk the main boardwalk to the Swamp Rot Inn, its pet alligator, and that single room available for rent. At the far end of the plank-walk, on a picturesque set of rocks, Mad Marty's stranded laundry ship provides clean clothes to all, and constant amusement to the three exceptionally famous Men of Low Moral Fiber frequenting it.

Outside the seaworthy downtown of Woodtick, on the humble shore, lie the unremarkable huts and homes of the residential part of town, although in reality, Woodtick, being the only settlement of the island, has in a way been scattered all over Scabb. Outside the strict town limits, and provided one is willing to cross not particularly perilous jungles and row over swamps in coffins, one—preferably a tourist—can find the Voodoo Lady's International House of Mojo, some lovely beaches, several secluded piers, a slightly mysterious lighthouse, and a picturesque cemetery proudly featuring the quarantined tombs of green tongue fever victims. Or one can simply stay at the Bloody Lip, have a grog with a nice straw, and enjoy Jojo the monkey's excellent piano tunes.

DESIGN INSIGHTS

It is impossible to come up with anything more pirate-y than a town made of half-sunken ships, and Woodtick is exactly this. Not only does it perfectly fit the theme and game logic of one of the finest adventure games ever made, but Woodtick also conveys the weird theme-park-ride aesthetics and humorous-horror atmosphere *Monkey Island 2* was aiming for. This isn't a world designed for cohesiveness and realism, but a consciously otherworldly setting with bizarreness at its very core. Depicting an obviously fake, skin-deep reality allows the game to play with delightful anachronisms, unfathomable towns, and world-building moon logic, and, impressively, nothing ever feels random. Game designer Ron Gilbert's forethought is palpable even if the Secret of Monkey Island has still to be revealed—players know that things make sense, even if they can't quite understand how.

As for the particular successes of Woodtick, besides cleverly implying—not showing—the rest of town on a low-res map, one has to mention the quality of the high contrast, hand-painted artwork, the warmth of its locations, the vividness of its inhabitants, and the brilliant, dynamic musical theme of the place. Having Woodtick actively react to the Largo Embargo and its eventual cancelation was a clever touch too.

RUBACAVA

Grim Fandango

4

GENERAL INFORMATION ////////////////////

City: Rubacava

Game: *Grim Fandango*

Developer: LucasArts

Publisher: LucasArts

Release Date: 1998

Genre: Adventure

Platforms: Android, iOS, Mac OS, Linux, Windows, PlayStation 4, PlayStation Vita

You haven't died until you've visited Rubacava. The liveliest, most vibrant place throughout the Mesoamerican Hades; the town that never died. An extravagant, cheerful yet forlorn city where heartbroken lovers await their soulmates and the ancient dead dance wildly through countless nights. Rubacava: a city of long shadows, papier-mâché skeletons, bright lights, and unexpected fogs, where the biggest of the bone bands play the finest bebop tunes and jazz and mariachi get married to Andean melodies. This is the great postmortem melting pot. In this town, lost souls are bound to be found and hardened criminals can watch the occasional saint embark the *Nada Mañana* cruises toward a restful afterlife.

This high-life port town of the Land of the Dead is located on the coast of the Sea of Lament, and thus serves as a crucial way-station on the four-year journey to the Ninth Underworld and eternal rest. Reaching it means braving the Petrified Forest, and then, upon arrival, buying passage across the ocean as quickly as possible; yet somehow this almost transient place keeps on growing. Souls tend to linger here in waiting, after losing hope in a better hereafter, or by being swept away by this breathtaking urban embodiment of Mayan, Aztec, Toltec, and Mexican metaphysical beliefs.

Not being a theologically detailed location, Rubacava didn't always exist, but is far older than anyone remembers. Its turbulent history has a palpable weight to it as the dead refusing to leave the afterlife behind are always the more intriguing ones, and their city, teetering between a full-on mobtown and a revolutionary hub, could never be anything but fascinating. The moon of Rubacava has definitely seen much as the tiny transit town by the sea grew to become today's metropolis, and geographers have long argued whether nostalgia or allure is the main centrifugal force boosting its population.

Sense of loss aside, though, this is an undeniably stunning, intoxicating city. The sea laps mesmerizingly against lofty bridges, sublime bas-relief decorations can be discovered in the most unexpected of places, the shadows of imposing buildings hold countless secrets and drinking

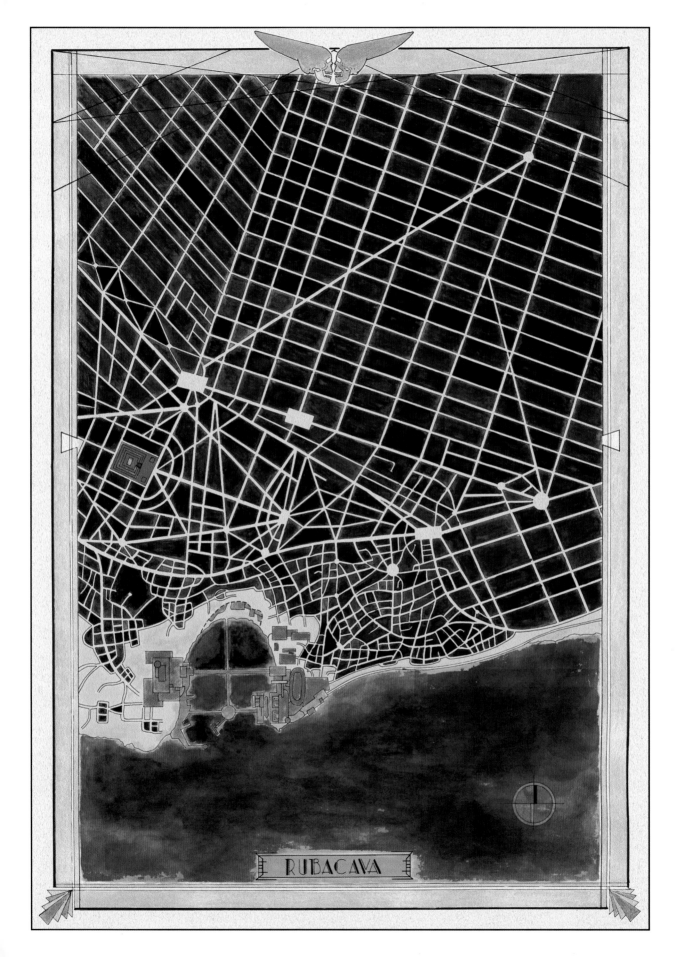

RUBACAVA

Tranquil moments at the Rubacavan harbor

holes, and sudden explosions of scale and spectacle regularly impress. Add in the blimps' sky-traffic, the gargantuan cat-racing track, an unrivaled nightlife, eye-catching sky signs, the lively masses of the dead, and a thousand promises, and the city's gravitational pull makes absolute sense. The sights are countless, the colors dizzying, the music perfect, and the scope awe-inspiring. The aesthetic experience of getting lost is worth dying for—one path might lead to an abandoned lighthouse, another to a forgotten pier, and a third to a cliff-carved elevator toward a new section of town complete with massive casino.

Rubacavan life isn't confined to holding a job or playing the kitties. Things often get exciting, dangerous, and even hopeless in this city of the poor masquerading as the cosmopolitan town of the rich. Demonic bouncers abound; skeletal birds mock; and betrayal, passion, and passionate betrayal are as common as tensions and stark divisions. Shattered illusions, shady schemes, the occasional miracle, an unashamedly corrupt police force, and the popular desire for postmortem justice make for an explosive mix that only temporarily abates during the Day of the Dead: the single day of the year when shows, clubs, and slot machines stand abandoned, and when the over-worked masses are allowed a moment of respite.

Walking the streets on any other day reveals a staggering menagerie of characters. Posh lawyers, hip club owners, exhausted or defiant workers, gangsters, agents of the Department of Death, artists, sailors, and gamblers roam the shadows of emblematic skyscrapers and gather around stepped pyramids and vast plazas. Rarely, the occasional former florists researching the forensic side of botany can also be glimpsed. Second death by sprouting is a notoriously flowery and complex affair; apparently, one only florists can analyze. Only mob bosses can turn into macabre gardens.

It is in the harbor district, though—the oldest part of town—where the vibrancy of unlife truly explodes. The gigantic Feline Meadows racetrack effortlessly dominates the area and sets the tone, even if locals know that the old town can offer more than bets and transit. Hidden in an old Scrimshaw tank, for example, lies the infamous Toto's tattoo parlor, where liquid nitrogen and drills are used to create stunning tattoos on bare bone, whereas up on the magnificent bridge connecting the two harbor clifftops—under the statue of Justice—hides a morgue. A steep climb down to sea level reveals the beautiful gold-and-blue art nouveau Blue Casket club owned by Olivia Ofrenda, the very heart of beatnik Rubacava. In a building nurturing defiance, and standing out in an art deco modernist city of gleaming towers, this is the spot to discuss revolution, drink coffin shooters, and recite poetry.

A fashionable couple outside Manny Calavera's aptly renamed Calavera Café

It's not just architecture that alludes to twentieth-century modernism. As the city grew past its initial waterfront core, it was almost certainly influenced by functionalist ideals, possibly even by Le Corbusier's Radiant City plans, and it adapted a predominantly gridiron structure with regularly spaced diagonal avenues to its needs. Wide boulevards allow unreasonably powerful demon-driven cars to achieve ludicrous speeds, and they connect pastoral suburbs with a bustling downtown that's developed both vertically and horizontally. Activities have been modestly organized; admittedly, the sheer fluidity of death's reality led to haphazard implementations, unfinished avenues, labyrinthine alleys, and clashing functions. Adding to the confusion, Rubacava's recent explosion in size has been driven more by speculation and money laundering than planning forethought, allowing for odd configurations and even unnaturally big crocodiles in badly maintained sewers.

With the exception of the few newer industrial areas, the labyrinthine harbor and its surrounding leisure district remain the city's core economic hub. Gambling and entertainment are soaking up the cash produced by the hardy Sea-Bees, who are working on ships suspended in thin air and gazing at the well-kept docks where opulent ocean liners await their lucky passengers.

Just as the harbor is divided between extravagant pleasures and hard toil, so is the rest of the city.

Art deco towers and impressive zeppelins dominate the city skyline

Death wasn't the great leveler after all—with class lines drawn, tensions rise as the rich continue to exploit the poor. Even the pious seem capable of suffering in this cynical economy when the chief of police is a notorious, bribable gambler, and upstanding crime lords such as Hector LeMans can seemingly do as they please. The police are only interested in running protection schemes and arresting striking union members, inadvertently fueling the flames of the fledgling resistance. And as the Sea-Bees, the workers' vanguard, come closer to the incendiary ideas of the beatniks, and the name of almost mythical revolutionary leader Salvador Limones keeps on inspiring defiance, it is evident that a revolution is brewing—just as the mob moves on to take over the town.

DESIGN INSIGHTS

When it comes to the setting of Rubacava, *Grim Fandango*'s triumph lies in just how grounded the city feels, how palpable its sense of layered history is, and how strongly players connect to the place. For once, they aren't mere wanderers passing through. Manny Calavera, their in-game avatar, gets to breathe this city in; after a short introductory sequence, a full year takes place off-screen in which Manny goes from sweeping floors to owning a club. As he establishes a connection to the place, so do players, and this is key in validating Rubacava and its culture as something real. It is indeed excellent game writing that conjures this initial illusion of civic reality.

Writing is what also provides the city's atmosphere and vibrancy, and is helpfully supported in constant dialogue with clever design choices, an amazing musical score, and Peter Chan's stunning art. The plot and narrative strongly influence, and in turn, are influenced by the place's sounds, art, and locales. A cohesive whole with a convincing atmosphere is crafted. Well-chosen references beyond the narrow world of pop culture and thoroughly researched inspirations allow Rubacava to present an imaginative mix of classic noir literature and cinematography, Mexican folklore, and Mesoamerican beliefs, masterfully assembled in one of the most memorable locations of gaming. Creating a unique brand of architecture based mostly on an Aztec reinterpretation of modernist art deco is also particularly apt, considering the influence of Mesoamerican step pyramids on early twentieth-century skyscrapers.

What's more, Rubacava provides players with spatial immersion on a grand scale. It feels alive and massive, bigger and more important than any individual. The achieved sense of scale is helped by the adventure genre's screen-by-screen navigation, which allows players to fill in any gaps, while the metropolitan size of this city of towers is mainly implied via backgrounds, brief but evocative cut scenes, and dialogue trees.

As every corner of each screen leads to new locations, *Grim Fandango* intentionally lets players get initially lost in order to appreciate its size, spectacular vistas, creative architecture, intriguing characters, and detailed backgrounds, while simultaneously helping them construct a mental map. Rubacava is dotted with landmarks, memorable districts, and logical connections that are easy to understand and remember. The elevator takes Manny up the cliff, the bridge leads to the other side of town, and the harbor's floating square connects everything on the sea level. Such sensible spatial relations and an abundance of shortcuts make sure that, by the end of Rubacava's chapter, players feel they've mastered the geography and secrets of the city.

5

THE CITY
Thief: The Dark Project

City: The City

Game: *Thief: The Dark Project*

Developer: Looking Glass Studios

Publisher: Eidos Interactive

Release Date: 1998

Genre: Immersive Sim, Stealth

Platforms: Windows

Nameless, for no name was ever needed, and vast beyond measure, the sprawl of the mythic City is a metropolis of countless people, rich banks, arcane powers, groundbreaking technologies, and ancient roots. Here, forgotten magic coexists with electricity and steam-powered machines. The hot fires and cold steel of the Metal Age have erected defiant towers atop sacred catacombs and forgotten settlements. The Baron's infamous City Watch patrol worn stone roads under the glow of electric lamps and floating orbs—to occasionally prevent crime, but mainly to police the poor. The rich, powerful, and corrupt city-state of the City is deeply divided by class and beautifully bisected by the Great River running through it from north to south.

Wide, arched stone bridges connect its banks. Auldale, the City's richest quarter; the densely populated Dayport; the modern New Quarter; Eastport's docklands; and Shoalsgate all lie to the river's east. On the older western bank, the lively Downtowne, the First City Bank and Trust of the North Quarter, Newmarket, mixed-class South Quarter, the warehouses of the Wayside Docks, and wealthy Hightowne are the districts dominated by the Clocktower of Stonemarket, the City's tallest building, which has stood for centuries. Its still-turning gears are as old as the once-thriving Old Quarter, around which the rest of the City eventually grew. Buildings there are packed close together and the streets are narrow and cluttered. Following the Cataclysm half a century ago that saw the undead pouring out of the Old Quarter to terrorize the City, a large part of it, the now-ruined Sealed Section, was quarantined behind tall stone walls to keep whatever still walks there at bay, and to better hide the mystical artifacts enduring in the vaults of the great old Hammerite Cathedral.

The Old Quarter's labyrinthine structure has deeply influenced the city surrounding it. Oppressive, rat-infested cobblestone alleys and uneven roads shadowed by stone balconies lead under arches and past gates into the unexpectedly spacious plazas of the City. Electric lights, torches

The roads of the city are shadowy and often dangerous

and oil lamps, hanging wires, and strange hieroglyphs proliferate below towers, keeps, ramparts, and spires. Castles and mansions dot the landscape in uneasy harmony with classic, columned buildings, intricate cathedrals with stained-glass windows, and edifices clad in metal. The dawning of the age of metal is increasingly evident. Pipes run alongside buildings, massive cranes, and iron scaffolding. The vast majority of buildings, however, are made of solid stone cut in an impressive range of ways, even if brick and timber-frame buildings also survive. Ornate Gothic stone

windows, floral motifs, and multistory houses blend into each other in a kaleidoscope of architectural and organic designs.

The City's imposing skyline

With the exception of the tiny, spartan, torch-lit houses of the many, the interiors of the City's buildings are as eclectic as the City itself. Aging baroque opera houses are equipped with elevators; maze-like keeps of large stone halls and vaulted corridors are protected by mechanical warrior statues. The obscenely rich have no flair for the functional. They enjoy colored marble floors covered with carpets, wood-paneled walls, and overly extravagant decorations. The distasteful opulence of Lord Bafford's manor, with its golden wallpapers, gigantic gongs, and reflecting pools, is infamous, if drunk servants are to be believed—and why shouldn't they be in a metropolis of hidden wonders? It pales, however, when compared to Constantine's mansion. This stately house is said to be a place where logic falls apart, where rooms and windows are skewed at bizarre angles, and where obscene, out-of-scale furniture, indoor forests, and the void itself challenge reality, gravity, and Euclidean geometry.

Below other keeps and guilds lie miles of caverns, and subterranean, archaic living quarters. Serpentine underground burial sites filled with supernatural horrors hide beneath ancient factories, themselves buried under prisons, whereas a whole lost city, covered and sealed, is only remembered via crumbling maps sold for a fortune. And yet life never really pauses to think of such wonders. Above ground—among food stands, shop windows, and horse-drawn carriages—day laborers, paupers, orphans, and pickpockets simply cannot afford the luxury of watching out for hooded figures and imagining cursed treasures. Life is short and hard. Disease is rampant, shelter rare, and health-giving potions too expensive for honor-bound traditionalists too proud to join the Thieves' Guild or betray their rich masters. Religion may forbid stealing, but for the starving masses, such spiritual matters sound intolerably philosophical.

The prevalent faith, the Order of the Hammer, an authoritarian techno-theological religion, has never been especially popular. Its sanctified inventions brought wealth to the City lords and not the poor. In its glorious temples, novices are not even allowed to speak, and the guards wielding massive war hammers are rightly feared. The Builder is a harsh but often inspiring deity promising endurance and eternity through human creation. The reclusive, all-but-animalistic Pagans on the opposite side have strong ties to their perverted idea of nature, and a deep hatred of civilization and all progress. They are avoided, often despised, and do not seem interested in preaching or bringing more followers to the worship of their eldritch god, the Trickster. As for the neutral, secretive Keepers, they strive to maintain all balance within the City. To them, the world is a great scale that must always stay in balance. Knowledge is but a set of weights to be added to one side of the scale or the other, and even the Devil walking the City's streets is something to be carefully balanced.

DESIGN INSIGHTS

Thief: The Dark Project defined both the immersive sim and the stealth genre. It was the first PC game to use light and sound as game mechanics, and featured complex simulation systems that allowed for emergent gameplay. Players were encouraged to focus on hiding, evading, and misdirecting in a world where innovative physics provided palpable gameplay and believably cast shadows acted as safe spaces. Sound was crucial in navigating levels. It allowed non-player characters (NPCs) to communicate their thoughts, states, and positions to the often-invisible players, while also helping said NPCs detect intruders. Walking produced quieter footsteps than running, and stepping on carpets was less noisy than on stone floors.

Added to these, the first-person perspective allowed for a personal, first-hand experience of the game's City; usually crouched still in the dark, waiting for a guard to pass by, or rushing from shadow to shadow. A sense of physicality was prevalent and added weight to civic spaces and architecture; a feeling of actual space was achieved. Levels were largely unscripted and maze-like, and offered freedom in choosing how to reach objectives, thus forcing players to appreciate and analyze the built environment from the point of view of a thief, demanding they consider which of its aspects could and should be used. Further emphasizing immersion was the lack of an auto-map feature. In-game maps did not track player position and were often too old and sketchy, pushing players to rely on landmarks and discover their own shortcuts, while meticulously exploring the City and learning about it via notes, environmental details, and overheard conversations. The setting and its mythology were therefore revealed organically, and glimpses of a larger world were provided, while cut scenes connected the discrete locations of the game's missions.

The medieval urban sprawl of the unnamed City itself achieved uniqueness and memorability by combining steampunk machinery, medieval Gothic sensibilities, and touches of both noir and high fantasy to create something entirely new. It positioned itself somewhere between the historical and the mythical, and fully developed its imaginary world and enriched it with culture, religions, dialects, fashion, technology, and a history that supported the wild variety of juxtaposed elements. All environments were heavily abstracted, suggestive, or even symbolic; in the ruined Sealed Quarter, for example, most houses were merely odd shapes implying crumbling buildings. And yet, even flamboyant surrealism managed to fit inside this otherwise sensibly constructed game world—Constantine's Escheresque mansion impressively proved this.

6

SIGIL
Planescape: Torment

GENERAL INFORMATION ///////////////////////

City: Sigil

Game: *Planescape: Torment*

Developer: Black Isle Studios

Publisher: Interplay Entertainment

Release Date: 1999, 2017

Genre: RPG

Platforms: Android, iOS, Linux, MacOS, Nintendo Switch, PlayStation 4, Windows, Xbox One

Sigil, a.k.a. the City of Doors and the Cage, is the eternal metropolis sitting at the crossroads of the multiverse. Floating above an infinitely tall spire in the center of the Outlands, it connects all. The center of the ring of the Outer Planes can lead to any place, and any plane of the Planescape multiverse: from Carceri or Baator to the Negative Material plane or the demi and inner planes; from the void of the Astral plane or the mists of the Ethereal plane to the Prime Material Plane, Krynn, and the Forgotten. The City of Doors, an impossible site, contains portals to all these locations and more. It is a gateway to everywhere, and the city through which everyone will sooner or later pass. More portals than can be imagined, permanent or temporary, locked or hidden, can lead from its dirty alleys to the expanses of the Abyss or to long-forgotten, ancient immaterial halls.

The Cage is huge, but not infinite. Wrapped inside the surface of a torus, it is a closed structure twenty miles in circumference and five miles in diameter (as officially measured by the Harmonium). Smoke and distance obscure views, and only artificial light illuminates the inside of the torus, becoming brighter during peak and dimmer on anti-peak. No matter the time, looking up reveals a city stretching above and around observers; it spectacularly curves away overhead.

In the City of Doors, there is no east and west, no north and south. Surveyors prefer the peculiar directions of radial and chordwise when attempting to map this incredibly complex place that's overwhelmed and literally covered with shifting, disappearing, and reappearing buildings. The major structures, the ones everyone believes in, are the more stable ones, acting almost as landmarks drifting over the centuries in a metropolis where the bizarre becomes mundane.

The Lady of Pain, the true lord of Sigil, and an entity of inscrutable motives, can physically enlarge or shrink the city as she desires. Those who gaze upon her visage are flayed to death, and her enemies are locked for eternity in labyrinthine demi-planes of her own construction. Her Serenity is an enigma wrapped in a mystery of absolute silence. The Lady never speaks, but her will

SIGIL, CITY OF DOORS
THE CAGE

LADY'S WARD

MARKET WARD

LOWER WARD

THE HIVE

GUILDHALL WARD

CLERK'S WARD

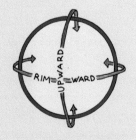

RIM

UPWARD

is always plain to her agents. Floating through the streets, adorned in shining, keen blades, she is the absolute ruler of Sigil, the creator and destroyer of planar portals, and the guardian of stability. Neither deities nor wars may taint the true neutral existence of the Cage. Even the bloodshed of the eternal Blood War is kept far from the City of Doors.

Spaces within Sigil do not always make sense

The sharp, multi-pronged silhouette of the Lady is mirrored in the city's spiky architecture of traditional ornamental blades and forbidding fences. The spikes combined with heavy doors, thick walls, and iron bar windows create defensible, safe interiors, as well as tortuous images of sharp and sinuous metal shapes entangled with each other. Sigil is imposing, and its architectural shapes extreme in their variety and obscurity of function. Radiant architraves and domes loom over countless mind-bendingly combined buildings and alleys of muted browns, grays, and greens. Iron and stone, usually conjured by magic, are the most common building materials, while unsettling faces and gargoyles are the most common ornamentation of pillars and rain spouts. Roofs of dark gray slate tiles cover houses huddled around interior courtyards in areas poor and rich alike. As buildings crowd over each other, streets are cut off from the sky entirely, although not necessarily forever. Sigil is alive. It breathes, grows, and shrinks, swallowing up whole streets and giving birth to new alleys. It changes and groans when the Lady of Pain rearranges its unmappable, dense surfaces. Young boulevards and courtyards are created by the city's masons, and buildings built on top of older ones form intricate catacombs and canyons of stone and iron—always balanced around the desires of the dreaded Lady. Her will dominates space, occasionally even allowing homes to shift from one ward to another.

The wards, Sigil's six districts, are the most straightforward way of keeping track of where things are. Their boundaries may be unclear and shift unexpectedly, but it is their inhabitants and activity that define them. If manufactories move out and rogues move in, an area is said to have moved from the Lower Ward to the Hive. The latter, home to the poor and unwanted of the city, turns its residents into thugs, thieves, and grave-diggers living under crumbling roofs and shanties stuck one upon another. Neither the Mortuary nor the Mausoleum, the Alley of Dangerous Angles, nor the Hive's Ragpicker's Square could ever be mistaken as part of the industrialized Lower Ward. Clogged up with the smoke from foundries and the sulfurous gases from portals to the lower planes, this is a center of craftsmanship and production. The Lady's Ward, on the other hand, famous for its fountains and a place of consumption, is the richest and most exclusive section of the city, whereas the Market and Guildhall Wards, the trading hubs of the multiverse, welcome traders, craftsmen, artisans, and the middle classes. The affluent Clerk's Ward of bureaucrats and middlemen proudly features the headquarters of the Society of Sensation, and Fall-from-Grace's wondrous Brothel for Slaking Intellectual Lusts.

Admittedly, the size of Sigil makes describing all of its wonders impossible, but among magical stores, clockwork buildings, and cavernous taverns, the Brothel for Slaking Intellectual

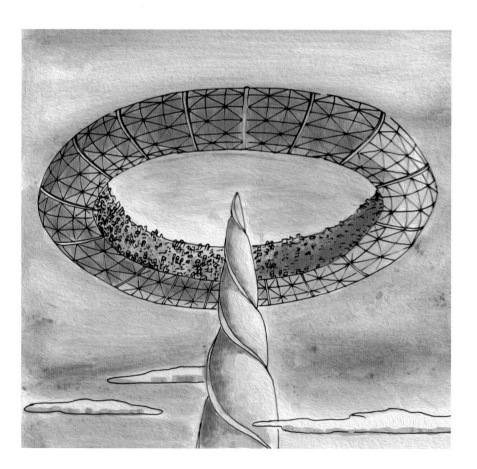

The torus of Sigil is a sight for the gods

An ancient scribe of the Dustmen faction inside the Mortuary

Lusts always stands out. It is a circular building around a lush garden where a chaste succubus and nine courtesans of the spirit engage patrons in fascinating conversations. The brothel's discourse even overshadows miracles such as the public wells refilling straight from the elemental plane of water, the lightless coffin labyrinths of the Weeping Stone Catacombs, and the fact that, despite the complete lack of sewers and the city's sheer size, the atmosphere somehow remains breathable.

Sigil has a population of over a million, and most of them were neither born there nor in the Outlands themselves. Strange folks abound. A constant interplanar bazaar fills the streets with any possible race. Clueless come from the Prime Material Plane to mingle, drink, and argue philosophy with the plane-walkers of the Great Ring. Elves meet the ghoulish Dustmen with their undead servants, or study spell-casting rat swarms—nothing is too unlikely for Sigil. It is a cage for beings from all walks of life—and unlife—although coexistence is not always easy. Sigil's fifteen philosophy-defined factions seem locked in eternal and often deadly political struggle as Athar, Sensates, the Revolutionary League, and others vie for power. Everyone in Sigil is a cynic after all, and this is a truly dangerous place. Even more so for the arrogantly ignorant. Living in an impossible city can never be simple, but the opportunities here are indeed endless, and one could hope to even discover what can truly change the nature of a man.

DESIGN INSIGHTS

Sigil is a virtual city based on one of the most detailed and famously imaginative fantasy cities of analog gaming: a confusing settlement from the pen-and-paper world of *Dungeons & Dragons* that summarizes the wild, multi-planar setting of *Planescape* into something almost comprehensible. A complex, constantly reshaping urban environment connected to every place in existence, it departs from traditional high fantasy and occasionally embraces science fiction elements. An alien place wonderfully reimagined in digital form that allowed *Planescape: Torment* to touch upon philosophical matters and tell a melancholy story. Watching 1998's *Dark City* and playing 1999's *Torment* was what convinced me that such whimsical, shape-shifting places could actually be visualized. Additionally, the latter defined the civic narrative opportunities for a whole medium, proving that a city is a setting that can tell infinite stories and is capable of introducing complex worlds such as Planescape. Having players start out in Planescape's signature location immerses them immediately in a video game setting refreshingly faithful to its printed counterpart.

The game runs on a modified version of the Infinity Engine, allowing its pre-rendered, isometric world to be filled with incredible detail, many characters, and an abundance of hotspots. The truly odd appearance of the city is based on an utterly unfamiliar architecture and descriptions of a geography that barely makes sense. Unique buildings with unexpected interiors and even more unexpected functions rob players of familiar references, and are brought to life and enriched by fine walls of text. Excellent writing and evocative dialogue capture the essence of Sigil, and do justice to its inner workings.

The atmosphere is further enhanced by a truly immersive soundscape. This city really does sound like a crowded place where drunks can be heard outside bars and auctioneers shout in the distance. Extra touches such as a local language, the Chant, based on an imaginary version of the cockney dialect, or a unique breed of spell-casting rat swarms really bring forth the uniqueness of a town where sometimes the undead are heartwarmingly sympathetic. As for the in-game map, it is aptly presented on sewn-together pieces of skin tattooed with locations, thus successfully tying in with the game's theme of inscribed bodies and representing the fragmented nature and uncertain topologies of *Planescape*.

7

CLOCK TOWN
The Legend of Zelda: Majora's Mask

GENERAL INFORMATION ///////////////////

City: Clock Town

Game: *The Legend of Zelda: Majora's Mask*

Developer: Nintendo EAD

Publisher: Nintendo

Release Date: 2000

Genre: Action-RPG

Platforms: GameCube, Nintendo 3DS, Nintendo 64, Nintendo Wii, Nintendo Wii U

Existing in a dimension parallel to Hyrule, the land of Termina was, according to legend, divided by four magic giants into four quadrants. The northern one, home of the Goron, consists of vast pine forests and the frozen Snowhead Mountain range, whereas to the east lie deep, desolate canyons plagued by the undead and the dark auras cast from the Stone Tower Temple. The aptly named Southern Swamp quadrant holds the Deku Palace and the Woodfall Temple, and, in Termina's west, the Great Bay meets the wild ocean and both the Zora and the Gerudo civilizations have flourished. At the exact center of the land, surrounded by the large city of Clock Town and the Termina Field, stands the colossal stone Clock Tower. Powered by a subterranean river and a water wheel, this ancient, cyclopean clock counts the days to the Carnival of Time, and acts as a lighthouse during nights.

In a culture revolving around the magical concept of time, naturally the Clock Tower itself has grown dominant, and the Carnival of Time is celebrated every year during a holy day revered by all the peoples of Termina. On the eve of the festivities, when the sun and moon align, the Clock Tower's doors open, and from its top, a ceremony to call the gods is held to the sound of age-old songs. Believers from all of Termina gather around the tower to celebrate and pray for good luck and bountiful harvests. To pay their respects to Nature and Time, they dance, sing, and revel, while wearing the traditional masks resembling the Four Giants, the four guardian spirits of Termina.

Clock Town itself is a holy site, a religious city built to worship the gods and to accommodate pilgrims from all four quadrants, to sit at the very heart of Termina and contain the essence of its culture. Growing into a major center of trade, leisure, and spirituality, and becoming the greatest settlement this world has ever known, was almost inevitable. Today, completely surrounded by tall walls, Clock Town protects the sacred tower, while its four guarded gates are always welcoming to peaceful visitors. The gates, each facing a different cardinal direction, are made of the materials

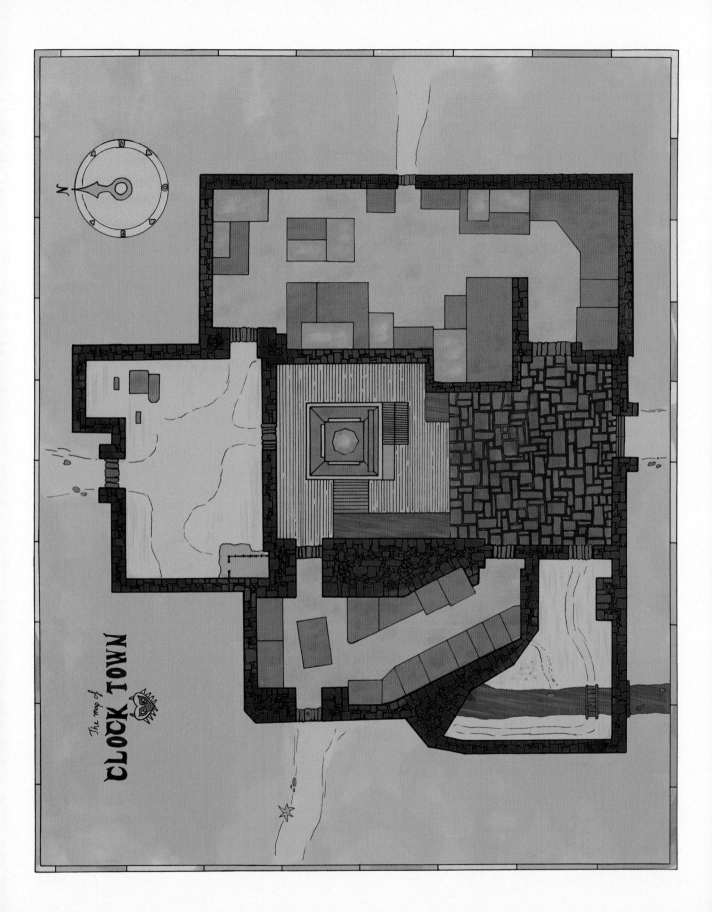

The map of
CLOCK TOWN

The stepped, lively road of Clock Town West

of their respective quadrant, and all lead inside the walls of a town overflowing with colorful decorations, finely preserved bas reliefs, and, of course, life and commerce.

The center of the city, South Clock Town, is not merely a civic hub but a regional one. Enclosed by the high stone walls of the town's other three districts, South Clock Town is actually a great ceremonial square surrounding the Clock Tower. There are no houses or other permanent constructions here. The Clock Tower stands alone, and monumental: the centerpiece of Termina. The plaza around it can hold large crowds and truly comes alive during the Carnival of Time, when wooden stalls with thatched roofs and colorful flags are erected, and when all of the world's races mingle in celebration and hope. Additionally, South Clock Town provides the only way toward the Laundry Pool, probably the most serene, pleasant place in the city. Tucked away in its quiet corner, guarded by ivy-covered walls, this small beautiful pool under the blue sky, where Clock Towners once did their laundry, attracts and calms the distressed among its trees, bright flowers, and neatly trimmed grass.

The three remaining districts of Clock Town, each named after their respective compass direction, reflect the region of the world they open out to. North Clock Town is thus the city's garden. A beautiful, large park dedicated to the recreation of locals and visitors, sporting a joyful playground for the children, it occasionally hosts outrageous mapmaker Tingle and his whimsical wares. There are no buildings here, but the northern wall hides the entrance to a fantastical fairy fountain. Clock

Clock Town's Clock Tower

Town West is much less spacious and much more focused on commerce. It is essentially one long, winding, stepped path lined with shops, stalls, and businesses such as the Bomb Shop, the Curiosity Shop, the Post Office, and the Swordsman's School. Clock Town East, on the other hand, is the town's vibrant core of everyday life, and the prime residential center. Its buildings are home to many of the town's denizens, including purple-haired Mayor Dotour, responsible for scheduling the performances for the Carnival of Time, and his wife, Madame Aroma. It is here that Clock Town architecture reaches its apogee with the finest of thatched roofs, the best stonework, the most intricate carvings, and the most elaborate wall decorations. It is also here that one can play exciting games and win weird prizes from establishments such as the Shooting Gallery and the Treasure Chest Shop.

Vibrant and beautiful though it is, Clock Town is in danger. The city is currently facing the greatest threat in its history. It is on the verge of destruction, threatened by a moon slowly falling from the sky, aimed squarely at the Clock Tower. Only the prophesied Hero of Time is said to be able to avert the catastrophe by playing fabled time-twisting, sky-bending tunes. But, as the massive Clock Tower ticks down toward certain doom, and the carnival is getting ever closer, no hero has yet appeared. And there are only three days left.

DESIGN INSIGHTS

Clock Town is a settlement that fully embraces the central theme of *Majora's Mask*: time. It is also a city built around a single definitive core function—hosting the carnival and covering its requirements—that holds together a whimsical and occasionally outrageous fantasy world. Additionally, each of Clock Town's areas leads to a major region of the game. This is the world's central hub, and, in typical Zelda fashion, not only does it show off its characteristic theme, but it also consists of symbolic representations of areas, as well as civic elements. This simplicity leads to a very clean layout that is easy to navigate, yet filled with side-quests, activities, characters, and shops.

With time being employed both as a theme and as a mechanic, players get to reset it and replay the exact same three days over and over. Everything has been fully scripted over said three days, and this is what makes the town come alive and feel like an elaborate, out-of-scale puzzle box. Every non-player character follows a very specific, beautifully thought-out timetable, one that can be fully accessed through the Bombers' Notebook. The location of characters and what they do is independent of player action, meaning they get to live out their choreographed lives, and, as a group, provide the impression of a breathing cartoon society. They do whatever it is they are supposed to be doing, interacting with one another, and never waiting for player input. The same applies to in-game events, meaning that Clock Town can live through three complete days on its own, and even let itself get destroyed.

8

ORGRIMMAR
World of Warcraft

GENERAL INFORMATION //////////////////////

City: Orgrimmar

Game: *World of Warcraft*

Developer: Blizzard Entertainment

Publisher: Blizzard Entertainment

Release Date: 2004

Genre: MMORPG

Platforms: Windows, MacOS

Fleeing the harsh alien world of Draenor, betrayed by their leaders, and enslaved to demons, the orcs were forced into Azeroth as the unholy vanguard of the First Burning Legion. The once noble tribes were corrupted and coerced into unspeakable atrocities, and it took a great shaman and noble leader, the legendary Thrall, to remind them of their true identity and lead them through a brave rebellion, all the way to freedom. Ancient clans were brought back together and united under Thrall's guidance, as the victorious shaman warchief guided the liberated orcs out of the invaded Eastern Kingdoms and into the continent of Kalimdor, the land of eternal starlight. There, they and their allies toiled hard for a hopeful future, and, in the northern valleys and caverns of the newly named lands of Durotar, built their great city of Orgrimmar.

Carved into the mountain, Orgrimmar is the greatest stronghold of the orcs and the capital of the Horde; a fortified complex guarded by stout walls, steep cliffs, massive gates, and tall towers. To its south lie the barren lands and deserts of Durotar, and to its north, Azshara's forests. In this city of valleys, orcs, trolls, tauren, goblins, and all other races comprising the loose alliance of the Horde live together. Behind Orgrimmar's immense walls, shamans pass on their knowledge, warriors spar in the gladiatorial arena, and war machines rest ready, in a town that manages to feel safe, vibrant, and even cosy, while serving as a major trade, military, and cultural hub. Orgrimmar is famous for its tauren, Winter Solstice festival, resident blue drakes, goblin-designed contraptions, scribes, merchants, warriors, bankers, and, rather unexpectedly, elaborate postal service.

The home of the warchiefs is an imposing city sitting at the center of a vast web of zeppelin routes, portals, and trade avenues. Its main entrance, the massive, heavily fortified south gate, is covered in iron plates and huge spikes to awe visitors and scare invaders. There are no soft edges here, and a snaking passage of fire and steel designed to break the momentum of any attacking army leads inside the urban fortress of Orgrimmar and to the Valley of Strength. In this city of layers, the sense of verticality is strong, and the architecture monumental, austere, and claustrophobic.

The long, vibrant alley of the Drag is an important path within Orgrimmar

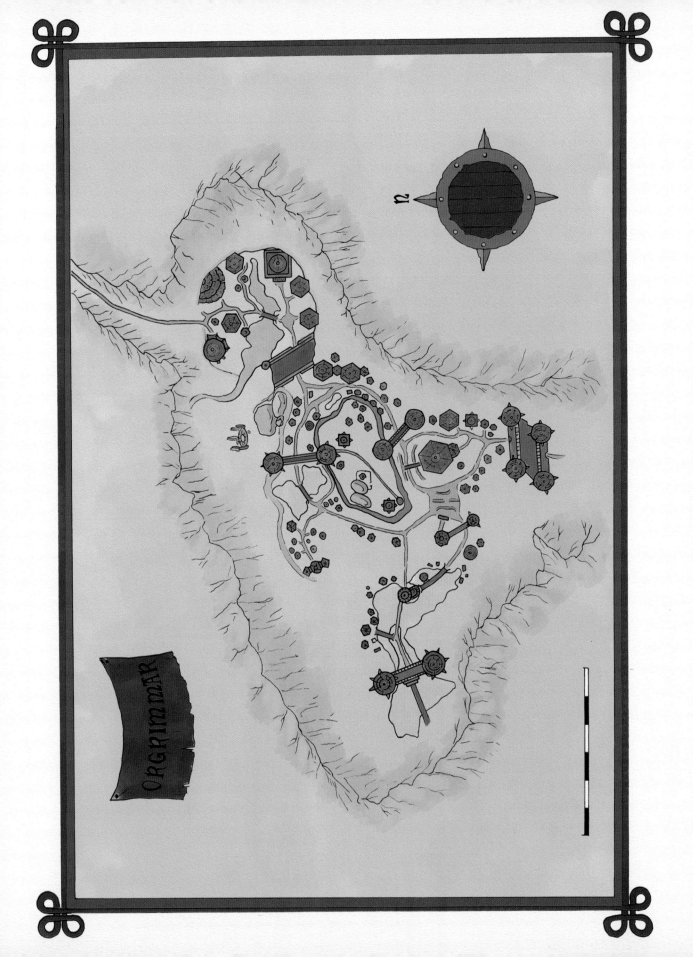

Thrall's old stone fortifications of the main Orgrimmar gate

The signature reds of the Horde can be seen on roofs and banners, among ornamental blades, tusks, and pyres that remain lit at all times, as contemporary towers of rock and metal coexist with the older wooden structures, alluding to a less militaristic, more optimistic past.

Orgrimmar has never known peace. Its turbulent, violent history has never stopped reshaping it. As it now stands, the Valley of Strength is its effective center, and the first area visitors will

Fire baskets light the gates of Orgrimmar

glimpse is between the giant arches of the main gate. There, at the mouth of Orgrimmar, lies the Horde's seat of power, the rebuilt Warchief Hold, defiantly welcoming all invaders, a testimony to its leaders' bravery and strength. Overlooking the dusty utilitarian arteries of the great city, its awe-inspiring, towering edifice is surrounded by major banks, great auction houses, and countless shops, forming a bustling hive of activity. On the steep hill above, the Orgrimmar Skyway is accessible via large elevators, and its two great zeppelin towers connect the city to most of Azeroth.

Linking the Valley of Strength to the Valley of Wisdom in the north and the Valley of Honor to the northeast is the Drag, a long, busy street running through a narrow valley. This beautiful, partly shaded, open-air marketplace is known for its myriad vendors and specialists, but also for the tunnel leading to the Cleft of Shadow: a subterranean district of perpetual gloom dominated by massive tents supported on bestial tusks, home to Orgrimmar's rogues, warlocks, and practitioners of the darker arts. The Cleft houses a portal to the Blasted Lands, and the only known entrance to the dreaded Ragefire Chasm is set deep below the city.

Past the Drag, between two gates, lies the Valley of Honor, defending the city's northern entrance by the Southfury River and providing barracks, training, and arms to the Horde's warriors and hunters. Here, along the small lake, rests the Hall of the Brave, housing warriors and battle-masters, while the Ring of Valor arena provides entertainment and combat experience. The Valley of Wisdom, on the other hand, where the hold of Warchief Thrall once stood next to the gigantic armor of Mannoroth the Flayer, is nowadays almost exclusively populated by the peaceful tauren. Their totems and huts among the remains of the hold and the pools the Cataclysm created make this a uniquely serene district.

Partly sunk during the Cataclysm too, the Valley of Spirits to the western end of town is a deep, narrow valley ending at the Talon Gate. It is the long-standing seat of the Darkspear Trolls, and a showcase of their unexpectedly whimsical architecture of elaborately decorated tribal tree houses, lake towers, and hanging sky bridges. Next to the Valley of Spirits, and where the Goblin Slums for the Bilgewater goblin refugees were once located, a Horde embassy has been constructed, complete with its own sub-district of traders, diplomats, and the headquarters of allied nations.

It is beyond evident that Orgrimmar's geography has been continuously, and often violently, sculpted and re-sculpted by its history. Since its founding in honor of Warchief Orgrim Doomhammer, it was meant as a great warrior city, but one dedicated to defense, prosperity, and survival. The city was forced to protect itself against the Scourge and the Legion, played a key role in the war against the Lich King, and was even attacked and set ablaze by raging fire elementals, suffering serious damage to its fabric. As a result, Garrosh Hellscream, appointed to lead the Horde by Thrall himself, was also tasked with rebuilding Orgrimmar for war.

His sweeping transformations ensured the city's fortresses now rank among the most powerful of Azeroth. Spiked metal towers line the streets and the banners of the Horde wave from every post. The zeppelin towers that once stood outside the gates were demolished and rebuilt inside the town on the safety of the Orgrimmar Skyway. The old stone fortifications have been turned into a citadel of metal, and most of the rustic wooden architecture of yore has given way to reinforced steel and iron. The rural, inviting town of optimism, a celebration of the Horde's unity, was segregated into distinctly racial quarters, even as more gates and portals were opened to the outside world. As for the intimidating main southern gate, it took on the appearance of a mighty weapon, adorned with enormous iron spikes and two foreboding towers, ensuring the increasingly tyrannical, xenophobic, and paranoid Garosh would hold onto his power.

But the orcs and their allies could not endure any form of slavery anymore. After a lengthy, devastating siege, Orgrimmar was liberated, and once again partly rebuilt. All races of the Horde began moving back to the city, and trade routes were restored as Warchief Vol'jin fought hard to bring back normalcy and prosperity. Only his mortal wounding at the battle on the Broken Shore has brought worry back to Orgrimmar's alleys.

DESIGN INSIGHTS

As is the case with all World of Warcraft cities, Orgrimmar lacks a sense of scale appropriate for a metropolitan-level hub, a problem the now-aging engine could never hope to overcome. The place looks tiny for what is essentially an imperial capital, residence is effectively missing, and its functions are exclusively game-focused. It is still beautiful, mind you, and sports some brilliantly evocative architecture and districts. And even if it only features a single barber, Orgrimmar feels alive, truly dynamic, and is teeming with players. Impressively, it keeps on changing, evolving, reacting, and occasionally defining the game's lore, while its structural and architectural revisions embody and showcase political and societal changes.

Also on the plus side, its landmarks, clearly defined districts, and sensible spatial differentiations, make it easy to navigate. The arrangement of activity centers brings activity, traffic, and life to the city, as players move back and forth between vendors, auction houses, banks, trainers, and quest givers. Interestingly, and whether intentional or not, Orgrimmar features spatial solutions proposed in Christopher Alexander et al.'s classic work *A Pattern Language*, which, not unlike MMORPG design, focuses on creating environments that stimulate social interaction, and proposes intuitive, welcoming spaces and easily navigable cities.

Alexander's work is not about single patterns but about the combination of several, and Orgrimmar seems to follow this particular logic too. On the regional scale, it is a major center on the edge of a zone as per Alexander's prescriptions, whereas high-level services (found only in larger settlements) have been clustered tightly, and all neighborhoods/districts have clear boundaries. (Alexander claims that a neighborhood without a boundary is a weak neighborhood.) Every district comes with its instantly identifiable character, and locally provides its community with the things it needs—trainers, vendors, banks, etc.—once again following Alexander's suggestions, or common planning sense.

MAP of Fallen London

9

LONDON
Fallen London

GENERAL INFORMATION ///////////////////

City: London

Game: *Fallen London*

Developer: Failbetter Games

Publisher: Failbetter Games

Release Date: 2009

Genre: CYOA, Interactive Fiction, MMO

Platforms: Android, iOS, Web

Welcome, delicious friend! Welcome to Fallen London, and the Neath. Welcome to the greatest port of the Unterzee. Please enjoy the smog, smoke, gaslight, and delightful gloom. We find ourselves one mile beneath earth's surface in the marvelous, dark, and expensive metropolis housing the Echo Bazaar. Here death is but a mild irritation, corpses love their tea, rats craft wonderfully intricate weapons, and devils are keen on discussing philosophy. Soft-hearted widows eagerly succor lost souls, ambitious barristers make their rounds, poets and models glower at one another, honey-addled artisans struggle to focus, and feral cats hunt snakes beneath the bell of the House of Chimes.

This leaning clock tower half-sunken in the Stolen River, rumored to be a perversely exclusive club, was once referred to as Big Ben. But, just as Baker Street became Moloch Street, Piccadilly is now called Lusitania Row—its name was changed over thirty years ago, back in 1861 when London was stolen by bats and dragged deep into the earth. The monarch, Her Enduring Majesty the Traitor Empress, is said to have sold the city to the Bazaar in exchange for her husband's life, and the metropolis now rests on the shores of the ancient black ocean. Hell is close, immortality is cheap, and the screaming has subsided in the former imperial capital and latest home of the Echo Bazaar. Londoners can, after all, get used to anything, and despite what anarchists claim, London was never better off. It's so peaceful, so beautiful here.

Preposterously, London was not the first city to be taken underground. It is in fact the fifth, although little is understood of its evidently lesser predecessors. We do suspect that the silver tree of the Forgotten Quarter was a living birch during the Fourth City, and that the Gods of the Third City still walk among us, but know little else. Obviously, the preceding cities were also located in the Neath—in the very same cavern of impossible size, that is, and probably close to the Bazaar's contemporary location by the tremendous sea of the Unterzee. There is no sun here, plants scoff at photosynthesis, and during the "day" Londoners simply light more candles under the phosphorescent artificial stars of the cavern roof. Seasons do not exist, yet it occasionally snows, gentle rains aren't unheard of, and sometimes the weather does become hotter and suspiciously more humid. Oh, and although not strictly a meteorological phenomenon, stalactites do fall daily—handily into the Stolen River for the most part. Formerly known as the Thames, the city's river now passes through neighboring Hell, effectively connecting the realms and making devils populous enough to maintain an embassy. The dream realm of Parabola is quite accessible too, as is the surface world, although most of the city's contacts lie within the wider Neath. From the lawless islands of its now drowned southern suburbs and its colony on the Elder Continent, to the nations of the Unterzee, the Bazaar tries to know all, and its agents reach far beyond London. It keeps in touch with the Khanate of the Fourth City's descendants, the Tomb-Colonies of the semi-dead, the devil-ruled Iron Republic, and, crucially, Polythreme, where objects become sentient and Clay Men are created to be used as cheap labor.

Looking below Fallen London, one would discover hints of the previous cities in a labyrinth thousands of years old, but also the hatcheries of the Rubbery Men and the tangled mazes of the Clay Quarters. Deeper still, below the phosphorescent slugs, lie the gigantic sleeping beasts drugged to prevent their cataclysmic awakening, and slightly above those the Masters of the Bazaar's summer homes. Speaking of Masters, it is Mr. Veils, Mr. Spices, and the rest who curate the surprisingly sentient Bazaar. Each one controls part of the city's economy; Mr. Apples, for instance, guides agriculture, Mr. Wines deals in entertainment, Mr. Fires rules industry, and Mr. Pages regulates the printed word (and taxes love stories). We don't quite know what the Masters are, but anything between angels and sentient fungal colonies sounds plausible. Besides, what actually matters is that trade and industry thrive, even if the occasional pauper joins the revolutionary ranks, or is forced to trade their soul.

One has to earn one's keep after all, and sometimes trading one's soul is preferable to becoming a zailor, and definitely much easier than having the Quizzical Auditor and the Office of Public Interests pay money for one's tales. Of course, mud larking, scavenging, rat-catching, working as a journalist or an archaeologist, and becoming a candlemaker are all valid options too, even if the way to affluence is paved with the trade of secrets and rumors. Alternatively, and as constables seem to be holding a grudge against the homeless anyway, the dangers of a criminal or artistic career shouldn't be ruled out.

Then again, danger is a very relative concept. Death in the Fifth City is merely an inconvenience. Get stabbed and someone will sew you back together; drown and a couple of days' rest will get you back on your feet; contract exotic diseases yet never face the hereafter—but know that once you die down here, you'll never be permitted on the surface again. Such a profound change in life's essence has led to mostly empty graveyards, and several quiet and unacknowledged revisions of certain passages in the city's bibles. Churches still hold services, bishops still exist, and the Empress is still the head of the Church of England, but theology had to become more flexible, and people are definitely more polite toward Hell. Many holidays and festivals remain too, with Christmas and Hallowmas in particular being very popular across the political spectrum.

Inspired by the endurance of such traditions, London's urban geography never changes dramatically. In fact, early Victorian, pre-Bazaar maps can still be surprisingly useful, even if declared contraband. The twisting streets of the old city were further bent into a labyrinth with the Bazaar at its heart when the city fell, and every mayor feels the need to move buildings around, but the changes aren't profoundly confusing. Thankfully, fine drinking and dining establishments are

always easy to discover. Dante's Grill serves an excellent deviled kidney, the Royal Bethlehem Hotel has at least one brilliant chef, Beatrice's Tea Parlour is still widely respected, the Medusa's Head is a perfect drinking hole for rat-catchers and spider-crushers to enjoy a pint, and the Singing Mandrake, famous for regulars such as the Sardonic Music-Hall Singer, is *the* place to be in Veilgarden despite competition from the area's honey-dens.

Of course detailing, let alone visiting, all of the metropolis's districts would be impossible, but a quick introductory tour would have to start from the imposing prison of New Newgate. Carved into the body of an immense stalactite, the prison is only accessible via dirigible, and only slightly more agreeable than Watchmaker's Hill. The latter, renowned for the blind men running its observatory, is a fungal wilderness by the river where the Department of Menace Eradication subcontracts adventurers to deal with things slithering out of Bugsby's Marsh. To its northeast, across the river, are the Wolfstack Docks where steamers dock, and where Mr. Fires keeps his office among warehouses, rowdy pubs, and dueling arenas.

Farther north, by the Mahogany Hall and between Doubt Street and Childcake Street, lies the old market of the Spite known for its twisty alleys, silk-weavers, pickpockets, and acidic fog. From there on, follow Doubt Street past Fiacre's Foot to reach Mrs. Plenty's lively carnival beside the Prickfinger Wastes, and witness the relaxation of polite society's rules. To skip society altogether, mount an expedition to explore the final remnant of the Fourth City, the Forgotten Quarter, on the other side of town. Its silent, un-mappable avenues are lined with ancient statues, and its crumbling buildings are alternatively empty or overflowing with snakes. On the north bank of the river, past Lusitania Row and surrounded by majestic gardens, is the Empress's Shuttered Palace, and close by, one finds Ladybones Road, with its surrounding narrow streets hiding the Moloch Street Underground Station leading to Hell, the spy-infested Clathermont's Tattoo Parlour, and the emblematic Hangman's Arch.

What most slumming enthusiasts actually miss, however, are the swaying ropes of the Flit, the rooftop kingdom above the city ruled by the incoherent king of thieves, home to beggars, urchins, revolutionaries, and the forgotten. For all its criminal squalor, and the constant danger of a slightly fatal plummet, it's actually very pretty up there. Gas lamps and candles twinkle below like lost stars, and you can see all the way to the black mass of the Unterzee, freely observe the city's predominantly human masses in their daily flow, and keep tabs on the exceptional characters making London truly delectable.

Enjoy your stay, delicious friend!

DESIGN INSIGHTS

Fallen London is a very rare beast. It is a sprawling, constantly evolving nineteenth-century metropolis made of over one million words, home to dozens of fleshed-out characters, and hundreds of fascinating stories. The writing on offer is frankly sublime, and the detail pored into the city staggering. If there's a single lesson for the aspiring designer of game cities, here it is: the power of the written word still holds. Additionally, text allows for an unprecedented amount of elements, situations, and locales to flesh out the city without requiring a triple-A budget, as the game embraces the flexibility and comparatively low cost of text to provide a well-rounded urban experience. Glimpses of almost every aspect of civic life from the humble to the flamboyant are offered. Politics, architecture, road layouts, bars, activities, and even the surreal but believable economy are described, while all sorts of little touches, such as the intricacies of scholarly life, imply that truly complex structures are in place.

Fallen London blends Lovecraftian monsters with romantic themes, the literary versatility of Poe, Penny Dreadful aesthetics, and a darkly hilarious wit to create an entirely original world that's familiar yet also utterly strange. The recognizable but bizarre setting is based on a brilliantly reshaped, stylized version of Victorian London that provides the new lore with a rich history and a concrete preexisting socioeconomic background. Adding devils and a few imaginary historical layers, and substituting the pound with the echo doesn't really change too much, but instead inspires an imaginative retelling of a cohesive history. Crucially the city's history is far from over. Being a living game's setting, as opposed to being a novel, Fallen London is a dynamic, evolving city that has been changing and expanding for over a decade. Each "storylet" and vignette simultaneously encompasses and enriches the metropolis, while each mayoral election helps players feel like an active part of it.

As for the game's visuals—the beautiful map, a select few evocative illustrations in a cohesively Victorian style, a simple interface with elegant elements, and a collection of tiny pieces of art— they are more than capable of supporting the atmosphere and defining the style of *Fallen London*. The avoidance of trite pop culture references, the importance of the townspeople in the grand scheme of things, and a masterful framing of the city between Zee, marshes, and sunken suburbs are also worth noting.

ANOR LONDO
Dark Souls

10

GENERAL INFORMATION /////////////////////

City: Anor Londo

Game: *Dark Souls*

Developer: FromSoftware

Publisher: BANDAI NAMCO Entertainment

Release Date: 2011

Genre: Action RPG, Horror

Platforms: Nintendo Switch, PlayStation 3, PlayStation 4, Windows, Xbox 360, Xbox One

In the beginning, there was no fire. No life, barring the immortal dragons among the Archtrees, until, suddenly, the First Flame came into the world. With it, four powerful Lord Souls came into existence, and were claimed by Gwyn, Gravelord Nito, the Witch of Izalith, and the Furtive Pygmy; the progenitor of humans. It was Gwyn who decided to go to war against the dragons, and Seath the Scaleless, a mortal dragon, who tipped its balance, joining the new Lords to usher in the Age of Fire. Following the defeat of the dragons, and the end of the Age of Ancients, the victors declared themselves gods, and decided that Anor Londo would be the glorious capital of their lands. A long prosperity followed, and humans flourished. Lord Gwyn ruled from his home in Anor Londo as centuries and millennia passed, but, over time, the First Flame began to fade. With it, the power of the Lords withered, darkness rose, and Gwyn sacrificed himself to prolong the Age of Fire. But, with the flame artificially rekindled, the undead curse emerged to plague, and corrupt, humanity. Demons now walk the world, and men and women are slowly dying or, worse, following an eternity of death and rebirth, turning Hollow: empty, insane, and violent. The balance of death and life has been disrupted, harmony shattered. The kingdom of Lordran, and the city of Anor Londo, withered and died.

Eons before its fall, the unreachable city of the gods had become legendary. Sitting atop the highest peak in Lordran, this city of giants was conquered by Lord Gwyn, who enslaved them and led them in constructing their greatest achievements. Rebuilt under its new leader, Anor Londo served as his throne. Gwyn was surrounded by the other gods, and his army of Silver Knights ruled the greatest city in the world, and the most powerful kingdom. Conceived by brilliant human minds, and constructed by the incomparable strength of the giants, Anor Londo was the manifestation of a single god's will, and destined to serve as his tomb after his sacrifice. But Gwyn's doom did not save Anor Londo, and the resident deities have long forsaken the cursed city, with the exception of Gwyn's youngest offspring: Gwyndolin.

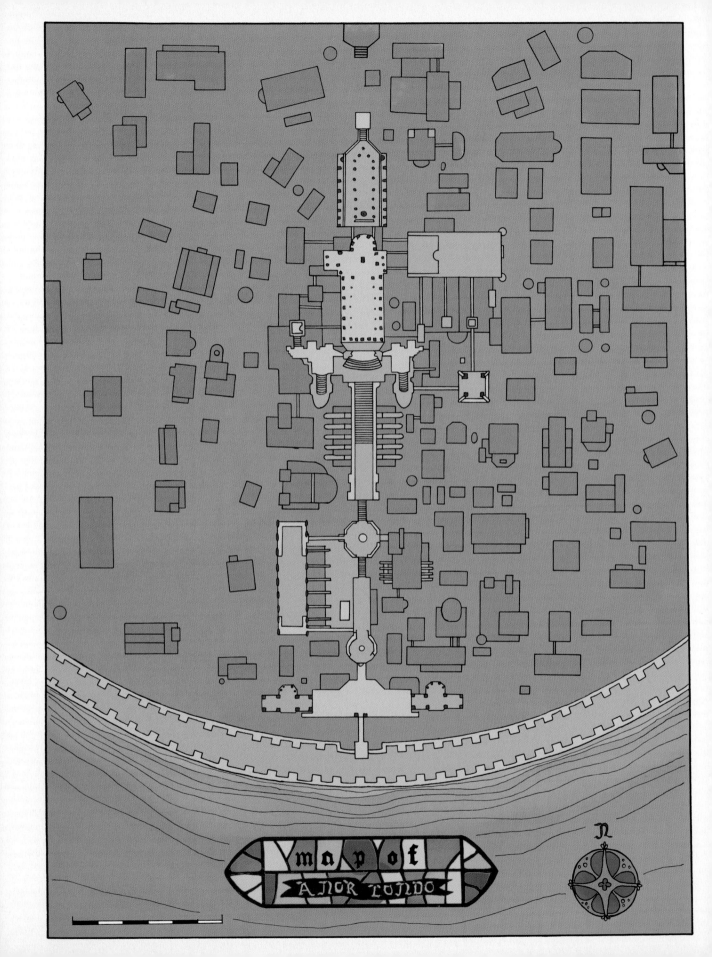

map of
A NOR LONDO

Anor Londo is lost and bereft of all life, but if any hope may be allowed back into the world, the Chosen Undead must walk upon its deserted stone paths. Locked away in the Asylum of the far North among the Hollow to await the end of the world, the Chosen Undead will, if legends are to be trusted, escape the eternal prison and attempt an impossible pilgrimage. Tasked by Kingseeker Frampt, the primordial serpent, with retrieving the Lordvessel from Gwynevere, Princess of Sunlight and last remaining deity in Anor Londo, the Chosen will have to reach Anor Londo. To do so, she or he will brave Sen's Fortress, survive the Iron Golem, and discover the fate of the Undead by ringing the Bell of Awakening. Obstacles will be overcome and impossible walls scaled if the city is to be reached, and a new Great Lord crowned.

Up the side of a sheer cliff face, secure in the steep, fortified mountains overlooked by the Duke's Archives, and shielded by massive walls, lies the radiant, desolate city of Anor Londo. The full awe of its splendor is evident from the first glimpse. Surrounded by a bleak world starved of warmth and light, its beauty, radiance, and perpetually setting sun are said to profoundly aston-ish. Illuminated ornate structures of white stone and gorgeous architecture stand as a testament to Anor Londo's enduring glory. An arresting vision of an almost forgotten world survives among intricate bas-reliefs, large plazas, mechanical spiral staircases, imposing towers, and beautifully grotesque statues, even if any sense of tranquillity is deceiving. This place looks as heavenly as it is deadly. Sunlight flooding over the city's ocean of cathedral spires is an almost unbelievable sight, as the superficially serene city does not lie in ruin. Angelic beauty goes hand in hand with

Dominated by the Grand Cathedral, the eternal Anor Londo is a mesmerizing city

Intricate staircases connect the city's levels

the demonic fiends walking between elegant castles, and even infesting the city's great axis: a majestic bridge towering over residences and cathedrals alike, and leading to the Grand Cathedral.

Climbing the steep steps that lead to this ancient, foreboding edifice, one is struck by its sheer power. A complex Gothic structure, a massive basilica veiled under thousands of spires and statues, the Grand Cathedral is dramatic in its ornamentation, and mesmerizing in its presence. Still standing proudly in the very center of Anor Londo, this was once Lord Gwyn's castle, and its stunning rose window, strong walls, and flying buttresses took centuries to complete. Flanked by an ornate temple hosting the statue of Gwynevere, and an incredibly large painting made by Ariamis, the detailed behemoth defines local architecture. Anor Londo's buildings share its cream-colored exteriors, exquisite carvings, and strong Gothic elements. They form a stunning forest of buttresses: an intricate pattern of nooks and crannies with secrets hiding in ribbed vaults and under pointed arches. Huge armed statues guard abandoned terraces, marble galleries, and holy chambers, while ancient elevators connect chapels, courtyards, and balconies.

But as the Chosen Undead is bound to discover, neither artisans nor peaceful citizens live here anymore. Where humans once toiled and created, gigantic sentinels now patrol. The current denizens of the city—gargoyles, mimics, demons, and cursed knights guarding dead gods—pale before

Dragon Slayer Ornstein and Executioner Smough, who bar the way to Gwynevere's throne room. A handful of non-hostile characters such as a forgotten giant blacksmith cannot guarantee the Chosen's safety. Nothing can be truly known about Anor Londo these days. It is the capital of lies—a trap of alluring beauty, where mercy could never reside. Only an unflinching, uncaring test of merit awaits all who enter this eternal testament to the hubris of the gods. In this age of nihilism, even sunlight itself cannot be trusted.

DESIGN INSIGHTS

Dark Souls is rightly counted among the best games ever made, and the city of Anor Londo may be the exact point where it shows off its brightest colors, most exuberant architecture, most deceptive illusion, and most demanding boss battle. Excellently designed, the level, inspired by the city it takes place in, is an elaborate set that encompasses all that makes *Dark Souls* unique—a brutal challenge set in an almost optimistic environment, starkly contrasting the previous dark, depressing areas. The full majesty of the city's wonder is thrust upon players, and initially feels like an intimidating, impressive, mysterious reward following the bleakness of Sen's Fortress.

Dark Souls' darkly atmospheric world feels coherent and believable, as does Anor Londo, and one of the reasons for this is the many roots it has in the real world. Besides drawing inspiration from the common spiritual iconography of demons, and liturgical chanting, the Grand Cathedral in particular was directly inspired by the stunning Duomo di Milano. Its innumerable spires grab attention, and make it instantly obvious that this will be the level's ultimate destination. The rest of the disturbingly convincing city, despite not being open for exploration, has been built to scale, and beautifully bathed in sunlight. With the minimalist plot of *Dark Souls*, it is up to the environment to truly tell the world's story, but never explicitly. FromSoftware has been consistently more concerned with theming, and its lore of fallen gods was centered on Anor Londo, where everything is too large, too intricate, and too beautiful.

The introduction to the city is also breathtaking. Soaring up the side of a cliff, and over Anor Londo's battlement, the cut scene introducing it is both staggering and successful in showing off the city's size and glorious complexity. Wisely, players get to experience the beautiful architecture first hand, as the castles of Anor Londo require balancing across precariously thin walkways while avoiding arrow bolts. A medieval, armored version of parkour over narrow buttresses, roofs, and ledges can be experienced through a magnificent, uninviting place, where the environment constantly reminds of how threatening an entity the city is. Even its sunlight is false, and if players disbelieve and kill "Gwynevere," Anor Londo will sink back into darkness.

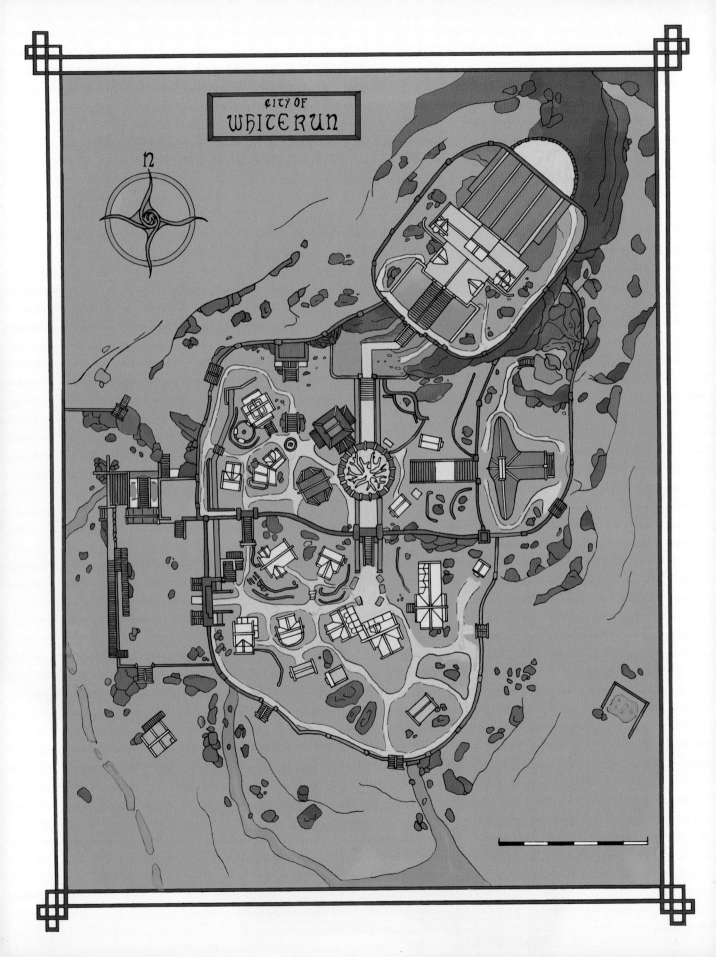

11

WHITERUN
The Elder Scrolls V: Skyrim

GENERAL INFORMATION ///////////////////////

City: Whiterun

Game: *The Elder Scrolls V: Skyrim*

Developer: Bethesda Game Studios

Publisher: Bethesda Softworks

Release Date: 2011

Genre: RPG

Platforms: Nintendo Switch, PlayStation 3, PlayStation 4, Windows, Xbox 360, Xbox One

Whiterun, *Ahrol-Se-Dovah* in the language of dragons, is the capital city of Whiterun Hold, the greatest of all nine Skyrim Holds. Sitting proudly at the center of the northernmost imperial province, this is the ancient seat of the Nords, where the proud race still live their simple, harsh lives rooted in tradition. The deeply religious men and women of Whiterun take up arms when duty dictates, and live communally in what Mikael the bard described as the Jewel of the North, surrounded by windy, freezing tundra plains, snow-capped mountain ranges, deep valleys, and dark forests.

The climate and heavy snowfall profoundly influenced the quintessentially Nord architecture of Whiterun. Steep, lavishly decorated, hand-carved, and often tiled roofs keep the snow away, while constantly burning hearths at the center of each building keep people warm. Most houses are made of wood, a few wealthier ones of stone, and each building is distinctive in its layout, size, and decoration. The consistent architectural style across classes, featuring ornate entrances, carved pillars, and narrow windows, gives the city a unified, cohesive look, with the legacy of the ancestral longhouse evident in buildings housing extended families—most impressively in the ancient Jorrvaskr.

Jorrvaskr, the honored mead hall of the Companions, is the oldest building in town, and its underground communal living quarters the largest. Built by Jeek of the River, the captain of the longboat *Jorrvaskr*, and his twenty-two men upon discovery of the Skyforge, the construction was based on the ship crafted for the Return of the Five Hundred Companions of Ysgramor, and has existed alone in the mountains since long before the first town was built around it. The Skyforge itself, a great ancient forge said to be older than the Elves, was feared for eons as a relic of the gods. It is shaped as an eagle with its majestic wings spread out and its eyes looking at the rune-covered anvil.

View from the Winds District

Jorrvaskr: the mead hall of the Companions

Although less ancient, it is the towering fortress of Dragonsreach that has always sat at the center of Whiterun. The great castle at the top of the hill was built following the war with the Snow Elves, the Night of Tears, and the sacking of Skyrim's first human capital. The city has roots going back to the First Era, when, as legend has it, King Olaf One-Eye bested the fearsome dragon Numinex in the duel of Thu'um, and brought the worship of dragons to an end, cutting all ties with the old roots across the Sea of Ghosts and declaring the Nord a new people. Dragonsreach was rebuilt to hold Numinex captive, and the beast's gigantic skull still adorns its great hall. Nothing is eternal, however, and Whiterun, once considered equal to the Imperial City, has, in recent times, suffered and diminished. The raging civil war, excessively harsh winters, raids, dynastic feuds, and attacks of frost trolls have all taken their toll.

Just as Whiterun retained the feel of a Nord village during its peak, it still holds on to the spectacle and organization of a true capital. Impressively occupying the three plateaus of its proud hill, and protected by its still formidable walls, the city is unique in its verticality. Dragonsreach takes up the highest plateau, the Cloud District, below which continues the almost exclusively residential Wind District, followed by the lively and commercial Plains District at the bottom. Outside the keep, people stay in detached houses, walk on paved roads, and live among fine statues, standing stones, and braziers that are always lit. Flowing from the top and forming waterfalls, canals, and serene pools, water adds much to Whiterun's character, whereas the city's hinterland adds more to its economy. Outside the walls, Whiterun Stables, the largest in all of Skyrim, as well as farms and hunting grounds, provide for the city's residents.

The Plains District contains all major shops and several residences. Its gate is Whiterun's sole point of entry, and the road crossing through it leads to the marketplace around the well, and then through the rest of the city all the way to the castle. The stalls of the marketplace sell everything from fruits and meat to books and jewelry, and are harmoniously co-existing with Arcadia's Cauldron alchemy shop, the Bannered Mare tavern and inn, friendly Wood Elves selling general goods, and the equally Elven Drunken Huntsman, catering to the needs of hunters with bows, arrows, and fine drinks.

The Winds District, Whiterun's ornate, mostly residential area, is home to the Jorrvaskr mead hall, and was named after the mountain winds gusting through it. Living there is not a designation of class, as the home of poor, elderly seer Olava the Feeble is right next to the wealthy and ancient household of famed clan Battle-Born, and actually closer to the center of the city's spiritual life: the majestic, slowly dying, holy Gildergreen tree. The sacred tree of Kynareth, the oldest living thing in Skyrim, overlooks the spacious Temple of Kynareth and is surrounded by running water. The house of the prophet of Talos, a secret temple for a forbidden god, is nearby, as is the funerary Hall of the Dead. Whiterun's mausoleum provides a home to a priest and a shrine to the god Arkay, and rests above catacombs buried deep in the mountain, hosting generations untold of Nord dead, as well as the occasional undead. Thankfully, those buried in the graveyard outside the Hall do rest peacefully.

Ascending toward the keep and the Cloud District, one passes by the stunning waterfalls before arriving at the imposing Dragonsreach. Past the gothic archway, and showcasing how little separates Nord nobility and common folk, lies the always welcoming entrance to the political heart of the city. In the awe-inspiring great hall of Dragonsreach, the Jarl holds court among intricately carved columns and elegant arches. The Jarl family quarters and suites for other residents are in the stone-built rear of the keep, where Numinex was held captive. Inspired by the logic of the long-houses of old, Dragonsreach also includes a blacksmith, a wizard's laboratory, servants' quarters, kitchens, barracks for the city guard, and a jail underneath it. As for the old dragon cell, it offers majestic views of the still lively city.

Despite the harsh climate and the interesting times Whiterun has found itself in, its energetic economy and life endure. The town's central location in Skyrim makes it the province's major commercial hub and a waypoint for caravans, providing protection against giants, brigands, and gigantic brigands. Being a hub has also enriched Whiterun's population with Wood Elves, Dark Elves, Imperials, and even Redguards, but has placed it in the middle of a human civil war between Imperial Legion loyalists and Stormcloak rebels. Jarl Balgruuf may be trying to maintain the city's neutrality, but as war approaches and dragons have awoken, the city's fortifications will soon have to be restored to their former glory—if only to enforce said neutrality.

DESIGN INSIGHTS

Whiterun, being the definitive Nord city of the Elder Scrolls world, succeeds in creating a convincing, cohesive, and evocative architectural style. It wears its Rohirrim and Viking inspirations proudly, and implements them masterfully. Decorations, materials, roofs, tiny windows, the centrality of the hearth, and the dialectics of stone and wood help craft a built environment reminiscent of genuine historical places. What's more, the city manages to look recognizable and impressive from all angles, but best from the angle the vast majority of players will approach it from. Its hill, castle, and walls provide it with a very distinct silhouette.

Being sensibly organized, and not having missed anything glaring, Whiterun also gets the feeling of a small, living, breathing town right. It thoughtfully provides with all the necessary urban functions. Religion, economy, residence, politics, death, transportation, and access to goods, food, and water are all taken into account, while even the hinterland's functions haven't been ignored. Seeing a fantasy city spill outside its walls is, sadly, still a rarity in video gaming.

There's also an implied history in Whiterun's architecture, with wood and stone emphasizing the contrast between newer and older constructions, whereas the foundations of collapsed buildings outside the city fit the in-game lore of the civic and regional decline. Parts of town lie empty and parts of the defensive walls have not been rebuilt, yet still the ancient grandeur is evident. Enemies would have to break through three gates, overcome successive fortifications and bridge moats, and survive winding pathways exposing them to the city's defense towers in order to storm it. And thankfully, players get to actually test these evidently well-researched, historically accurate medieval fortifications, either as defenders or attackers.

Details aside, the only thing that would improve Whiterun would be a larger size—probably unfeasible for such an already huge game—and a few more inhabitants. Whiterun's imaginary society feels a bit too complex and its role a tad too significant for its modest scale. Sadly, not all technological and cost constraints can be overcome with clever writing and planning, although even a few abandoned houses instead of empty spaces within the walls would have worked wonders. Finally, worth mentioning is the wise choice of making all major buildings bigger on the inside in order to conjure impressive architectural sizes without eating up too much precious real estate.

Left: The Great Hall of Dragonsreach

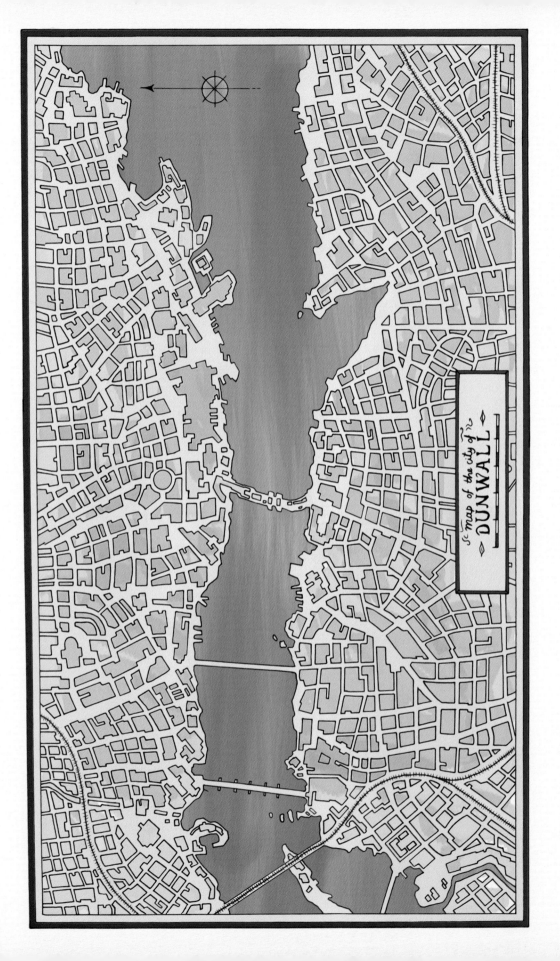

12

DUNWALL
Dishonored

City: Dunwall

Game: *Dishonored*

Developer: Arkane Studios

Publisher: Bethesda Softworks

Release Date: 2012

Genre: Immersive Sim, Stealth

Platforms: Windows, PlayStation 3, PlayStation 4, Xbox 360, Xbox One

Walking through claustrophobic alleys, breathing in smog, and passing by barely standing homes, one could have trouble recognizing Dunwall for the imperial capital it is. The city has admittedly seen better days, but there is still beauty here. Especially during dark nights, when the chimneys belching out smoke stay hidden, Dunwall looks magnificent with its countless lit windows, angular roofs, and spires mirrored in the wide river. A thousand years ago, a forgotten town lay at the spot where today the capital of Gristol and the Empire of the Isles dominates the Wrenhaven River. A modern whaling city of wonders built upon the remnants and vestiges of what had come before, it somehow retains its archaic atmosphere despite crass technologies and the ruckus of 200,000 souls.

Dunwall has ruled the empire for over two centuries, but now the empress lies dead, assassinated at the hands of her Lord Protector, and the princess is missing. Awaiting the murderer's beheading, and the rescue of the heiress, the Lord Regent and the High Overseer are governing the city and filling Coldridge Prison with their enemies. Corrupt politicians struggle for power. Maneuvers in the Gristol Parliament go hand in hand with violent plots, and the muted masses powerlessly despair. Dealing with a lethal, unprecedented rat plague is what truly troubles the great city, however, and what has led to general upheaval and widespread chaos despite the recent militarization of everyday life. Quarantines and martial law have been aggressively enforced by the Lord Regent to fight the disease depopulating whole neighborhoods and filling the sewers with mindless weepers.

Hellish scenes are played out daily as the plague ravages every corner of the city, slowly overcoming class barriers, and, as the rest of the Isles fear, maybe even the seas of the imperial archipelago. A naval blockade has effectively quarantined Dunwall, cutting off its increasingly sick and virulent population from hope, while the bandage-wrapped carcasses of plague victims are thrown in the sea or simply left for the rats to devour. The elixirs needed to protect the general populace are too costly for most, and with the oldest strains of the plague discovered in the slums,

Sunset at the industrialized river bank

A view of the affluent Estate District

many have wondered whether this isn't God's wrath at all, but some sort of perverted eugenics or population-control scheme.

Dunwall is, after all, notorious for its extreme class divisions, cynicism, and xenophobia. Such deeply embedded notions have survived the stench of death, as life attempts to simply carry on. Loudspeakers still broadcast propaganda, and there's money to be made by killing rats. Streets remain lively and dangerous, although poster advertisements tend to focus more on remedies or extravagant ephemeral entertainments such as those offered by the Golden Cat's sensual hostesses. Graffiti has taken a turn toward the more apocalyptic, and gang activity has gone rampant, yet urchins keep on jumping between roofs in the night fog, ignoring the deadly "walls of light" the City Watch has installed to control flows. The upper classes, on the other hand, hoard elixirs, enjoy extravagant masked balls, play political games, and sink ever deeper into intoxicating debauchery.

Surrounded by the finest architectural delights of Dunwall, they have elected to ignore all danger and stay hidden in heavily guarded manors, lush apartments and estates of marble staircases, and meticulously landscaped gardens. The more cunning prefer armored, modern residences covered in metal that try to blend in with rows of stone and brick buildings. The angular rooftops, narrow facades, and characteristic chimneys are common throughout Dunwall, contrasting the austere, imposing brutalism of state buildings, the functionalism of industry, and the art nouveau domes of establishments such as the Golden Cat bathhouse. Even in the poorest quarters, among collapsed masonry and sheets of corrugated iron, the functional innards of town are usually evident for all to see in the form of pipes running between buildings. Dunwall's City Planning Department keeps them functional, but also historically perpetuates class contrasts by zoning massive factories in densely packed workers' districts, and by ensuring the wealthy continue living on the secluded, well-lit, airy positions of the city's numerous cliffs.

The Wrenhaven River, the main thoroughfare for whaling and commercial ships, bisects the town and meets the sea to the west, past the fortified Kingsparrow Island and its monumental lighthouse. The harbor spreads along each shore of the Wrenhaven with numerous docks serving riverside districts, and tall bridges allowing the passage

The whale oil industry can be particularly cruel

of large vessels inland. This watery linear center divides the city into a wealthier north and a poorer south. The imperial seat of the Dunwall Tower, and the Estate District, home to the aristocracy and the majestic Clocktower, define the northern shore, whereas the slums of the Distillery District and the Slaughterhouse Row's smell of blood define the southern. Other districts include the Drapers Ward, the aptly named Civil Services District, the Rust District and its Berrington Ironworks, suburban communities such as Mutcherhaven, and the now-flooded Rudshore Financial District, where plague victims, dead or alive, are being dumped amidst cultists and feral wolfhounds.

Many practitioners of the occult gather around Wyrmwood Way as well, where, despite the occasional raid, charms and runes can be traded. The High Overseer of the Abbey of the Everyman, the leader of the ecclesiarchy, has been uncompromising in his enforcement of the Seven Strictures, and the religious police have been fanatically torturing and branding supposed heretics and hunting down the cultists of the Outsider. Worshipping the Outsider is considered anathema, but the shrines and scribblings dedicated to Him betray a widespread desperate hope for an interventionist god. Unlike the Abbey's assertions, He has proven His existence and chaotic power. This unique being of the Void, whose name is spoken as a curse and blessing both, was born a man over 4,000 years ago and absorbed in the Void; His mischievous influence has been felt through history ever since. Many attribute all magic to Him, or at least to the all-consuming Void.

Even the learned professors of the Academy of Natural Philosophy acknowledge and study the ruinous supernatural powers of the Outsider and the Void, occasionally experimenting with the mathematical beauty of melody against their creeping chaos. But for all its advanced technologies, metaphysical anxieties and knowledge, the Academy too remains indifferent to the plight of the many, and actually adds to an increasingly sophisticated arsenal of oppression tools, including energy bullets, arc pylons, and blinding searchlights. Deadliest of all is the heavily armored, almost insectoid tallboy, which fires explosive arrows and walks above terrified crowds on its motorized stilts.

Dunwall's entire technological infrastructure and economy are based on two pillars: the exploitation of workers providing the profits, and the whaling industry providing the required whale oil to power machines, utilities, and residences. It is crude electricity that brings lighting and heating, enables audiographs, powers production, and allows for the transportation of goods and people via trains, railcars, and, should the need arise, armored vehicles. And it is the hulking whaling trawler that provides the source for this energizing oil—whales whose slaughter is not merely industrialized but beyond brutal. These majestic, intelligent, gentle creatures have their fat sliced from them while still alive, invoking, according to most spiritualists, the fury of the Outsider himself.

DESIGN INSIGHTS

It may be fictional, but Dunwall is a city that could exist. It is a historical place functioning independently of players. Born centuries ago, recently reshaped by an industrial revolution, fearful of its prehistory, and ravaged by a rat plague, Dunwall is more than a background connecting levels. It is a convincing, cohesive, and occasionally stunning illusion, consisting of detailed urban environments and architecture. A virtual city that does not exist in a vacuum, but as part of an empire in a much wider imagined world.

The beautifully realized, stylized art adds a tone of storybook unreality to the proceedings, and provides a strong graphical identity while avoiding the structural demands of a photorealistic world. Dunwall's oranges, browns, and blues paint a uniquely vibrant yet decaying and often austere reality, circumventing steampunk clichés.

Based primarily on Edinburgh and London, the city implements elements of both and follows their blend of historical buildings with contemporary constructions. Interestingly, its inspirations move beyond well-known landmarks and all the way to researched history, class divisions, back-alley aesthetics, weather, and sky colors. Tweaked by an obviously talented team, the result feels delightfully odd, yet familiar and grounded in reality, as the layers of history and technology, plus a very distinct economy at the heart of everything, produce a uniquely built environment. Architecture and planning mutate around whale oil technology, while real-life references provide a recognizable atmosphere and a scale we are familiar with. London's smokestacks and rooftops have been adjusted to a wholly original electro/steampunk world where almost-modern technology has been married to a strong Victorian-era aesthetic.

By not being an open world, *Dishonored* affords the meticulous design of its relatively small areas, filling them with often unexpected details and letting them tell the story of the world via their environments. The size of the city is mainly implied by way of majestic views, maps, and, of course, the cunning use of dialogue, whereas using the river to travel between places connects them all in an immersive whole. A dynamic whole, too, as Dunwall responds to how players treat it. Wanton murder, for example, will lead to more rats and zombie-like weepers, whereas a stealthier approach will intrigue the general population.

This is also a city fit for supernatural assassins, enabling and supporting different styles and speeds of play. Every area allows for many spatially sensible routes over roofs and ledges, or via tunnels, sewers, and intricate pipe networks. Every element of the setting seems functional and ready to serve the preferred style of play, while the plot tours players through Dunwall's defining rich, destitute, industrial, derelict, and militarized districts.

YHARNAM

13

Bloodborne

GENERAL INFORMATION ////////////////////

City: Yharnam

Game: *Bloodborne*

Developer: FromSoftware

Publisher: Sony Computer Entertainment

Release Date: 2015

Genre: Action RPG, Horror

Platforms: PlayStation 4

Over the years, many a valiant scholar or desperate parent ignored all warnings and ventured to shadow-soaked, secluded Yharnam, never to be seen again. Located deep in the strange eastern valleys by Moonside Lake, Yharnam is said to be cursed—a curse that erodes one's reason and turns men into feral beasts. Named after mourning Yharnam, the Pthumerian Queen, esoteric, forbidden texts and half-mad rogues alike warn of a town of degenerate heretics, a city of blasphemous, scandalous secrets enraptured by its excesses and overfed on ungodly ambition. The city is a temptation for the naive, offering naught but death and insanity; a terrifying presence reaching up to the skies willing to bury all that is righteous under its vain arrogance.

Alas, neither the stigma of heresy nor eldritch terrors can dissuade the hopelessly sick from seeking Yharnam's mythical blood cures. The clergy of the renowned Healing Church are said to employ ancient medical practices able to cure all afflictions and realize the most miraculous revivals. Rumors neither of communion with the unspeakable Great Ones nor of horrific experiments matter when the Church's blood ministrations bring vigor to all who accept them, and often grace them with godly visions. This Communion—a mysterious, euphoric blood concoction—has granted exceptional longevity to all Yharnamites and, in the process, attracted legions of addicted worshippers to the Church. Oblivious, doomed worshippers fated to face horrors worse than death itself.

Whispers of the terrible disease that has gripped Yharnam are growing stronger. Travelers claim that chained coffins now line its streets, and that the infected are mad with bloodlust. Plague is ravaging all, as an endemic affliction known only as the Scourge of the Beast is turning Yharnam's inhabitants into repulsive, murderous monsters. As wise sages warned, prolonged exposure to the healing bloods goes against human nature; it corrupts fundamentally, offering transcendence only via complete, unholy mutation. Twisted humans, werewolves, and sinuous skeletal beasts finally roam the streets, howling their chilling cries as hideous, lame carrion crows feast upon countless corpses, and legless, writhing bodies attack their still-human offspring. Unspeakable horrors have

The spires of Yharnam

been unleashed, it is known, but at least every night the cursed yet honorable hunters are seen rising up to cleanse evil and revel in the bloodshed.

Torch-bearing Yharnamites in torn garments—and even wheelchairs—help with these hunts. People with bandaged eyes—devout worshippers of the Old Blood—band together to roam the foggy alleys, ecstatically purging heretics, beasts, and interlopers alike. The souls unfortunate enough to be captured meet gruesome ends at the stake or the cross. But never forget! The barely human monstrosities hanging maimed and half-burned on bloodied walls were once men, women, and children who turned to Yharnam in their greatest, most desperate need. Their screams and their burning, rotting flesh were once human, just like the few remaining civilians that are not out for blood, and who are instead hiding behind locked doors and curtained, barricaded windows.

The blood-drenched city of metal and stone, now all but ruined, finally resembles the wild architectural fever-dream it always aspired to become. Its spindly cathedrals and aesthetic obsessions openly echo cosmic communions, whereas the chaotic arrangements of sharp roofs and impure religious imagery have long sacrificed order to strive for the sublime. Throughout history, Yharnam was imposing but bleak, sprawling but intensely vertical, haunted yet disarmingly beautiful. Now innumerable spires are piled on buttresses, arches, and great bridges, and its Gothic majesty

Abandoned Old Yharnam

is said to tower above mortals, a presence engulfing, oppressing, and threatening with ever-ascending slender castles and ominous bell towers. Even now, it must be awe-inspiring to look upon the edifices and ornate gables suffocating the skyline, and to appreciate the exquisitely grotesque craftsmanship evident on rich facades, detailed gargoyles, and disturbing etchings.

The oldest part of town, Old Yharnam, was the first to be ravaged by what historians have called the plague of Ashen Blood. It was eventually abandoned and put to the torch, leaving little more than burnt-out, forsaken ruins none dare visit; the howls of the beasts inhabiting the old town are a mournful reminder of ancient sins and the terrors awaiting the once affluent Central Yharnam. There, in the barely beating heart of the city, tiny pockets of sanity cling on to a precarious existence in a labyrinth of twisting roads and majestic bridges. In Central Yharnam, massive churches still stand proud, Iosefka's blood clinic still administers cures, and the Tomb of Oedon still manages to fill hearts with dread. Eastward, provided cardinal points retain their meaning in such a region, lies the gated Cathedral Ward, home of the Healing Church and the splendor of the Grand Cathedral, where rumor has it an obscene bestial skull lies on its only altar.

The dank, cobblestone, canyon-like streets of the city, lit feebly by lanterns and candles, eventually lead past flooded quarters and through foggy courtyards to the dreaded Hemwick Charnel Lane, and from there to Hemwick Graveyard and outside Yharnam. The dangerous town environs, infamous for hiding rituals dedicated to unknowable gods for centuries, are also believed to be home to a deep, foreboding forest hiding a village of Yharnam's outcasts—a village other than Yahar'gul, whose entire population is dead and where corpses are said to have been melded in the walls. Farther out, the once noble Cainhurst Castle has collapsed into a frozen-over ruin, its deserted regal silhouette still beautiful against the dark waters.

We can never know why Cainhurst Castle was abandoned, just as we can only hope to learn but a fragment of Yharnam's mysteries. We must accept that this hellish place will curse all who lay eyes upon it, for it is a manifestation of Hell itself where reality, dreams, delusions, and nightmares fuse. We must see its healing promises for the destructive temptations they are. Even its very own, once-famed Byrgenwerth College openly admitted that utterly alien, impossibly ancient ruins were discovered below Yharnam. Its scholars described them as tombs of the gods and curses of the Pthumerians. The Daughter of the Cosmos, false prophecies of life eternal, and warnings of celestial beasts shredding the fabric of reality were also mentioned. I implore you all, no matter how hopeless, to never set foot in the dreaded city.

DESIGN INSIGHTS

Bloodborne's eclectic and masterfully combined inspirations provided Yharnam with a strong foundation to build its unsettling world on. Lovecraft's cosmic horror, the romanticism of Bram Stoker, Gothic and Victorian architectural and planning notions, preindustrial European aesthetics, High Renaissance Mannerism, and obvious surrealist influences crafted a sublime, singular world for the dark fantasy city of Yharnam to inhabit. Real-life inspirations were thankfully always subtle and never directly referenced—the exception of a religious terminology of choirs, clerics, and churches was present to underline a parallel with recognizable institutions. Narrative, after all, was deeply embedded within the imaginary geography of Yharnam; a town built on horror, and apparently directed by an almost familiar but definitely alien spatial logic. Spires upon spires upon spires don't make practical sense, but definitely feel geomantic in purpose and thoroughly inhospitable.

Yharnam is essentially an open world where storytelling is sparse and atmosphere lush. Its modest size allows constant subtle changes, alternative perspectives, an incredible level of detail, and well-thought-out shortcuts. Besides, this decrepit Gothic city is more than a mere battleground. It allows interactions with strange non-player characters, extensive exploration, and an almost archaeological piecing together of the plot. Every aspect of the game—characters, items, weapons, locations—tells the story of this place. Players must make inferences and rely on their own interpretation to figure it out. Interestingly, the world the game presents them with evolves as they experience it—the higher a player's "insight" level, the clearer they will perceive the eldritch reality superimposed on a city essentially existing in parallel universes.

The surroundings are appropriately alive, reacting, and constantly aware of player presence; always unpleasant, never safe. Even the non-bestial characters add to the atmosphere, whispering from their boarded-up homes, coughing in dark corners, and being puzzles unto themselves. Save them, befriend them, heed their increasingly ominous dark mutterings behind closed doors or endure their accusatory screams. If *Bloodborne*'s beauty is in its world, its horror lies within its inhabitants. Diseased mobs patrol the city in convincing ways instead of merely spawning, monsters haunt appropriate locations, and even inexplicable patterns seem to be locked into some sort of ritual.

The stellar execution, excellent cinematography, striking visual consistency, and a soundtrack requiring a full orchestra and a thirty-two-member choir obviously helped to bring Yharnam to glorious life. Its visuals were rendered in extraordinary detail, and their romantic imagery remains unparalleled in triple-A gaming. Yharnam is packed with repellent majesty. It is a place that disapproves of player meddling, and yet constantly tries to lure players in. A shining, regal locale-turned-charnel house allows them to witness something grander than themselves in a degraded state: to experience the vertigo of the sublime in its civic form.

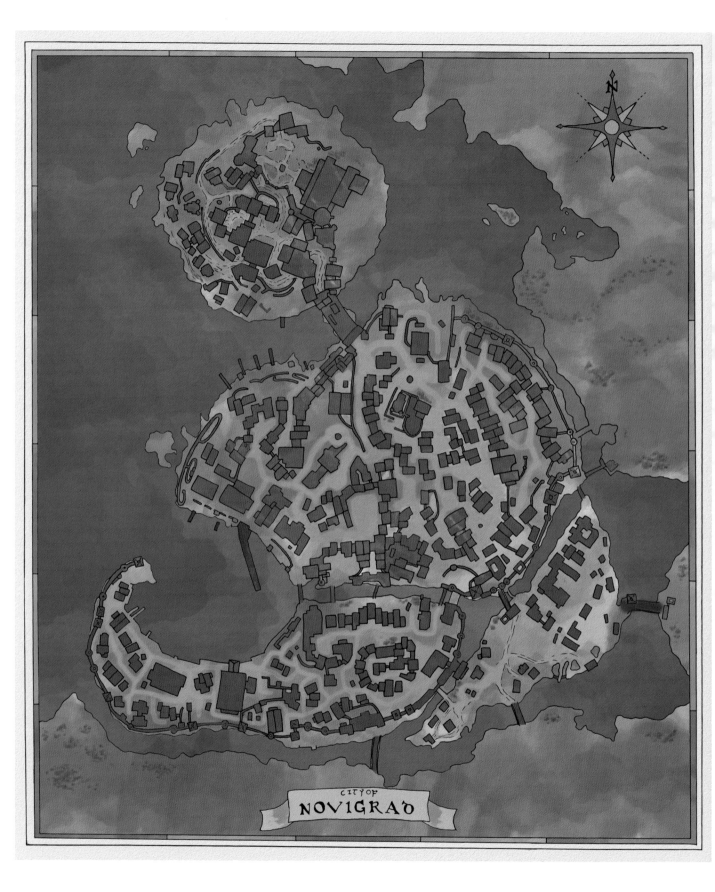

CITY OF
NOVIGRAD

14

NOVIGRAD
The Witcher 3: Wild Hunt

GENERAL INFORMATION /////////////////////

City: Novigrad

Game: *The Witcher 3: Wild Hunt*

Developer: CD Projekt Red

Publisher: CD Projekt

Release Date: 2015

Genre: Action RPG

Platforms: Nintendo Switch, PlayStation 4, Windows, Xbox One

The Free City of Novigrad may not be an imperial capital, but it most definitely shines brighter than any other city. With a staggering population of nearly 30,000 souls, Novigrad is the bustling heart of the North. Its eight banks, twelve brothels, nineteen temples, thirty-five inns, and four watermills, its countless stores, slaughterhouses, guilds, and manufactories have turned it into a powerful center of commerce. A place where all crafts and wares are available, and scholars and artists thrive under a wonderful skyline of red-tiled roofs and proud towers; a city where opulent buildings sit alongside mud-spattered, humble quarters in the shared safety of the town walls. Wraiths, giants, ghouls, griffins, and the spectral riders of the Wild Hunt could never hope to breach the massive fortifications constructed by the Oxenfurt Academy architects and be blessed by the holy flames of the Eternal Fire.

The town's characteristic red-tiled roofs

Built where the Pontar Delta meets the Great Sea, the hilly isles comprising Novigrad provide the natural canvas for its stunning cityscape. Water-bound trade passing through its harbor and a strategic location have nourished the city's tremendous economic and political power, making it a force both the kingdoms of the Northern Realms and the Nilfgaardian Empire must respect. It is in Novigrad where all goods traveling the great river are transferred from river barges to seafaring vessels, and vice versa.

Novigrad would be invaluable to any great nation. Its coin, weapons, mighty fleets, and control of the river would allow whoever controlled the Free City access to the keys of the North. Spies, criminal organizations, and trade guilds wage brutal but subtle wars here for power and influence. Conspiracy, assassination, blackmail, and bribery thrive within its walls as the city is beset by enemies, and the bloody conflict between Nilfgaard and Redania, already straining its resources, draws ever closer. With Novigrad's freedom threatened, moods are on edge. The city has no standing army but for the ranks of the ever-present Temple Guard and the strong deterrent of the powerful Temple Fleet. However, the ruling hierarch can always hire scores of mercenaries to defend

Typical masquerade ball accessories include elegant masks

the town, and serve the increasingly fanatic Church of the Eternal Fire. Political turbulence has incited a wave of witch hunts, and allowed the Church to take advantage of prevalent fears to point out and purge the supposed guilty: elves, dwarves, and especially mages and sorceresses.

It is on Hierarch Square that heretics are burned. At the very core of Novigrad's central island, where noble houses are perfectly situated to enjoy the regular executions conducted by the witch hunters, it is here that the well-to-do mingle with the rabble under elegant residences—and the few abandoned houses once belonging to mages. Hierarch Square is a busy marketplace throbbing with life, and merchants, beggars, craftsmen, thieves, and aristocrats rub shoulders by Butcher's Yard theater and the ironically dwarf-owned Vivaldi Bank. Just off the square, the Kingfisher Inn is famous for beautiful bard Callonetta and her songs of romance, whereas the aptly named hub of the Fish Market lies to the southwest. The eastern section of central Novigrad, the Bits, is an overcrowded, pauperized district with rows of dilapidated houses leaning over narrow, muddy streets. Muggings are not uncommon at the Bits, although, among petty thugs and desperate beggars, one finds that flickers of humanity persist. Less poor or crowded but still struggling, Silverton lies to the central island's northwest, and is constantly packed with merchant stalls.

For the select few located north of Hierarch Square in Gildorf—the city's most affluent district—life is sweet. Literally elevated above the slums below, Gildorf is home to an elite of nobles, rich traders, ambassadors, and the high clergy, who enjoy stunning villas and large mansions and savor the vaulted marble interiors of Sigismund's Bathhouse or the hedonistic delights of the Passiflora brothel. There are no beggars or cutthroats here; only fine establishments protected by the Temple Guard, who also monitor access to Temple Isle through the arched St. Gregory's Bridge. Temple Isle, the religious heart of the city, holds an impregnable citadel and the Great Temple of the Eternal Fire. The stately marble tower, whose ever-burning flame can be seen from miles afar, is decorated with golden flames and protects the sarcophagus of Prophet Lebioda. Under the tower, the faithful pray, and priests deliver sermons among the merchants of Electors' Square.

Industry and commerce thrive in the specialized southern areas of town, and the southernmost of its three islands. Harborside, the busiest harbor of the continent, serves ships from all shores of the Great Sea, bringing in tons of goods. There are no residences among the docks, warehouses, rowdy taverns, and rowdier seagulls in this district of stone piers, transport canals, cranes, and ships of all sizes. Sailors, merchants, and dockhands work under a forest of masts, ignore the stench of fish, and often find themselves in adjacent Glory Lane. A major workshop and manufactory area, Glory Lane is notorious for Lacehalls, where affordable love and abundant wine hide the Putrid Grove from the eyes of the witch hunters and provide a haven for the persecuted nonhumans and magic users under the protection of Francis Bedlam, the King of Beggars.

Underneath Novigrad, a cavernous network of monster-infested sewers, storm drains, and brick tunnels betray the town's origins: men built on top of an ancient elven city. Sections of the Free City's sewers are actual hallways and chambers constructed by the Aen Seidhe long before the First Landing and the human invasion of the Pontar Delta, and eons before Novigrad earned its independence as a city-state. Nowadays, elven aesthetics are frowned upon, and local

Densities in Novigrad can be pretty high

architecture is defined by great cathedrals, imposing bell towers, and the emphatically human technique of half-timbering. Structures of proudly exposed wooden frames, plaster, brick, and tiled roofs, as well as a few usually administrative stone buildings, paint the city's characteristic image. With property taxes based on street frontage, it is common for townhouses to be narrow and expand their living space with a wider second story jutting out over the street. The large residences seen by bustling paved streets or cobblestone squares belong exclusively to the aristocracy, and contrast starkly with the immense misery of the famished countryside—as does city life in its whole.

Novigrad is a world of its own with plenty to discover around every corner. Entertainments are numerous and diverse; music is played publicly, and finding a table to play Gwent, the ancient dwarven card game, is easy. Employment options are numerous too. Pubs, taverns, shops, armories, slaughterhouses, workshops, and, of course, the harbor are always in need of tireless hands ready to work hard and spend on countless little luxuries. All citizens dress in colorful clothing, placards advertise theaters and carnal pleasures, and kids play among bandits, impressed visitors, and roaming pigs. Nothing, however, could conceivably compare to the opulence of the nobles' masquerade balls—they are indeed legendary. Almost as legendary as the city's xenophobia.

DESIGN INSIGHTS

Novigrad is one of the biggest, most thoroughly fleshed-out fantasy towns in gaming. It is an immersive, believable yet exotic urban environment absolutely worth exploring and studying. The level of detail is astonishing (with stones even holding roof tiles in place), and combined with the obvious historical research pored into it, the rich world of Andrzej Sapkowski's *Witcher* novels and well-selected real-world inspirations help create a lived-in, sprawling city. It is an authentic-feeling town combining Central European myths, architectural and planning elements from the Middle Ages, and details of Polish tradition, while also drawing from the docks of Gdańsk, the towers of San Gimignano, and old Amsterdam.

Distinct class-based and functionally differentiated districts, along with the natural divisions of a city built on islands, make Novigrad legible, its form similar to recognizable historical layouts, and compatible with the city's seemingly chaotic roads. The dreadful lives of the poor majority are convincingly portrayed and uniquely contrasted with the even more desperate peasants of the countryside. The existence of in-town wells is another rare touch of realistic, functional design, although admittedly, the otherwise lovely city walls wouldn't be too defendable in reality. Public spaces, a rich soundscape, and an intriguing topography haven't been forgotten either, adding beauty and vivacity to the town. Historical realism extends to Novigrad's hinterland too, from where a working world economy supports the town, crafts its wooden carts, and grows its food. This is a big city in a big game world, and you'll first hear about it and note its presence hours before approaching its bridges.

The massive scope of the production is also evident in the 250-plus unique buildings comprising this virtual city, which—even if incapable of holding a claimed population of 30,000—means the city never feels smaller than it should. Interestingly, the people inhabiting it have personalities and sensible schedules too. Different types of residents or visitors mix in each zone, all following distinct but varied fashion trends and all conveying the overall atmosphere of colorful, vibrant Novigrad. This is a densely populated place where non-player characters sneeze, walk to work, gossip on player actions, shop in the morning, and mind their own business. They even react to rain.

15

NEKETAKA
Pillars of Eternity II: Deadfire

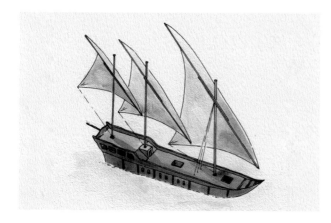

GENERAL INFORMATION ////////////////////////

City: Neketaka

Game: *Pillars of Eternity II: Deadfire*

Developer: Obsidian Entertainment

Publisher: Versus Evil

Release Date: 2018

Genre: RPG

Platforms: Linux, MacOS, Nintendo Switch, PlayStation 4, Windows, Xbox One

To the east of Dyrwood, the dangerous seas of Deadfire are contested by the Royal Deadfire Company of the Rauatai Empire, the Vailian Trading Company, the Príncipi sen Patrena federation of pirates, and the tribal alliance of the Huana. The largest, and strategically most important island of the archipelago, is Neketaka, home to the ancient Huana city of the same name. A great, mountainous port city controlling the crucial harbor of the island's eastern gulf, Neketaka is a metropolis so ancient, its foundations are said to predate the great cataclysm of legend that once almost led to the extinction of the Huana civilization. But where the continental Engwithan vanished, leaving only ruins, the Huana persevered and, guided by the powerful Kahanga tribe, rebuilt and resettled Neketaka, which rose to become the prime commercial hub of the archipelago. The respected tribe still rules the city with Queen Onekaza II, a shrewd strategist, as its monarch.

Neketaka, the city of the twin peaks, has been constructed on the rocky slopes of two majestic mountains. Buildings and terraces hover on the edges of cliffs, and plazas and patches of green dot the landscape. The city is a majestic spectacle, offering spectacular views of the sea from every spot. Its beauty, prosperity, and opportunities have drawn many Huana from their traditional settlements over the centuries, although in recent years, it has also welcomed Vailian and Rauataian traders and allowed them to carve out their own spaces within it. The majority of Neketaka's over 120,000 inhabitants remain Huana, but many Natlan humans, dwarves, elves, and even a few godlike—still feared for their aberrant head shapes—can be found in this multicultural settlement. The city is a major exporter of koiki fruit, rice, palm oil, cocoa, teak, pearls, and luminous adra. It is also very noisy as barbarians, paladins, druids, wizards, ciphers, sellers of summoning figurines, and magical performers mingle between taverns, factories, mansions, and bathhouses.

Neketaka's sibling mountains, the larger one with the mythical waterfall on the west and the humbler eastern one, are connected by two great bridges, with a smaller one far below them. The

Galleons are a common sight in Neketakan waters

stone lanes, towering structures and cleanly divided districts for the city's artisans, priests, or laborers contradict traditional equalitarian Huana societal norms, but the prevalent architecture does at least keep up with tribal tastes, showing a preference for nature-inspired rhythms and shapes.

At the foothill of the western mountain, Queen's Berth forms the commercial backbone of town. An expansive port district of wooden and stone docks daily welcoming newcomers and vast numbers of ships to the city, the Berth brings in wealth and increases the might of queen and city both. Among shipyards and busy streets, Ivorr the Bright preaches in the market square surrounded by countless stores, the extravagant headquarters of the Vailian Trading Company, and the company's newly constructed luminous adra mill with its huge waterfall-powered grindstones. The route to the east, overlooked by the Valera and other estates, leads past Sanza's renowned Map Emporium, through the plaza facing Peddler's Canal, past the Wild Mare's noisy sailors and courtesans, and past narrow roads lined with small houses into the Gullet.

Suspended against the tremendous waterfall, essentially between the two mountains, the Gullet, Neketaka's slum, hangs above the chasm at the heart of the city. This is where the destitute and the hopeless barely survive in shanties and hastily converted caves. Home to the Roparu caste, the lowest in Huana society, as well as to myriad colorful, desperate, and often unsavory figures, food here is distributed for free according to tradition, and as the queen sees fit. It is never enough though, and locals are known to starve to death or get killed while attempting to rob fully armored passersby. The historic Hole is the sole tavern in the Gullet, a place as foul-smelling as the hidden Delver's Row black market. Interestingly, the district's justice system revolves around forcing the condemned in rusty cages and dumping them into the Old City below, into a large, undead-infested cavern where the remains of the ancient sunken metropolis that fell during the cataclysm have collapsed.

Further east, past the tunnel and its short bridge, and below the eastern mountain, lies the fortified Brass Citadel. The Great Kingdom of Rauatai's heart of operations in the Deadfire archipelago is packed with cannons, mortars, soldiers, and fortifications, and acts as a naval base for the kingdom's military operations. Allowed to exist on coastal Neketaka, the Brass Citadel is primarily used to keep sailors fed, armed, and paid. Above its docks, warehouses, and barracks, above even the Imperial Command building, thickly clustered residences lead to the Sacred Stair. Possibly the first part of Neketaka to be settled, the holy district of the Sacred Stair is an open area with temples dedicated to all the gods worshipped by the Huana and the other major cultures residing in the city. Its centrepieces, the great temple dedicated to Magran and the tower of the Sacred Stair, are surrounded by temples to Gaun, Berath, and numerous other deities. The Hanging Sepulchers nearby consist of an ancient network of catacombs and mausoleums, serving as the ceremonial resting place of venerable Huana leaders.

At the western end of the two bridges spanning the Neketaka chasm, beyond the waterfall, and above the Gullet, lies the affluent artisans' district of Periki's Overlook. Named after explorer Periki, who founded the Watershapers Guild and lived most of her life here, this is a beautiful place of intricate carvings and colorful, spacious mansions, including the one belonging to Archmage Arkemyr. Terraces overlook the lower parts of Neketaka, while the luxuriant Luminous Bathhouse,

The Brass Citadel of the Royal Deadfire Company

Cuitztli's Exotic Herbs, and the famed magical emporium Dark Cupboard are clustered around a lively mercantile plaza.

Farther up, perched at the top of the mountain, the Serpent's Crown is the richest, most arresting district in Neketaka, from where the Kahanga Palace commands breathtaking views of the city and the archipelago below it. Here, Queen Onekaza II rules, and gathers her allies among persistent rumors of a reborn vengeful god who razes keeps and settlements to the ground. She knows that no civilization could ever hope to survive two apocalypses.

DESIGN INSIGHTS

Being the radiant metropolis of a pirate-themed fantasy RPG, Neketaka had to become an expansive, detailed port city built upon centuries of lore and imagined history. Its size is initially overwhelming, and the two mountains it rests upon awe visitors. The largest city in *Pillars of Eternity II* is a complex, varied urban center organized in functionally and architecturally distinct districts, each with their own soundscape and style. It is filled with quests, characters, and distractions, ready to entertain burglars, fighters, and wizards. A city carved by nature and society, whose dungeons simply make geographical sense and where Deadfire's major forces compete, Neketaka functions as a showcase of the game's lavish backgrounds, detailed setting, and intriguing planning concepts. Visiting the temple district and seeing the rest of the city below its steep cliffs, for example, provides a sense of depth and three-dimensionality rarely seen in isometric games.

Neketaka never stands still. Residents have individual lives, jobs, routines, and schedules that carry on regardless of whether they are being observed. Moreover, it presents a reactive world that is actually elegant. Rob a regular citizen, and instead of them blindly attacking the player, they will attempt to call the town guards or simply flee. People here react to player activity in different ways depending on who they are: criminals do not appreciate law-abiding heroes, factions and individuals seem to remember previous actions, and the strange godlike race still get odd looks. As for the competing factions, it is they who draw players into narratives within and about the city, allowing them to subtly change it over time.

Stellar aesthetics aside, the in-game map makes traveling between districts an exceptionally designed experience. Traveling is tracked on the map itself, providing a sense of real-time movement, which helps players imagine their party making their way through the dense, sometimes confusing urban tissue that hasn't been modeled; they also run into random encounters presented via text and sketches, which further flesh out the city. Isometric district levels do not flow into each other, and it is this map that implies the metropolis beyond the explorable areas; conjuring images of what has not been directly modeled in-game, further aided by illustrations, lore drops, and discussions.

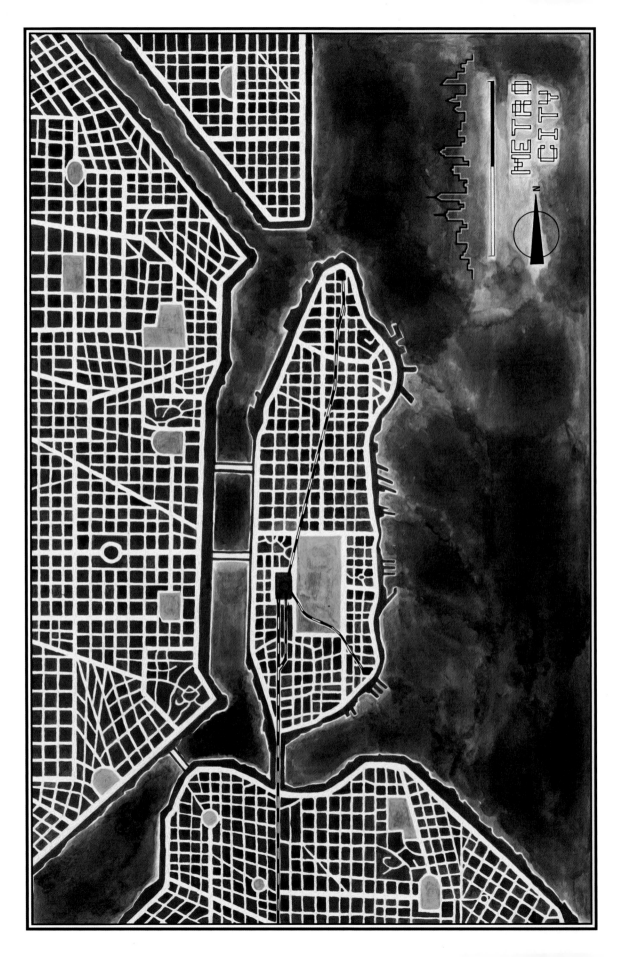

METRO CITY

METRO CITY
Final Fight

16

GENERAL INFORMATION /////////////////////

City: Metro City

Game: *Final Fight*

Developer: Capcom

Publisher: Capcom

Release Date: 1989

Genre: Beat'em up

Platforms: Arcade, Amiga, Amstrad CPC, Atari ST, Commodore 64, PlayStation 2, Mega-CD, ZX Spectrum, SNES, X68000, Xbox, Game Boy Advance, iOS, PSP

The year is 1989, and Metro City is fighting its never-ending war against violent crime. Newly elected mayor, Mike Haggar, the obscenely strong pro-wrestler turned politician, has been taking to the streets himself to stop wrongdoers and bring murder rates below the unacceptable rate of six per day. But curbing crime also means cutting into the profits of the Mad Gear gang, and its (suspected) industrialist leader: the notorious Mr. Belger. Attempts to clean up the city and protect the streets seem to have hit his operations hard enough to spark a full-blown syndicate war, which the mayor and his most trusted friends are fighting almost single-handedly. Most citizens, although thankful for the modest decrease in criminal activity, are too afraid to help, and the police are too corrupt or powerless to meaningfully join the struggle.

These are truly hard days for the metropolis, and yet, despite everything, Metro City remains the economic powerhouse of the Eastern seaboard of the United States. Its downtown, not unlike Manhattan, located on an island by the Atlantic Ocean and connected to the wider metropolitan mainland via trains and bridges, sees millions of dollars flow in every day. It is money that keeps the sprawling, dense cityscape expanding, but also money that fills the crime capital of North America with dread and decay. Cynicism is on the rise, and has fueled an equally rising interest in cage fighting, illegal blood sports, pro-wrestling, self-defense, and a small but sizable vigilante culture. Street fighting and ninjutsu academies are all the rage, even if in many cases, it is the supposed good guys that might wreck the average unsuspecting car.

Muggings, stabbings, and fights are far too commonplace in the rundown, gang-ruled streets of a town plagued with violence, murder, and the deep-rooted corruption of the ruthless, all-powerful Mad Gear gang. Criminals literally crawl out of the sewers, abandoned basements, and deteriorating downtown blocks. Buildings stand all but destroyed, waiting for the mercy of demolition,

The slums and, in the background, the great towers of commerce

West Side's Chinatown

and the old town hall has barely survived. The last subway line remaining operational is in dire need of repairs following years of vandalism, while its abandoned train tracks lead to Sodom and his infamous illegal underground fighting arena: the Ring of Death. No wonder, then, that people have taken a preference to chopper bikes and bulky cars. And it's not just the slums and workers' districts that have succumbed to this fate either; visible between crumbling walls, the rich areas of gleaming towers and posh mansions are only superficially safer.

The actual organization of metropolitan space, on the other hand, doesn't seem to have been deeply influenced by criminal activity. Downtown's island remains connected via trains and bridges to the three mostly residential areas of the mainland. These are the more suburban, less economically important parts of the region; somewhat calmer, and, in places, parochial. They surround the heart of the city that beats on the island, which mainly consists of five unimaginatively named boroughs and a massive park at its very center.

The Slums—a jungle of ripped power lines, broken phone booths, boarded-up windows, barely standing residential complexes, rotting cars, burning tires, and derelict mansions at the southern end of the island—are a living hell for the destitute souls trapped there, but also for the poor petty criminals preying on them. The West Side has a slightly more middle-class air to it, even if it features a couple wrestling rings and some really tough bars. Its selection of decent restaurants and spirited Chinatown are enjoyed by a population willing to brave the streets and have some fun. The Industrial Area, deserted during nights, has an almost sci-fi look to it courtesy of all the factories, metal constructions, and active building sites, whereas the Bay Area waterfront offers a stunning if dangerous promenade and an excellent view of the Statue of Liberty. Finally, Uptown—the rich, chillingly dangerous part of town—is where criminal masterminds live in shiny art deco skyscrapers and enjoy wonderful parks with swimming pools in a place where even the fluffiest, poshest, tiniest of dogs can observe street brawls unfazed.

DESIGN INSIGHTS

Final Fight is a scrolling beat 'em up, and its city could have simply been an elaborate backdrop. And yet, Metro City is an important, even iconic element of the game that directly serves the narrative, visuals, and character design, and inspires its set-pieces. The '80s paranoid fear of rundown downtowns, as expressed in countless action movies of the era (including 1984's *Streets of Fire*), inspired the developers and defined the atmosphere, while many antagonists were named after rock musicians such as Axl Rose, Gene Simmons, and Sid Vicious.

Metro City was evidently not treated as an afterthought. Cartoony and pop culture–inspired though it was, its locations do not exist in a vacuum. These are not just disjointed neighborhoods or unconnected backgrounds—a wider city was imagined. *Final Fight*'s six stages take players through a guided tour of said city's downtown, and are seamlessly, often physically, connected to each other, creating a linear, cohesive continuity.

With Metro City's cinematic Manhattan influences, this is an instantly recognizable place, which draws heavily from its source material and makes sense within the context of the game. New York and Metro City share common elements, a similar layout, roughly equivalent boroughs, a large park, and, interestingly, a Statue of Liberty. The setting is further supported by some impressive graphics and excellent backgrounds that, although two-dimensional, attempt to convey three-dimensional spaces. Behind crumbling slum buildings, Uptown towers can be glimpsed, and perpendicular alleys leading into the screen add depth to Chinatown.

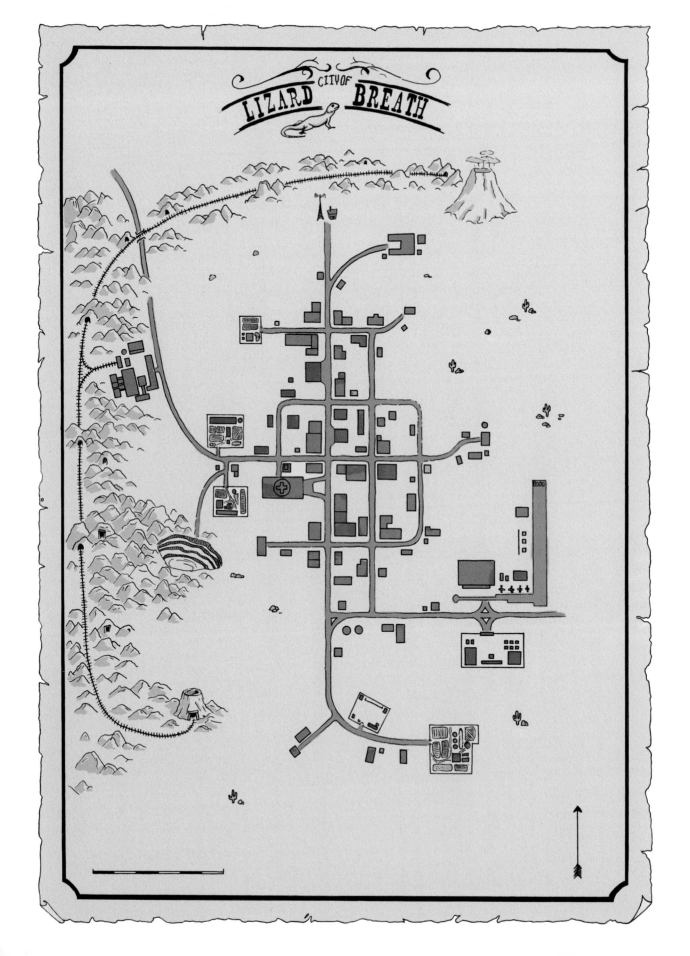

CITY OF
LIZARD BREATH

17

LIZARD BREATH
It Came from the Desert

GENERAL INFORMATION ////////////////////

City: Lizard Breath

Game: *It Came from the Desert*

Developer: Cinemaware

Publisher: Cinemaware

Release Date: 1989

Genre: Action-adventure, Interactive Movie

Platforms: Amiga, MS-DOS, TurboGrafx-16

A tumbleweed truck stop in the unchanging desert, the sleepy town of Lizard Breath would have remained hidden deep in its Californian valley, dying the slow death of a mining outpost were it not for the events of June 1951. This parochial, mostly friendly town of fewer than 500 inhabitants has a legendary tale to tell: one of saving the entire world, as the surrounding ancient desert witnessed a biblical prophecy nearly come true. The meekest of the meek, the humble ants, rose to inherit the earth, and only a man of science, geologist Dr. Greg Bradley, stood between them and the survival of the human race.

Dr. Bradley had arrived in the town he would help make famous to study the region's fascinating meteor fragments, when, to his initial excitement, the large meteor Stohlheinz A221357 came crashing down. Studying the meteor with the help of a college kid and a local prospector, the geologist quickly noticed its unique radioactive properties, but wasn't alarmed. After all, nobody was hurt, radiation levels were low, the town made the news, and people seemed happy with the new space rock. Even if animals refused to approach the volcano it landed in, enthusiastic talk of a cosmic-themed festival only abated when a railroad trestle collapsed over the highway, effectively cutting the town off. Then came the first sightings of strange lights, reports of unsettling noises, and the mysterious wiping out of crops by something eating them clear to the dirt.

Only after cows with sawed-off heads, and crucially butchered miners were discovered did the locals really get spooked, yet still they stuck to scary stories regarding old graveyards and ghosts around pump stations. It was Dr. Bradley who recognized the threat for what it was, and eventually managed to convince the town to prepare its defenses against an implausible but very real army of gigantic ants. Radiation from the meteor had mutated regular harvester ants into huge lumbering monstrosities capable of crushing buildings, and, provided they spread, possibly taking over the world. The good doctor also led the fight against the Atomic Age horrors on Main Street, and finally took on the ant queen in her lair, bringing an end to the end times.

Mutated ants on the fields of JD's farm

Main Street at dusk

A year on and the scars of these battles are still visible on crushed cars rotting in the desert and damaged buildings, but the town has largely gone back to its everyday routine. Curvy muscle cars and pre-World War II pickup trucks have returned to the roads, adding to the image of the now proud municipality. The city feels as natural as the bald surrounding mountains, red earth, green cacti, and harsh desert sun. The occasional violence of knife fights has also returned, as has the roughneck sociopathic trio of the Hellcats thugs, but, for the most part, life in Lizard Breath is pretty similar to that of the average little town in the fifties. The townsfolk rise early, labor hard until the sun sets, drink and retire early, and, nowadays, answer many a journalist's questions. Most places still close down after dark; work at the flashy Hot Springs construction site has resumed; the McWilliams Dairy and JD's farm are back to normal; and the mines are once again fully operational and relatively safe.

Interestingly, mine safety woes go back to the town's founding in the early 1880s. Ants weren't involved, but deaths were far too common, wages too meager, and the escalating strikes led to extreme violence in 1917, as private police deported over a hundred miners at gunpoint. It was the Roosevelt Administration that finally intervened in 1933, and, since then, things have been mostly peaceful. The current mayor, despite his poor handling of the ant crisis, is actually very popular, as his commitment to festivals and unwavering optimism seem to reassure everyone. Besides, the man did lose a car to ants, and kids do love Ant Evacuation Day and its sparkling ant queen. Even the Neptune Hall cult seems to like him.

However, Lizard Breath can be truly odd. It lacks a proper school, yet Platt University's lab is renowned, and it desperately needs a fire department, but only got a National Guard Armory. Cold War paranoia and the perceived strategic importance of quarries, mines, and the Jacob Minerals plant seem to have shaped this sparse, low-density town that's equally difficult to bomb and traverse. Watching Rocket Ranger at the drive-in and then dropping by the KBUG radio station at the other side of town can easily take up the better part of an evening. With the mine's pit railroad being the most modern transportation system around, many roads remain unpaved, and reaching remote places such as the weather station or the picturesque Hilber's airfield for antique biplanes can be taxing.

The linear downtown centered along Main Street is much easier to navigate. It sports a pharmacy, post office, police station, county court, Lizard Breath market, the *Lizard Breath Star* newspaper offices, Elmer's Service Station, and O'Riordan's Pub with its 25-cent tap beer. The Melville Memorial Hospital, known for its strict patient release policy, is also found on Main Street, whereas the mayoral office is just off to the east. The rest of the town's simple grid is dedicated to residences, while a small church, a local cult, and an ancient fortune teller cover any spiritual needs.

As for Lizard Breath's fittingly simple, rustic architecture, it is based on wood, and consists mostly of humble single- or two-story buildings, the occasional Western false front architecture, a few gingerbread houses, some newer brick structures, and Pueblo-style homes. The buildings' uniformly weathered appearance ties everything together, and allows the pale colors of the local fashion to stand out.

Hilber's Airfield

The town derives much of its charm from a cast of almost too vivid inhabitants, such as its stoic sheriff, naively optimistic garage mechanic, tough farmhands, hardboiled reporter, stout workers, overbearing nurses, occasional moonshiners, and even educated youngsters such as the brilliantly named Biff and Dusty. These people may have been initially skeptical of science, or at times downright rude to Dr. Bradley, but surviving the ants has really enlightened them, whereas the attention of national broadcasters simply dazzled them. Everyone is now looking forward to a bright future and the miracles of the 1960s. As for the mayor, he sees modern Lizard Breath as a family community with incredible potential, ready to host futuristic festivals for the entire state, and exhibit its monstrous carcasses to all mankind—provided a second ant queen hasn't survived, that is. The doctor has expressed his fears, but frankly, he should be more worried about the commies and less about those ants.

DESIGN INSIGHTS

Attempting to simulate a completely functioning town with the relatively primitive technology of 16-bit home computers, let alone presenting it in a cinematic way, was an overly ambitious goal, yet Cinemaware managed to come really close. Getting inspired by the pulp B-movies of the fifties—the 1954 film *Them!* in particular—was a masterstroke of originality, and Lizard Breath being unusual made it memorable, and allowed history to be kind to its outrageous ants, screaming girls, iconic cars, Wild West setting, and occasional oversights.

Admittedly, the town is too sparse, and lacks crucial civic functions such as education or residence. Anachronisms haven't been avoided; its roads are unrealistically rectangular, and its plan often nonsensical, but Lizard Breath does evoke a sense of place. The stylized art allows the player's imagination to fill in any blanks, named establishments add character, the protagonist has personal ties to the place, and a combination of top-down and first-person views add a three-dimensional element to the proceedings. Locations and characters such as Mac at the construction site or the National Guard sergeant, although not directly useful, flesh out the world and add complexity, while also acting as red herrings.

More importantly, the simple clockwork-like yet groundbreaking real-time simulation animating the game's non-player charachters (NPCs) creates a rather convincing, dynamic illusion of a realistic, living world. Impressively, said NPCs panic, react to certain choices, and even be convinced of things and act accordingly.

Moving around costs time, places shut down for the night, the drive-in cinema opens at 6 p.m., and in-game characters have distinct schedules. The passage of time is depicted via an in-game clock and changing location graphics show setting suns, night skies, and the bright desert; it is felt by the mounting pressure on the town, the movement of characters, and unavoidably scripted events. Everything is happening on a rather generous timer, but events will take place regardless of whether players are present. The feeling achieved is that of a world moving around players, rather than players simply moving through a predetermined world.

18

NEW ORLEANS
Gabriel Knight: Sins of the Fathers

GENERAL INFORMATION ////////////////////

City: New Orleans

Game: *Gabriel Knight: Sins of the Fathers*

Developer: Sierra On-Line

Publisher: Sierra On-Line

Release Date: 1993

Genre: Adventure, Horror

Platforms: Mac OS, MS-DOS, Windows

New Orleans is a sensual, dangerous city. The elegant Louisiana birthplace of jazz may be past its prime, but even if no longer the third-most-populous US city, this is a place filled with promise and allure. The patina of time has added grace to the crescent-shaped Mississippi port town, and mystique to the lasting traditions born of a turbulent history. From its founding as La Nouvelle-Orléans in 1718 by the French Mississippi Company on Chitimacha land, followed by its purchase from the United States in 1803, the American Civil War, the abolition of slavery, and all the way to the Civil Rights movement of the 1960s, New Orleans has always been an explosive melting pot of American, Creole, African, and European cultures.

Tellingly, the rich Creole, descendants of the old slave masters still consider themselves the only true Orleaners in a city where class and race divisions are consistently stark and destitution crushing. The recent deindustrialization and an increasing dependency on tourism have further suppressed wages; poverty rates are soaring; the population is declining; and violent crime has reached unprecedented levels, but, just like floods, deep-rooted social problems must remain hidden from paying visitors. Tourists are thus kept busy and entertained by the vibrant streets, regional delicacies, and jazz parties, while poverty is masked by the world-famous Mardi Gras and the beauties of the historic French Quarter.

The French Quarter is known for its centuries-old gridiron plan, traditional Creole architecture, wonderful balconies, and wild nightlife focused around the celebrated Bourbon Street. To its southwest, just beyond Canal Street, lies the American Quarter, the city's Central Business District. Interestingly, every road crossing Canal Street into the French Quarter changes its name, with St. Charles Avenue, for example, becoming Royal Street. Other downtown neighborhoods include Marigny and Bywater, whereas uptown ones—beyond Canal Street—include the Warehouse and University Districts, the Irish Channel, Fontainebleau, and the Garden District, with its majestic mansions of old powerful families. City Park, with its historic oaks, is also worth exploring,

Historic Jackson Square and the Saint Louis Cathedral

St. Louis Cemetery No. 1

as is Bayou St. John, an in-city bayou arranged into a narrow, leafy park ideal for couples seeking privacy and for colorful rituals on the Magnolia Bridge.

From bayou residences and shotgun houses to bungalows and remote swamp houses, New Orleans' districts are rich in architectural delights. Creole cottages, double-gallery houses, townhouses with large courtyards and intricately wrought-iron balconies line the streets of the emblematic French Quarter and house the Museum of Death, the Napoleon House, and mystery novelist Gabriel Knight. St. Charles Avenue, on the other hand, is famed for its large antebellum mansions, and, since the very first towers in the 1960s demonstrated the viability of the Orleanian skyscraper, the city's skyline was redefined along Poydras Street and the CBD.

Adding to the ambience are European-style Catholic cemeteries and lush parks, among which the Louis Armstrong Park proudly hints at the town's musical traditions. The Jazz and Voodoo Fests are excellent showcases of New Orleans' unique musical heritage, born of brutal colonialism and a fusion of European instruments with African rhythms. Being the only US city allowing slaves to gather and publicly play their music in Congo Square—nowadays within Louis Armstrong Park—New Orleans gave birth to its own indigenous music: jazz. The local sound was further influenced by Cajun, zydeco, and the Delta blues, only to eventually embrace rhythm and

Bourbon Street

blues, rock and roll, funk, and eventually hip hop, embedding them in the culture that birthed the jazz funeral.

Also marrying death to music and born of the terrors of slavery, voodoo is a deeply rooted pillar of New Orleans' culture, and has for centuries provided the downtrodden with strong communal bonds. As slaves and their customs began pouring into New Orleans following the Haitian Revolution, they bonded around the grassroots religion of voodoo, worshipping ancestral spirits, snakes, and the Great Zombi. Artists' renderings of voodoo dances on the Congo Square date back to the early 1800s, although depictions of the hidden, less refined meetings in the Bayou St. John and on the shores of Lake Pontchartrain are much rarer. Despite brimming with Catholic imagery, Orleanian voodoo always terrified plantation owners.

The ritual knives, whips, dolls, and Sekey Madoule coffins currently on display at the Historical Voodoo Museum offer a glimpse of the city's hidden practices, and were never paraded in public view. They were meant for vodooiene eyes only; for powerful bokors, mamaloa high priestesses, and the faithful to use in unseen Honfours and for holy rituals. According to voodoo beliefs, the loa—powerful spirits—could effectively possess humans during rituals performed around bloodied altars made of exotic materials such as elephant skulls and dedicated to gods such as Damballah or the dreaded Ogoun Badagris. The voodoo kings and queens of yore set up totems, drew veves, and the faithful danced wearing animal masks, soothing their shared hardship.

It was around 1830 when a woman known as Widow Paris and Marie Laveau emerged to rule and popularize voodoo in all of New Orleans. A hairdresser for rich Creole ladies, she employed a spy network of servants to provide her with secrets used to intimidate and blackmail the affluent, while simultaneously organizing phantasmagoric rituals. After emerging as the sole voodoo power in the city, she redefined voodoo into its uniquely New Orleanian version. She invented hundreds of charms, spells, and potions, held dramatic ceremonies by Lake Pontchartrain, and wasn't above selling tickets for her events to the curious. Her daughter, Marie Laveau II, took over as Widow Paris when Laveau got old, and encouraged the notion they were the same individual, leading many to believe that the original Marie Laveau continued to rule. Only a select few ever suspected that both Maries were nothing but mere puppets of a real queen.

Regardless of rumors, Marie's tomb in St. Louis Cemetery No. 1 is incredibly popular with tourists and the faithful, even if no one really knows which Laveau is buried there. Gruesome offerings and Xs on and around the tomb are common, as is customary with all voodoo graves. It is far from surprising that New Orleans' ornate, maze-like cemeteries are filled with significant voodoo tombs, and thus also with a menagerie of bull hearts, candles, and bloodied flowers adding to their disturbing ambience. As for the aboveground tombs, those are mostly due to the high water table.

Voodoo, initially a desperate sanctuary for the oppressed, has witnessed its influence grow to enthrall popular imagination and even reach the former slave traders. Fearing curses, walking around with hidden gris-gris, searching for love spells, drinking good luck potions, and consulting with fortune tellers are practices embedded in everyday culture, defining the local identity. Establishments such as the Dixieland Drug Store specialize in selling supernatural protection in the form of cures, spells, and advice regarding ghostly pests, while the Sister Cross radio ads promise to leverage the power of Jesus against curses.

On the fringes of voodoo, folk and pop culture whispers of a dark, necromantic cult are stronger than ever, as some of the city's daily murders come with flamboyantly ritualistic aspects very similar to the killings of 1810. There are still old people alive who claim to have witnessed deadly rituals by real voodoo queens, and will happily explain to anyone willing to listen that a *cabrit sans cor*—a goat without horns—can only refer to a human sacrifice, and that human blood has always been the guiding power shaping the city's fate. Actually, overlaying voodoo over the town map transforms New Orleans into a very particular, haunted space, where every locale hides dark puzzles alluding to the dark powers flowing through the city.

Especially in the Old Quarter, and around the inconspicuous St. George's bookstore, one can't help but feel an ancient story unravelling, as Rada drummers play louder and more passionately than ever. Their ominous sound seems to almost convey meaning, and could be connected to Tulane University's recent interest in African religions or the increase in cultist gatherings on the shores of Lake Pontchartrain. These days even looking at Jackson Square and its pattern of concentric circles conjures strange feelings and raises suspicions regarding the secrets buried beneath St. Louis Cathedral and the former La Plaza de Armas—suspicions that all the square's Cajun bands, tap dancers, merchants, and mimes cannot dispel.

DESIGN INSIGHTS

As is the case with most great game cities, Gabriel Knight's New Orleans is part of an excellent, innovative game; the first in a trilogy of well-loved, well-researched adventures aiming to tell mature stories. Setting it in the city of voodoo, Mardi Gras, blues, jazz, and whiskey was thus a very apt, very adult choice. The masterful realization of the urban setting and its strong ties with the plot and puzzles were achieved by embedding an abstracted, supernatural version of an existing place into the game; by socially, urbanistically, and culturally grounding *Gabriel Knight* in 1990s Louisiana.

Designer Jane Jensen famously hadn't visited New Orleans before tackling it, categorically showing that first-hand experience is not always necessary. It is thorough research and great writing that imbued *Gabriel Knight* with its unparalleled sense of authenticity. Realism backed by first-rate production values allowed players to immerse themselves in a game world of accurate Lucky Dogs stands, the *Times-Picayune* newspaper, beignets, and Spanish moss hanging from trees. It was this thoughtful attention to detail that added a concrete sense of locality.

Superimposing an over-the-top but essentially realistic version of voodoo on the fleshed-out city changed it into a scary, haunted place, whereas retaining a believable civic texture was supported by a treasure trove of information on local history and customs. Allowing players to non-violently interact with their surroundings and piece together its history helped further establish spatial immersion, as did the demand for frequent revisits to the game's locales and the thorough questioning of characters who were ready to comment on the place, its stories, problems, and legends.

Being a game that expected players to look at everything allowed for details and historical tid-bits to be organically revealed. Countless short descriptions added layers of depth, while exploring the city's legends, architecture, and lore provided crucial puzzle-solving hints. There were hundreds of hotspots to interact with, dozens of characters to talk to, two lovely maps allowing access to hotspots in the French Quarter, and select locations within wider New Orleans. Perusing said maps revealed street and location names that were only there to support the illusion of complexity and weave game screens into the fabric of a greater city. Immersion was further served by each in-game day opening with a paperboy delivering the paper, and Grace arriving at St. George's bookshop as the sun rose above the French Quarter.

FOURSIDE
EarthBound [a.k.a. *Mother 2*]

19

GENERAL INFORMATION /

City: Fourside

Game: *EarthBound* [a.k.a. *Mother 2*]

Developer: Ape Inc., HAL Laboratory

Publisher: Nintendo

Release Date: 1994

Genre: RPG

Platforms: Game Boy Advance, SNES

Past the Dusty Dunes Desert, far from the lure of the mole-infested gold mines, over the great beam bridge, and next to a wonderful if fully commercialized lake, lies the city of Fourside. It is the greatest, richest, and most populous urban center of Eagleland. An aspiring metropolis and a rising global city of finance, Fourside boasts a population of exactly 313,003 residents, and an overdeveloped tertiary sector that has somehow turned it into a place that can be both terribly exciting and mind-numbingly dull. Its cityscape does not betray its modest civic size, and presents a contemporary, imposing skyline that promises a bright future for the colorful populace. Megalomaniac Fourside strives to ape all aspects of New York City, yet lacks the history, size, and culture required, and to this very day remains embarrassingly parochial. Whereas the Big Apple is famous for its delicious bagels (among countless other delicacies), the finest bread of Fourside is, according to its very own bakers, spectacularly plain, sporting a nondescript flavor.

Admittedly, the Hippodamian grid of Fourside does indeed faithfully imitate sections of Manhattan. Wide, long boulevards and narrower local streets intersect at right angles, defining some properly modern rectangular blocks while thankfully leaving a lot of space for the city's many large parks. Despite its Big Banana nickname, and despite being officially called Fourside, the city is neither curved nor four-sided. It resembles a cross instead, which provides it with a distinctive outline that urban image-makers have hoped can evolve into a local cartographic trademark of sorts. Relatively bland high-rises, a selection of mildly intriguing skyscrapers and large, generic apartment buildings are brightened up by a few art deco and art nouveau buildings that enrich the town's architectural image. Commercial and residential areas are never too far apart—nothing really is—but Fourside is one of those precious few cities where cafes are filled with patrons ready to assign outlandish missions to random strangers.

Evidently, in the year 199X, Foursiders, not unlike New Yorkers, can use all the help they can get. Cruelty is on the rise, businessmen and politicians are forming shady alliances to redefine reality,

Fourside's still underdeveloped waterfront

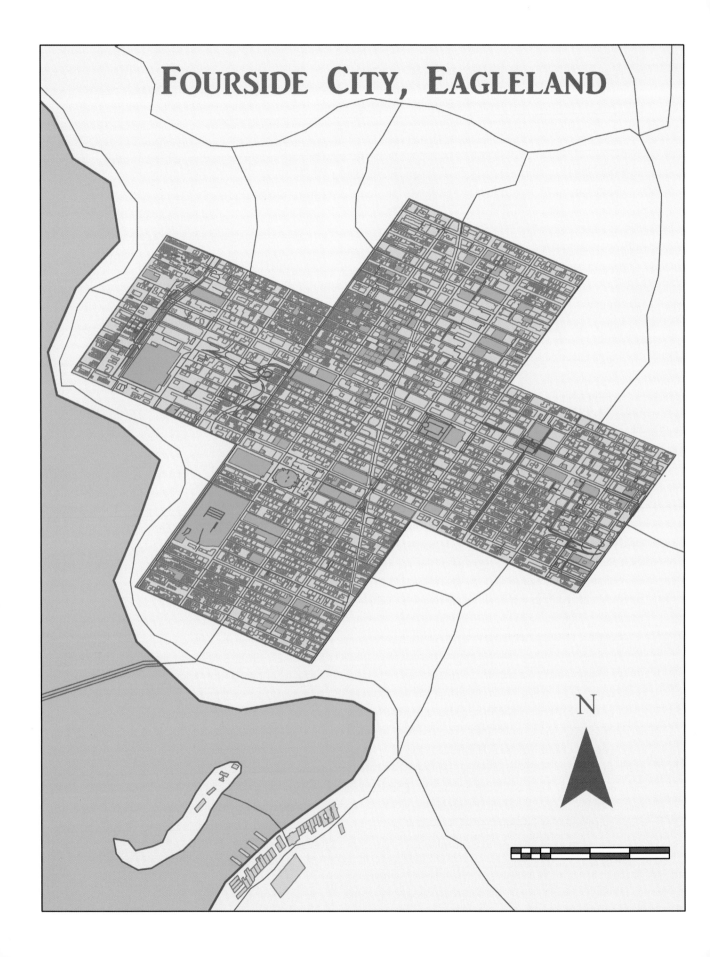

FOURSIDE CITY, EAGLELAND

N

The skyscrapers of Fourside look
more impressive at night

and the hopeless Escargo Express courier service really isn't helping much with the economy (or anything else). Even worse, street salesmen, clerks, and shockingly also tourists are being harassed by increasingly odd killer coffee cups, clumsy robots, sentient and obviously malevolent street signs, and extra-cranky old ladies. The police are apparently too busy evicting people from their homes to serve and protect anyone that is not a real estate businessman or the power-mad and inexplicably popular mayor, Geldergarde Monotoli. Crime of all sorts—and not merely the awareness thereof, as the mayor claims—is on the rise, but criminals are easy to recognize thanks to their strangely pale green faces. Still, the police remain focused on the safety of Monotoli and his lush offices in the modernist, forty-eight-story Monotoli Building. Satisfyingly though, the latter is not the town's most beautiful edifice.

This is an honor reserved for the newly opened Grand Department Store, affectionately known as "the Grand," which sits near the lake on the east side of town. This art deco tower looks a lot like a modestly sized version of the Empire State Building. A premium emporium, and a true monument to consumerism, the Grand is so large that even the clerks working there get lost, and is so labyrinthine, no one can disprove the legend of the dreaded Department Store Spook. Most interesting to first-time visitors, however, should be the downtown Dinosaur Museum with its large, not entirely authentic but very impressive dinosaur bones. Its manager, Mr. Spoon, has set the price of admission at a very reasonable $5 per person, which comes in much cheaper than watching a performance of the Runaway Five jazz band at the Topolla Theater. Of course, being an ambitious city, Fourside not only features a quality jazz band but also comes complete with its very own *Fourside Post* newspaper. There are lots of things to do and visit here. There's the Monotoli Grand Hotel, all the restaurants, shops and wonderful gardens, and the sidewalks are always so lively—just never spectacular.

Then again, UFOs have been spotted flying above town, and anyone brave enough to explore through the back wall of Jackie's Cafe will enter Moonside: a bent, nightmare version of Fourside where no means yes, and up means down. The sanest denizens of this bizarre place make no sense whatsoever, and cackle maniacally at the brain-erosive qualities of their environment. The less sane are mainly melting, lurking clocks. Everything is strange, backwards, and abstracted, and seems to be made of beams of light surrounded by deep darkness, as Moonside either exists on the flip-side of Fourside or is an illusion conjured by the ancient golden statue of pure evil known as the Mani Mani. Or both.

DESIGN INSIGHTS

EarthBound offers a very cartoony, two-dimensional pixel-art world composed of isometric villages, towns, and dungeons, with Fourside as its big, thoroughly abstracted metropolis. Themed around an idiosyncratic take on American culture and urbanism, *EarthBound*'s great city feels like a parody of an oddly perceived New York City. Just as the game subverts popular RPG tropes in an almost surreal way, so does Fourside play with its inspiration by turning the Empire State Building into a shopping center and populating its roads with killer taxis and crazed sign monsters. Interestingly, even the name Fourside doesn't mean anything in particular; it is simply the fourth city that the protagonist and his group visit, which is rather apt for a settlement consisting entirely of the archetypal symbols of a metropolis. Fourside is most definitely not a detailed, realistic representation of even a simplified city. A few blocks and some well-chosen landmarks are enough to stand in for a city of three-hundred thousand where only popular culture's staples of contemporary urbanism have been detailed: the city hall, the hospital, the mall, the museum, the hotel, and a few coffee shops and stores.

20

RACCOON CITY
Resident Evil 2

GENERAL INFORMATION /////////////////////

City: Raccoon City

Game: *Resident Evil 2*

Developer: Capcom

Publisher: Capcom

Release Date: 1998

Genre: Survival Horror

Platforms: Game.com, GameCube, Dreamcast, Nintendo 64, PlayStation, Windows

Nestled deep in the foggy but wonderful Arklay Mountains, Raccoon City was a typical American city in the Midwest. Surrounded by a craggy countryside of lakes, rivers, and ravines, as well as the old-growth Raccoon Forest, the city was part of nature's beautiful, diverse tapestry. Picturesque Victory Lake served as its freshwater reservoir, and the nearby dam provided it with cheap electricity. The great Circular River ran through town, while the Marble and Aimes Rivers flowed in its outskirts. Over 100,000 people once lived, worked, and occasionally prospered in Raccoon City, but nobody does anymore. The city has been a necropolis since 1998. It was bombed and burned to the ground by the US military, finally fulfilling the fate that was weaved into it.

Both Raccoon City's unexpected birth and tragic death were inextricably tied to the rise of Umbrella Pharmaceuticals: the world's largest pharmaceutical company and a gigantic multinational concern. Umbrella's success was built upon the ancient progenitor retrovirus, which laid the foundation for innovative viral treatments alongside the less publicized but more profitable development and sale of biological weapons to NATO countries. Umbrella contributed much more than employment to the city. It funded welfare, built infrastructure, paid to maintain public order, and became the cornerstone of the local economy, while the city in turn became Umbrella's playground—and experiment. Under its factories, the corporation built an expansive, complex facility for its network of secret laboratories that researched viral weapons, vaccine synthesis, cryogenics, and combat-focused mutations.

When the US government launched its sterilization operation to eradicate the town and contain the biohazard Umbrella had unleashed, the city had already turned into ground zero for an unprecedented zombie plague. The initial signs of impending doom came early in the spring of 1998 as bizarre murders started occurring in the Arklay Mountains and Raccoon Forest, eventually moving closer to the suburbs. Victims appeared to have been mauled by dogs or, worse, partially eaten

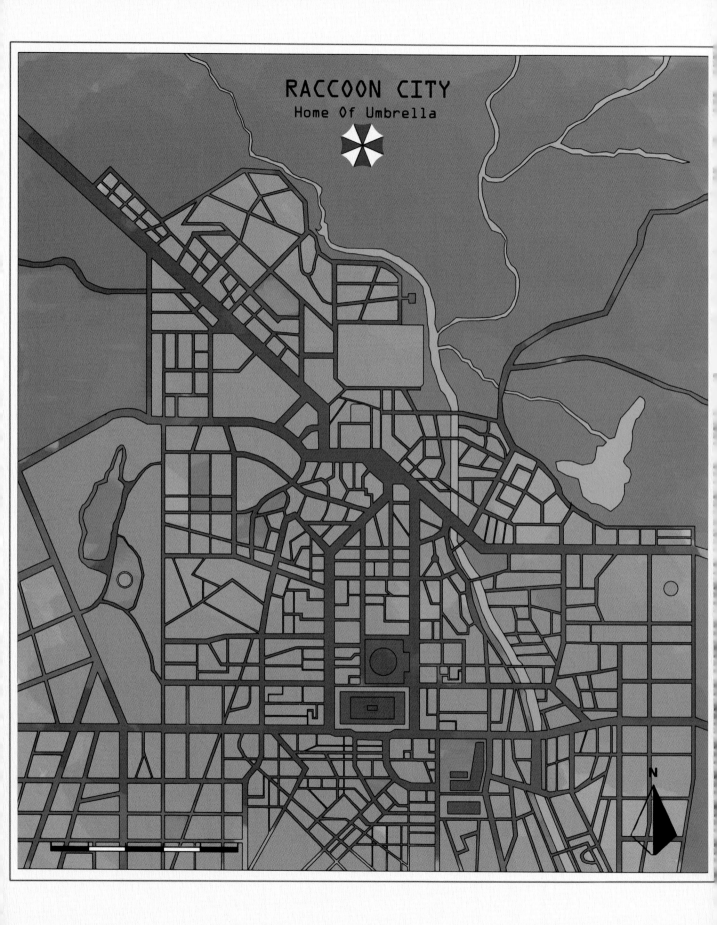

The train platform of the Raccoon City Underground Laboratory

by humans. Then, the huge forest fires came, and the incidents were forgotten until the water reserves got contaminated by Umbrella's viral biological weapons. Infections began as subtle skin rashes, before the virus quickly took over central nervous systems, killing its victims and reanimating their cadavers. By the end of September, the epidemic had transformed most citizens into zombies. Town officials and the police, too deep in Umbrella's pocket, were slow to react, and mostly preoccupied with hiding evidence of the company's wrongdoing.

Such a criminal failure to mobilize should not have come as a surprise. The city always belonged to Umbrella. It was the company that, during the 1990 to 1991 recession, funded the Bright Raccoon 21 city revival project, built the new Raccoon General Hospital, and even established the Special Tactics and Rescue Service police division. Besides, Raccoon City would have remained an insignificant rural settlement if, back in the 1960s, its isolation hadn't attracted the attention of aristocrat Oswell E. Spencer, the co-founder of Umbrella. Urbanization took off rapidly in the late 1960s when Umbrella Pharmaceuticals established its massive factories in town, and it even took it upon itself to construct the tram and subway systems. Umbrella always owned Raccoon City, even to its end.

Above: A rather average zombie
Right: The deteriorating, deadly
streets of Raccoon City

It was only after its officials and top researchers had fled the now useless city that the US Army was called in to start evacuating citizens and enforce the quarantine around the city's perimeter. Life in Raccoon City was over, and the only thing left to do was attempt to stop the contamination and hide any incriminating evidence. Few of the souls trapped in the city managed to escape before the bombings incinerated everything. Those lucky survivors have spoken of fires and explosions among collapsing buildings, crashed choppers, and burning buses; overrun barricades; and how those trapped in the heavily fortified police station all died, overwhelmed by the sheer numbers of the undead. It wasn't only flesh-eating zombies that roamed the streets, but other, worse horrors too. Terrifying, bulbous monsters, wall-crawling mutants, and ferocious skinless dogs were the rulers of the once successful mountain town during its final moments.

Raccoon City's spectacular death was a most profoundly atypical end for an otherwise average company town. This had been a calm industrial municipality, happy with its football team, local soft drink, and popular rock band, where nobody ever noticed the mutated beasts or toxic byproducts destroyed at Disposal Plant P-12A. Umbrella's presence brought jobs, after all, and sustained the elevated highways and long, straight roads. It supported life on streets lined with pay phones, billboards, and mailboxes. Raccoon City had everything it believed it needed. Gas stations, roadside cafes, shopping streets with colorful tents, booming industrial parks, bars, diners and restaurants, nice offices, gun shops, and even some decent graffiti. The St. Michael's faux-Gothic Clock Tower in town center featured in postcards, and was considered a local treasure alongside the zoo and city hall, even if most visitors were probably more impressed by the extravagant, massive

Raccoon Police Station. This repurposed art museum was an eclectic building, sporting neoclassical, baroque, and art deco elements, with a fountain in its entrance hall and, rather shockingly, a fine collection of art.

Another odd thing about Raccoon City was that, despite being divided by the Circular River, industrial, residential, and commercial activities seemed to have piled upon each other, and seemingly always revolve around Umbrella. Then again, almost half the population was employed by Umbrella Pharmaceuticals and its subsidiaries, and nobody ever imagined the town going so explosively wrong. On the bright side, though, state and corporate agencies will now have a fine chance of studying the city's ruins in order to gain unique insights into both the T- and the G-viruses.

DESIGN INSIGHTS

Raccoon City was originally mentioned in the first *Resident Evil*, but only visited by players in its 1998 sequel. Even then, little of the actual city was shown, and yet players and critics were too satisfied to notice. Building up excitement apparently worked, as did the pre-rendered backgrounds that allowed for higher resolutions and greater detail than would have been possible in real-time 3D. These backgrounds lent the world its distinct feel, and permitted controlled framing and the effective setting up of scares. Any inconsistencies that could not be hidden was easily attributed to the far-fetched plot, and an admittedly eccentric approach to architectural and civic design. With Raccoon City being an extreme example of a company town gone bad, every business or building could plausibly hide an Umbrella lab, and sewers and underground trains could lead to secret facilities, following a spatial logic that only makes sense when viewing the city as a gigantic laboratory, and its residents as a population of guinea pigs.

The most important lesson *Resident Evil 2* has to offer is that, before destroying a city, one has to actually build it. Raccoon City feels as if it actually existed before the zombies; it is deeper than a cardboard prop connecting indoor levels. Its varied zombies are representative of a wider population, and the few roads shown are rich in street furniture, architectural variety, and activity. They feel both typical and representative enough to paint images of a wider town before the catastrophe. Besides, the skyline of Raccoon City (glimpsed in the main menu) was modeled after Montreal. The vast police station, on the other hand, seems iconically odd, as it was housed in a former art museum in order to explain the bizarre puzzles scattered throughout the building. Overlapping influences, restrictions, and sensibilities have shaped Raccoon City: an intriguingly skewed vision of American Midwestern urbanism crafted by Japanese game developers using late-1990s technology under the influence of 1970s and 1980s zombie movies.

Welcome to beautiful
Silent Hill

population: 30,000

21

SILENT HILL
Silent Hill

City: Silent Hill

Game: *Silent Hill*

Developer: Konami Computer Entertainment Tokyo (Team Silent)

Publisher: Konami

Release Date: 1999

Genre: Survival Horror

Platforms: PlayStation

Silent Hill, Maine, was once a quiet resort town renowned for its serene ambiance. Surrounded by rolling hills and split by a calm river flowing into Toluca Lake, for decades, this archetypal tourist town was an essential destination for nature lovers who enjoyed snowy winters. It was a lovely place perpetually enshrouded in scenic fog. At some point, somehow, it simply slipped away from reality and into legend. Reaching it today is apparently not impossible, but most prefer to imagine the city based on fragmented, often incoherent narrations, blurry photographs, and old, undated maps. Very few still heed its call, and even fewer return. Those who do so speak of a deserted place of dread where it rains ash and where an unnatural, merciful fog obscures unholy hallucinations and unfathomable horrors.

Choosing to believe rumors of a spooky, secluded town supposedly built on ancient burial grounds feels almost parochial, even if the more fanciful ones are indeed intriguing—and persistent. Ostensibly, this city of almost 30,000 souls now stands deserted. Snow is falling even during summers, and, after reaching it, one is somehow bound to find all roads exiting the town blocked. Phones and radios are dead. Abandoned cars are rotting on empty streets, and broken windows, washed-out walls, exposed bricks, and deteriorating architecture paint the bleak image of a ghost town. Typical diners remain empty among solemn, unoccupied buildings, rusting mailboxes and fire hydrants, bent street signs, dead street lamps, and boarded-up stores. Meat is perpetually rotting in out-of-power store fridges. Barely standing fire escapes lead to leaking water tanks, and, where once life filled a normal city, only the trees lining the disproportionately wide roads remain alive—that and the mold growing on walls.

It has been pointed out that, for an unspectacular town with a pretty standard park-filled grid, Silent Hill always boasted some unexpectedly odd and ominous street names. Surrounded by Midwich, Finney, Ellroy, and Bradbury Streets, the town's main residential quarter, Old Silent Hill, features spacious single family homes, modest apartment buildings, cafes, burger joints, and

Retail in Silent Hill has died a gruesome death

convenience stores, retaining a structure reminiscent of normality, a last vestige of sanity. Spooked visitors now speak of backyards stinking of death, chilling otherworldly sounds, ceremonially severed animal heads, roads collapsing into chasms, and blood drying under garage doors. Whispers of someone, or something, still residing at the austere Balkan Church at the corner of Bloch and Bachman pale when compared to descriptions of the quintessentially American Midwich Elementary School. Through its old clock tower, it is claimed, one can enter a hellish dimension; a rusted world covered with viscera and strewn with corpses. Promises of a darkness that will bring the choking heat are scribbled on disturbing blackboards, and child-shaped abominations roam the halls.

Unnatural aberrations have also been witnessed on the bridges spanning the river to connect Old and Central Silent Hill: the collapsed Finney Bridge and the Bloch-Sagan Drawbridge. Central Silent Hill, the town's business district just east of Old Silent Hill, is decidedly more urban, packed with derelict stores, offices, banks, and restaurants. Disturbing, writhing vines rise through grates, and deadly horrors lurk in the expansive basements of the central police station and the town hall. As for the Alchemilla Hospital on Koontz and Crichton, it is haunted by deformed, decaying nurses and doctors looking for victims. Not that the Resort Area, the touristy waterfront by Toluca Lake, is any safer. Its scenic lighthouse, once lively docks, half-sunk boats, and creepy amusement park are described as extremely deadly.

Scholars of the occult can trace Silent Hill's unique oddness throughout history. Ancient indigenous tribes called the area it occupies "The Place of Silenced Spirits," whereas a centuries-old secretive cult known as the Order has supposedly marked the city with its continuous efforts to revive a primeval, dark deity. Admittedly nothing short of demonic manifestation could perhaps explain the abrupt transformation of Silent Hill to an empty husk of a town devoid of all human life save for a handful of wanderers lured to the city, and a few residents trapped among vaguely humanoid monsters, winged demons, impossible lizards, and skinless, twisted dogs. In alleys, around blood-curling altars, in maintenance tunnels, and even on the open road wild delusion manifests, horrid beings stalking their incomprehensible prey among broken wheelchairs, writhing flayed bodies, and a ghostly girl walking on thin air. A darkness seems to be devouring the town, transforming it into a hellish nightmare. And when the blaring sirens are heard, skies suddenly turn black, tiled pavements turn to rusted gratings, city walls morph to bloodied metal meshes, and the shapes of too many hanging bodies define an even darker realm to the sounds of grinding metal and an inhuman cacophony of screams.

The nature of Silent Hill itself becomes uncertain as rust and flesh fuse. Living walls drip blood on metal floors, and, if any of this is even vaguely true, it does appear as if this small city has found itself at the epicenter of clashing realities, a merging of alternate dimensions. Silent Hill may not be a dream, but distinctions between reality and dream seem to lose their meaning there. Space warps, exposing gruesome scenes, and spatial and temporal disturbances profoundly confuse. Could this be a hallucination, or is it someone's tormented nightmare of arcane symbols and immense pain? Could such a bloodied purgatory of weeping lost children and wrathful creatures ever exist?

Above: The few remaining residents of Silent Hill are not very talkative
Below: The signs of bloody violence are too common in the foggy streets

DESIGN INSIGHTS

It is rare for a late-1990s 3D console game to age well, but *Silent Hill*'s terrifying fictional town has done so brilliantly—as has the game itself. Based on a properly planned, functioning resort settlement, the titular town's decay, surrealism, and horror were layered on strong, believable foundations, while the game's design embraced the era's tech limitations. *Silent Hill* renders an essentially open-world city in real-time on the original PlayStation. Despite limited draw distances and slow CD-ROM speeds, it manages to offer a seamless experience, and mitigates limitations via the liberal use of fog and darkness, which also add to the sense of dread and allow for dramatic civic surprises. Muddy, low-res textures, limited visibility, and a camera prone to switching to disorienting, expressionistic angles enhance the dramatic effect of the already bleak atmosphere. Freely roaming around Silent Hill combined with pre-scripted camera changes provide a masterful, curated, cinematic glimpse of the city.

The quality of the genuinely disturbing writing and world-building elevated the game above tiresome survival-horror clichés. *Silent Hill* was never intended as a B-movie type of horror experience. Instead, it presents its town both as a core character and as the atmospheric stage for a melancholy supernatural drama; a psychological head-trip in a fascinating interpretation of small American communities as imagined by a Japanese team and influenced by the works of David Lynch, Stephen King, and Dario Argento. *Silent Hill* is almost the equivalent of an interactive, explorable *Twin Peaks*, albeit with streets named after horror authors and a school referencing *The Midwich Cuckoos*.

The implied size of the town is another success, as is a playing area aptly circumscribed by chasms, collapsed tunnels, and foggy lakes. Out-of-scale road widths and a limited view distance let players imagine a much larger place, and saving assets by only allowing a few buildings to be entered makes perfect sense. The major, meticulously designed buildings that can be visited further influence the players' sense of scale with their labyrinthine interiors. As for the town's three districts, they are realistically distinguishable (even within the fog) by offering different building volumes, densities, and repeated details. Architecture makes functional sense too, and schools and hospitals seem based on real-life blueprints. In the game's weird, conflicting but well thought-out world, subtle connections and references abound. The pterodactyl-like enemies make sense when players discover Alessa's copy of *The Lost World*, while the in-game religion borrows real-life elements such as the angelic name Metatron and the demonic Flauros.

Finally, one simply has to mention the excellent map system tying everything together. Besides conveying the layout of the city, this in-game map also keeps track of objectives and alludes to its physical nature by demanding that players pick the map (and its parts) up. Having the protagonist note things on it not only provides gameplay guidance, but effectively turns the map into a combination of journal, GPS, quest tracker, and storytelling device.

22

WAN CHAI
Shenmue II

GENERAL INFORMATION //////////////////////

City: Wan Chai

Game: *Shenmue II*

Developer: Sega AM2

Publisher: Microsoft Game Studios, Sega

Release Date: 2001

Genre: Beat'em up, Open World

Platforms: Dreamcast, PlayStation 4, Windows, Xbox, Xbox One

In ten years' time, bustling and overcrowded Hong Kong will be joining the People's Republic of China, officially ending its colonial era and ushering in a new and different epoch for over five million inhabitants. For now, though, life simply goes on. Merchants, tourists, workers, and clerks fill the streets as barges and green-sailed junks crowd the sea. British and Chinese culture fuse and clash, tradition meets modernity, and fully comprehending the uncaring, often cruel metropolis remains nigh on impossible. Hong Kong is wealthy, most of its inhabitants are poor, the Walkman is a mandatory fashion accessory, and Cantopop typically drowns traditional pentatonic tunes. Real estate prices are skyrocketing, Toys 'R' Us stores are flooding local malls, and Hello Kitty has grown into a cultural icon. Hong Kong cinema is going international with Jackie Chan and John Woo, and all of the city is rapidly moving away from manufacturing and into entertainment, services, and real estate.

Hong Kong's modern towers rise on top of hastily demolished buildings, yet still the character of the city's architecture persists. Red, blue, yellow, and green signs pile upon each other, bringing color to bare brick walls and flaking painted facades. The tong lau tenements remain ubiquitous, and a staple of the urban image. Most of them are up to four floors tall and narrow, usually less than 16 feet in width. They are typically mixed-use buildings with the ground floor reserved for shops opening up to the road, and the upper floors with their balconies remaining residential. Over the years, the tong lau have incorporated influences from Edwardian architecture, Bauhaus, and, of course, the traditional Cantonese style, while being built on increasingly denser city blocks. Lacking elevators is a common trait, and toilet facilities are not guaranteed, but the tong lau remain a Hong Kong mainstay. The more affluent districts of the city tend to favor more comfortable, European types of buildings, while surviving precolonial Lingnan-style upward-curving roofs and the even older gates of fortified villages and Tin Hau temples add historical richness to an already dense cityscape.

Outside the Man Mo temple, up on the Scarlet Hills

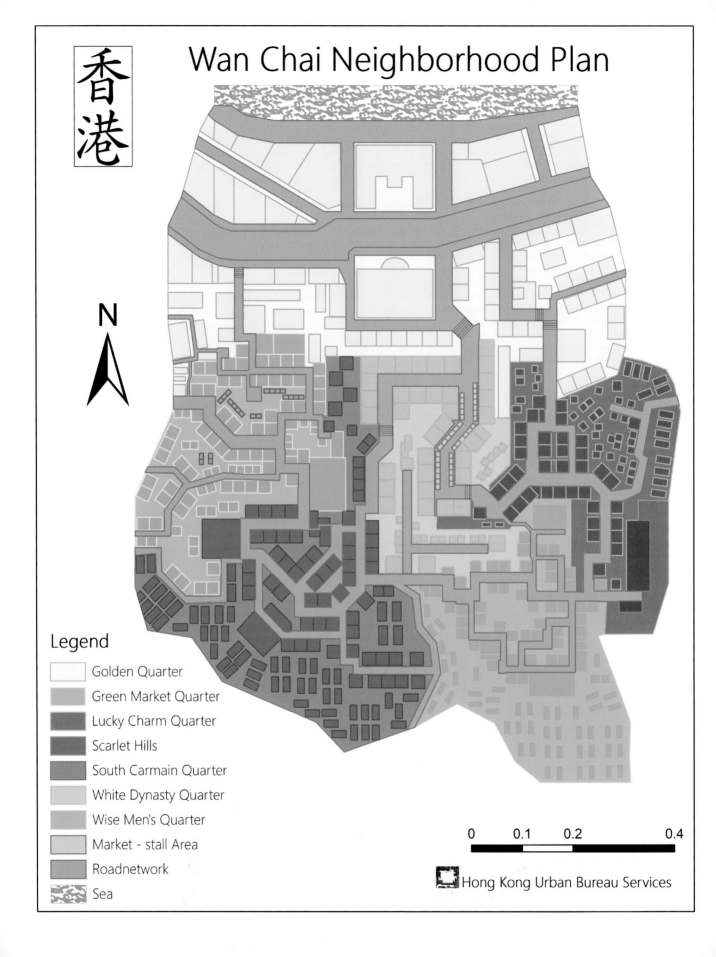

Wan Chai Neighborhood Plan

香港

N

Legend

Golden Quarter
Green Market Quarter
Lucky Charm Quarter
Scarlet Hills
South Carmain Quarter
White Dynasty Quarter
Wise Men's Quarter
Market - stall Area
Roadnetwork
Sea

0   0.1   0.2   0.4

Hong Kong Urban Bureau Services

The busy streets of Green Market Quarter

Wan Chai, which many consider the heart of Hong Kong, embraces all these influences, and represents the epitome of the city's lifestyle. Located at the northern shore of Hong Kong Island, next to Aberdeen, this is where tradition, old-fashioned trade, high-tech electronics, and ruthless finance meet with people of all classes. Overflowing streets and vibrant colors are characteristic of its markets, with the occasional tough guys, petty conmen, and pickpockets adding a threatening—if exciting—undercurrent to its impossible bustle. The streets are filled with stalls and bright signs in Chinese intersect above them. Bicycles, buses, businessmen, punk girls, and sailors with worn trousers traverse the sprawl of side streets and labyrinthine multi-story buildings that both Wan Chai and wider Hong Kong are made of.

Of Wan Chai's seven quarters, the northernmost, the Golden Quarter by the sea, is the most affluent. Fine, western-style apartment buildings, pricey cafes, glamorous shops, and cutting-edge neon signs line the busy avenue running down its middle. Streets are wide, automobile traffic heavy, and the area's jewelers famous—famously snobbish too, as anyone trying to enter Glamorous Jewelers in jeans is bound to discover. The spacious Golden Shopping Mall, with its varied clothing outlets, is way more accepting, even allowing musicians and martial artists to perform within it. The Juk Man Bookstore caters to local literary needs, while the multi-storied Pine Game Arcade offers the latest arcade video games—including the impressive *Out Run*—plus several jukeboxes and slot machines. To the Golden Quarter's southeast lie the snaking narrow roads of the overbuilt Green Market Quarter. Occupying its streets, one finds tong lau that have seen better days, brick and concrete buildings, and a mind-boggling variety of open-air stores and stands. Among red and green lanterns, colorful tents, and hanging meats, the greengrocers, butchers, restaurateurs, gamblers, hoteliers, and martial arts instructors make their business in a gambling paradise that has refined the thrills of duck racing.

The South Carmain Quarter is definitely worse off. Businesses here seem to be boarding up in dreadful anticipation of the realtors' bulldozers, even as many of the gray buildings' bravely stubborn tenants refuse to leave the houses they grew up in. The melancholy and dread of an inevitable future is broken up by Lotus Park. It may not be big but its red trees are exquisite, and the people calmly practicing t'ai chi under their shade seem to be doing so in defiance of the bamboo scaffolding hiding the transformation of ramshackle residences to modern high-rises. The forces of renewal seem intent on encroaching deeper, into the very center of Wan Chai. In the still lively White Dynasty Quarter, businesses are also closing, even if noticing this can be difficult. A wild menagerie of stalls selling spices, cooked food, fruit, birdcages, books, clothes, toys, tea, and medicinal herbs covers all, and the local bars, Bar Liverpool and Bar London, seem to be doing very well indeed.

Sega's impressive *Out Run* arcade cabinet

Doing even better, at the west end of Wan Chai, the Lucky Charm Quarter is where locals and foreigners alike shop for electronics and all sorts of clever appliances and gadgets. Commerce booms here, and has attracted all sorts of tea makers, cooks, tailors, and barbers, who seem to have gathered along the beautiful Three Blades Street as it steers away into the antique shops and pawnbrokers of the Wise Men's Quarter. But, past the latter's clusters of tong lau, past the humble shrines, traditional chemists, and religious stores lie the steep, long stairs leading up to Scarlet Hills. There, above the noise, above the greed of Wan Chai, serenity is generously offered to all at the Taoist temple of Man Mo and its beautiful stone yard. The monks are kind and patient, and the temple's precious book collection holds centuries of wisdom.

DESIGN INSIGHTS

Wan Chai is the urban open-world environment of a game that, at heart, remains an old-fashioned 3D beat 'em up. Thankfully though, much of *Shenmue II* is not meant to be spent fighting, but instead exploring its unique world, searching for clues, interacting with the economy, taking in the sights, and talking to non-player characters. These offer up clues and crucial information, while fleshing out the game's version of Hong Kong, providing backstory, and, more important, directing players toward the places they are looking for. Asking for directions and occasionally following characters who offer to act as guides are the most efficient ways of navigating Wan Chai; said directions are usually very clear, and involve recognizable in-game landmarks. Asking about reaching the district itself at the beginning of *Shenmue II*, for example, will have locals simply pointing toward a gate that needs to be crossed and reminding players to then take a left at the (unmissable) fountain.

Wan Chai condenses an iconic version of Hong Kong that combines reality and pop imagination, and is brought to life by day-and-night cycles, changing seasons, a weather system and residents with scripted, believable daily schedules. As time passes, non-player characters wake up, go to work, eat lunch, and return home. Shops open and close at set times, and further grounding players, survival in this setting costs money. Gambling, arm wrestling, street fighting, getting a job, or running a pachinko stand are all options for earning some, in a world of impressive detail that surpasses anything that had been attempted up until then. Wan Chai is a characterful, often humorous, stunning impression of 1980s Hong Kong with life purposefully flowing through its markets and packed roads. Sega even went as far as hiring specialists to decorate its interiors and design its furniture.

Unlike most open-world games before it or since, *Shenmue II* chose a more relaxed, almost hypnotic pace. Players help straighten shop signs, engage in simple everyday tasks, buy candy, talk with dozens of characters, and are allowed the time to dwell on details and take in the ambience. New side-quests and objectives do not keep on cluttering the flow of the game, and speaking to strangers doesn't launch even more quest-lines; it adds color and context instead. It is simplicity and elegance that make experiencing the tight, believable societal web of Wan Chai a delight.

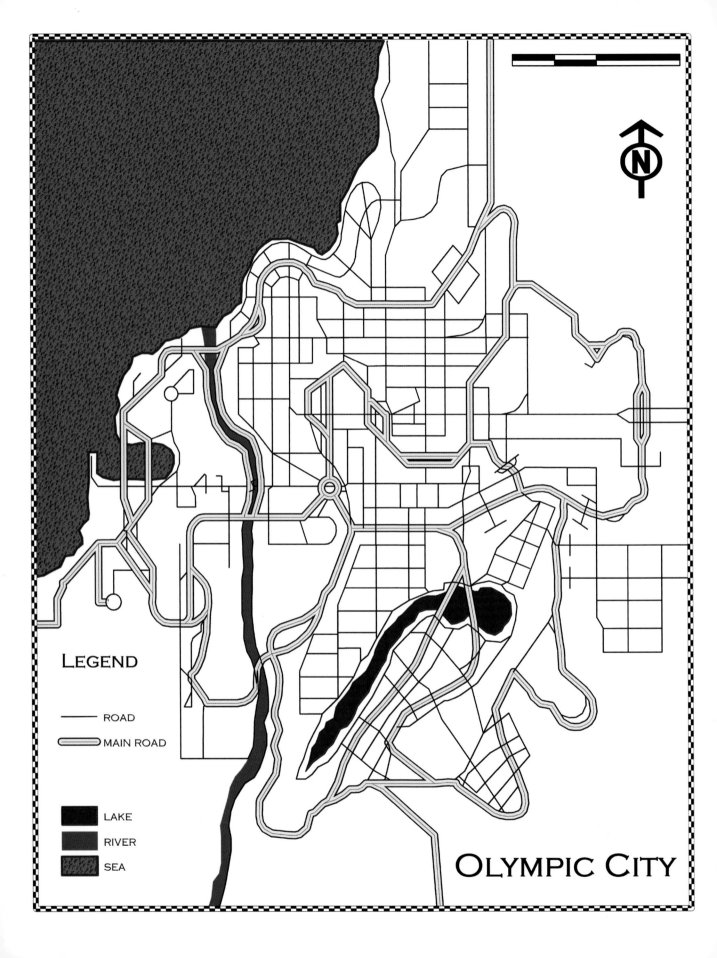

LEGEND

—— ROAD

◁▭▷ MAIN ROAD

■ LAKE

▬ RIVER

▨ SEA

OLYMPIC CITY

N

23

OLYMPIC CITY
Need for Speed: Underground

GENERAL INFORMATION ////////////////////

City: *Olympic City*

Game: Need for Speed: Underground

Developer: EA Black Box

Publisher: EA Games

Release Date: 2003

Genre: Racing

Platforms: Game Boy Advance, GameCube, PlayStation 2, Windows, Xbox

Olympic City, the major US port and flourishing coastal metropolis, is as decidedly unextraordinary as its climate is temperate. Olympic City, you see, never experienced a turbulent history, never starred in a movie, and the closest it ever came to overshadowing New York City was the construction of its most recognizable landmark, the one everyone keeps referring to as "the Empire State Building Halved." On the other hand, life here can be modestly pleasant, simple, safe, and, on occasion, rather lively, too. Jobs are plentiful, violent crime a rarity, and the local economy is booming. Oil refineries and factories are thriving in the expanding industrial districts, while new corporate headquarters keep appearing around the gigantic stock exchange. This otherwise unremarkable city is a financial powerhouse of countless shops, bright lights, well-kept parks, fancy billboards and a high-tech new stadium.

What truly sets Olympic City apart, though, and what has given it worldwide fame among certain circles, is something entirely unexpected: car racing. Not the sort of racing mainstream press covers, of course, but underground illegal races without sponsors or checkered flags. Dangerous races in heavily tricked-out cars, on public streets, lend an unprecedented edge to this average city. Shockingly, and rather crucially too, local police do not seem to mind these races, whereas the subtly varied geography of the town—its few hills, river, and intriguing coastline—allows for a great variety of impromptu racing tracks. Long, straight stretches of road are combined with broad boulevards, freeways cutting across town, perfectly curved interchanges, and narrow park streets. Tunnels, frequent roadworks, river drawbridges (allowing for amazing jumps), and dry riverbeds add a dangerous touch of extra excitement.

Not that underground racers consistently keep away from the downtown avenues of meticulously gardened trees and easy-to-terrorize peaceable citizens. Pedestrians themselves may be protected by some of the sturdiest bollards and pavement railings worldwide, but wisely prefer the relatively safer options public transportation has to offer. The demand for decent alternatives

One can't help but wonder whether such sinuous streets were actually made for racing

Street chandeliers are an Olympic City novelty

to driving and walking alongside traffic has been strong across all classes for decades, and Olympic City now enjoys a thankfully extensive subway network, decent bus services, and efficient picturesque trams. The train station, harbor, and airport serve long-distance traffic, and admittedly, provide some intriguing thematic backgrounds for underground races too.

Unsurprisingly, while pleasing and nicely varied, the architectural sights in Olympic City are never groundbreaking. Tall modern and postmodern buildings, and Chicago- and New York-influenced skyscrapers, are dominant, with an occasional cyberpunk aesthetic. The Verona Hotel bridging over a chandeliered tunnel stands out among a multitude of other massive hotels, whereas buildings such as the domed arts center and the old, colonial-style elementary school add flair to the predominantly steel, glass, and concrete downtown. Farther out, across workers' districts and petit-bourgeois suburbia, single- or two-story apartment buildings of brick and modestly sized McMansions are common, adhering to a rather typical structural pattern.

The city itself consists of a dense central business district, surrounded by a wider, varied downtown area, residential zones, and several suburbs and specialized sub-centers. It is essentially a small system of separate grids connected to each other via highways and freeways. The centrally located and ever-busy downtown, a favorite late-night racing circuit, features impressively lit buildings, the widest boulevards, the Grand Station, and far too many neon signs, especially on the lively Market Street. Its older, more touristy sections sport interesting churches, a small lake, and cosy cafes, and interact heavily with nearby Chinatown. The latter brims with retail activity, restaurants, and housing complexes, and is home to the popular City Plaza urban mall. The wider civic core includes further housing districts, as well as the corrugated iron roofs and obvious poverty of a few under-lit slums.

Port Royal, the town harbor, with its adjacent industrial Atlantica district, is located in the western part of Olympic City, where complex industrial facilities and the flames of oil refineries coexist with the city prison, a massive car graveyard, and some sinuous tunnels made for drifting. Posher suburbs with lush parks, pastoral park roads, fine public sculptures, and the occasional hotel or corporate tower are mostly located in the southern and eastern regions of the metropolitan area. As for the persistent rumors concerning the zoning for a specialized district focused on the sale, modification, and maintenance of exotic and very fast cars, they remain, for now, mere rumors.

DESIGN INSIGHTS

Need for Speed: Underground sold phenomenally, and achieved an unexpected level of critical appreciation despite Olympic City itself being unashamedly generic. Crucially, though, dominating the game was not the purpose of this particular city. It simply had to look right, feel plausible, support the game design, and allow for interesting courses and good level design. Olympic City was built to facilitate racing, and it achieved exactly that.

Choosing to use an imaginary settlement was another clever choice, as it was able to get away with many details that a depiction of Los Angeles, for example, wouldn't be able to, while simultaneously feeling familiar to most. Spatial variation and thematic courses were achieved by including recognizable, iconic urban sections—the slum, the suburb, the downtown, the entertainment strip—and arranging them sensibly. As for the visuals and style of the game, they were obviously influenced by the then-popular film *The Fast and the Furious*, typical US grid configurations, and the architectural styles mostly found in metropolitan New York and Chicago.

The elements and location archetypes used to create Olympic City's routes are obviously specialized, allowing them to be legible while driving by at top speed. So, the entertainment lane is packed with neon signs and bars, the slums are dark and dirty with narrow roads, and the Chinatown segments are simply unmistakable. Urban imagery and architectural typologies per district have been successfully abstracted into highly readable parts that can be assembled in repeatable but varied configurations. They are always recognizable, but never entirely the same. Special components such as the stadium or the train station obviously stand out, and help bring uniqueness to many of the game's 100-plus racetracks. Finally, the atmosphere of the races is enhanced in the night-time glow of the metropolis—all racing takes place during nights—which, combined with constantly wet roads, allows for the blurring of car and city lights and some appropriate reflectivity effects.

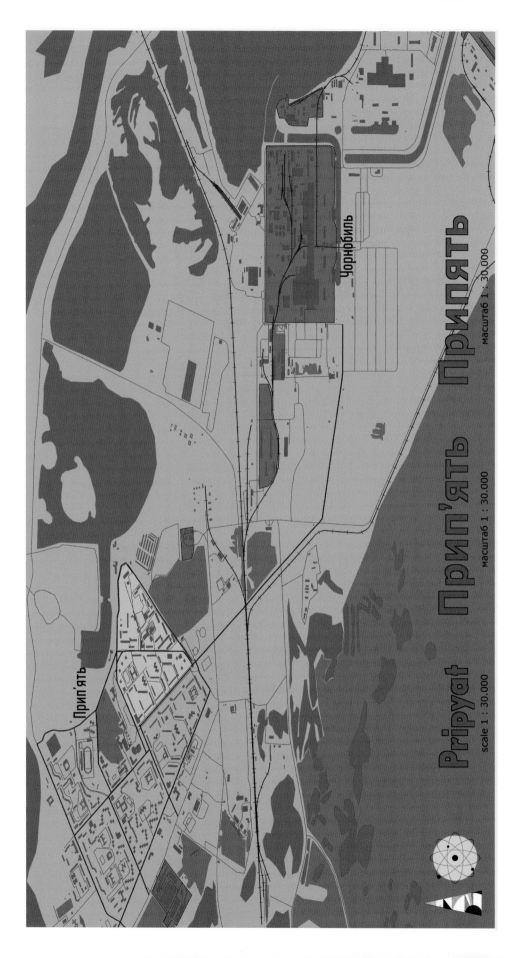

Прип'ять

Чорнобиль

Pripyat

Прип'ять

Припять

scale 1 : 30.000

масштаб 1 : 30.000

масштаб 1 : 30.000

24

PRIPYAT
S.T.A.L.K.E.R.: Call of Pripyat

GENERAL INFORMATION /////////////////////

City: Pripyat

Game: *S.T.A.L.K.E.R.: Call of Pripyat*

Developer: GSC Game World

Publisher: NA: Deep Silver, EU: Deep Silver, CIS: GSC World Publishing, WW: bitComposer Games

Release Date: 2009

Genre: First-Person Shooter, Open World, Survival Horror

Platforms: Windows

Named after the adjacent Pripyat River, the city of Pripyat was founded on February 4, 1970. It was the ninth nuclear city of the Soviet Union, and was built to house the workers and scientists of the brand-new ambitious Chernobyl Nuclear Power Plant. Constructed among the woods and marshes of the Polesie Plains, this was the largest power station in Europe, and its city quickly replaced the outdated village of Semykhody to encompass the Soviet vision for the atomic metropolis of the future. Pripyat was meant as a physical manifestation of a socialist-planned economy, a meticulously designed model city that achieved a population of 49,360 at its peak, and was organized along modernist lines to bring forth the triumph of humanist principles in urban planning.

Spanning roughly two square miles, Pripyat's structure consisted of eight residential micro-districts surrounded by industrial sectors, recreational zones, forest plantations, and areas reserved for future expansion. The city featured the central administrative core common to most Soviet plans, and generous open spaces; as buildings occupied less than a fifth of the total residential area, the rest was taken up by gardens, parks, forests, cultivated areas, and roads. District-level heating served the 160 typically modernist, functionalist apartment blocks that, with the exception of a few towers, ranged from five to nine stories in height and were notable for their flat roofs, waterproofed surfaces, and balconies. Public buildings, factories, and facilities were restricted to three stories in height, and all constructions were almost exclusively built from concrete blocks.

The commonly austere aesthetic choices of the USSR's architects were tempered by vivid murals, public art, lush flower beds, and the flourishes of color and uniqueness found in such places as the Prometheus Movie Theater, with its stained-glass windows and expressive statue of mythical Prometheus. On the walls of the Palace of Culture, bright murals praised brotherhood and abundance, and further lively splashes were provided by the signs of laundromats and

The statue of Prometheus still standing outside the Prometheus movie theater

Pripyat's Ferris wheel never turned

department stores. Eventually, the famous yellow Ferris wheel was erected to celebrate May Day 1986. And even if this Ferris wheel never turned, the city did come close to encapsulating what was officially regarded as utopia.

Pripyat was one of the most modern, most luxuriant cities of the USSR. It ensured all its residents had access to healthcare, education, art, nature, and leisure. Quality of life was provided by 13,414 apartments, 33,000 rose plants, fifteen kindergartens and elementary schools, playgrounds, secondary and technical schools, an academy of the arts, gyms, Olympic-sized indoor swimming pools and basketball courts, shooting galleries, libraries, three clinics, and a large hospital complex. Cafeterias, bars, and restaurants could serve up to 5,535 residents simultaneously, whereas two stadiums, several theaters, concert halls, and cinemas kept the thriving community entertained. Everything had been planned for, from fishing in the plant's cooling reservoir and sunbathing on the sandy beaches of the river to picking mushrooms in the forest, or watching the hydrofoils from the picturesque cafe of the port. Life here was good.

After disaster struck, everything just stopped. On April 26, 1986, at 1:23 a.m., the scheduled test of Reactor 4 in the Chernobyl Nuclear Power Plant went horribly wrong, and resulted in nuclear meltdown. A massive explosion scattered radioactive clouds across Europe, and, overnight, Pripyat's Ferris wheel became a monument to the worst man-made accident in history. Authorities evacuated 160,000 people living within 20 miles of the reactor, and Pripyat was emptied out. The Chernobyl Exclusion Zone—the Zone—was established to prevent all human activity in the area—with the exception of a network of laboratories covertly set up to research the effects of fallout on the human mind. Almost twenty years after the first incident and fifteen years after the demise of the Soviet Union, on April 13, 2006, a second disaster caught everyone off-guard. This new explosion, attributed to a mysterious AI called the C-Consciousness, filled the Zone with even more dangerous types of radiation, warping the landscape itself and spawning endless lethal anomalies, and with them, the Artifacts.

The strange, wonderful, and highly sought after Artifacts, said to possess miraculous powers and known to fetch incredible prices, have lit a beacon in the Zone's wastelands calling to all adventurers willing to ignore deadly risk for fortune. These people illegally roaming the Zone and hunting for Artifacts have come to be known as Stalkers. They are usually loners, but occasionally gather around common fires to barter, form groups and factions, and breathe life into the rudimentary society slowly growing in the empty villages, abandoned towns, and ruined farmhouses of the Zone. Sturdy, maintained shelter is, after all, crucial when the emissions occur: the ground shakes, the sky turns red, and lethal psychic energies kill anyone caught in the open while mutating unlucky animals. The populations of deer, elk, moose, and boar, which grew enormously after the evacuation of humans, along with the rising numbers of their natural predators, suffered severe genetic changes. Now, aggressive packs of pseudodogs, Cerberus-like chimeras, and tentacled bloodsucker monsters hunt alongside wild beasts, cruel groups of bandits, and telekinetic corpse-eating Burers.

Yet Stalkers keep pouring into the Zone. Especially since 2012, when the lethal psy-emitters, dubbed the "Brain Scorchers," were mysteriously deactivated, and the way to the center of the Zone, the fabled Wish Granter of Chernobyl and the city of Pripyat, was reopened. Nowadays, surviving the Jupiter Underground's deadly tunnels is possible, and leads to the heart of the former Soviet utopia: the decaying city of Pripyat now ravaged by radioactive contamination and reclaimed by nature. Rust has taken over, animals and mutants proliferate between rotting cars and collapsed walls, and residential slabs with smashed windows stand empty. The rising tide of trees has all but conquered streets, covered cracked plazas, and is gradually infiltrating buildings. Blocks rise above a dense forest, hiding deadly pockets of radiation, flaking frescoes, and old hammer-and-sickle—decorated lamp posts. The sound of dripping water coming through ceilings is a constant reminder of erosion eating ever deeper at the frames of Pripyat's structures, while anomalies, and with them those priceless Artifacts, have lured humans back to town to fight each other and die over the city's magical riches. Stalkers of multiple factions, the Ukrainian military, gangs of mutants, and Monolith cultists are being murdered around the Yubileiny Service Center— the erstwhile municipal center hiding Laboratory X-8 where the C-Consciousness first became self-aware.

DESIGN INSIGHTS

S.T.A.L.K.E.R.'s post-apocalyptic Pripyat is based on the very real city of Pripyat, and the equally real, globally infamous Chernobyl disaster. The game used the city's architecture and planning to construct its experience on believable foundations, and bestow it with an instantly identifiable atmosphere of dread. Abstractions were inevitably made and a few civic elements were moved around, but Pripyat remained close to its original image. Photorealistic depictions of the town, its landmarks, and the surrounding zone further pushed toward realism in a setting deeply influenced by the popular science fiction novella *Roadside Picnic* and its famous 1979 film adaptation in Andrei Tarkovsky's magnificent *Stalker*.

The layout of in-game Pripyat is for the most part modeled on the southeast area of real-life Pripyat, Microdistrict 1, where several important locations such as a middle school, a river port, a grocery store, a department store, a bookstore, and two kindergartens were crammed. The Prometheus Movie Theater was moved there from the city center, and the Yubileiny Service Center from Microdistrict 3. The buildings retain the layouts and uses of their real-life counterparts, and the urban environment, despite not truly being part of a cohesive open world, is believably constrained. The modest settlement size also allows for a certain dynamism, as Pripyat and its internal power relations change dramatically according to player choice.

The atmosphere is further supported by apt aesthetics, convincing recreations of the built and natural environment, and, of course, the built-in dread and nostalgia of a recent ruin. The soundscape plays a significant role too. It is never silent in Pripyat. The wind, the creaking doors, and the occasional groan or gunshot supply an unsettling ambient auditory environment that emphasizes potential dangers in dark basements and derelict apartments. Pripyat, beautiful as it might have once been, is sinister and tense, and the scarcity of foes is necessary to this balance. Familiarity breeds contempt, even among the game's gloomy stages, survival-horror sensitivities, and odd foes.

25

ARKHAM CITY
Batman: Arkham City

GENERAL INFORMATION /////////////////////

City: Arkham City (in Gotham City)

Game: *Batman: Arkham City*

Developer: Rocksteady Studios

Publisher: Warner Bros. Interactive Entertainment

Release Date: 2011

Genre: Fighting, Open World, Stealth

Platforms: Mac OS, PlayStation 3, PlayStation 4, Xbox One, Xbox 360, Wii U, Windows

More disturbing than Franz Kafka's most pessimistic thoughts, Arkham City is a hellish penal colony. A city-within-a-city, populated exclusively by Gotham's convicted population, was created only after a terrorist attack convinced Mayor Quincy Sharp that Arkham Asylum and the Blackgate Penitentiary simply weren't safe or big enough to contain crime. Sharp isolated a whole Gotham district, and converted it into a vastly expanded Arkham Asylum dubbed the Arkham City. All inmates have been relocated to this new facility, where Professor Hugo Strange is chief administrator and security is handled by the militarized law enforcers of TYGER. And as Gotham City's politics further degenerate into authoritarianism, all law-breaking or dissenting citizens are shipped to the prison district. Tax-dodgers, dissidents, and petty burglars are left to fend off crime bosses, serial killers, and deranged sadists in an environment where inmates are given free rein as long as they do not attempt to escape.

Arkham City takes up a significant part of metropolitan Gotham's heart, as an entire island with its existing infrastructure has been remodeled into this gigantic prison. Walled off and rapidly decaying, the vast new jail is worse than any slum. Located in uptown Gotham, Arkham City encompasses a major industrial area, many residential blocks, famous locales such as the Amusement Mile, Park Row, and Bowery, as well as numerous formerly important buildings. The First National Bank, the old Gotham Police Department building, the Solomon Wayne Courthouse, Gotham Cathedral, and a large section of the docks are all rotting alongside warehouses, hotels, bars, and countless residences. Not even the Olympus nightclub and the once-respected Natural History Museum were spared. Then again, Arkham City is not officially a prison; it is supposedly just a "quarantine zone" that, theoretically, enjoys security patrols, municipal services, healthcare, and parole options, even if, in reality, Arkham is a lawless war zone where the criminally insane run free.

The still-illuminated Krank Co. Toys sign against the Gotham City skyline

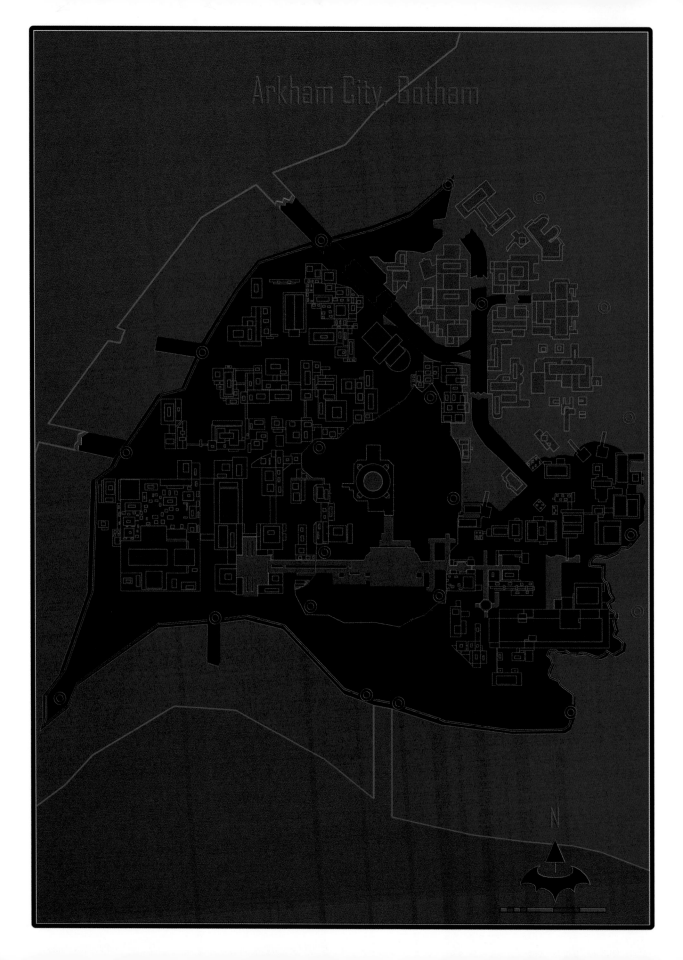

Arkham City's maddening, constantly monitored cityscape

As long as prisoners keep away from Arkham's restricted citadel, they rarely have to deal with TYGER's forces. From there, the Wonder Tower, a fortified urban panopticon and the tallest building of Arkham, runs the place. It keeps inmates in and interlopers out. It monitors the high walls surrounding the city, as well as its heavily fortified entry points. The perimeter walls are patrolled by helicopters, blimps, and ground teams, while the bridges connecting the prison to the rest of Gotham have been demolished or blocked off. Floodlights, searchlights, and TYGER's forces—the GCPD has no jurisdiction here—ensure nothing and nobody enters or leaves without Professor Strange's consent. This dense but still beautiful criminal ghetto, dwarfed by the skyscrapers of Gotham it can only glimpse beyond its walls, is under his complete control.

Gotham City's unique architecture evolved throughout the nineteenth century, and reached its apex during the twentieth century by combining Gothic Revival tendencies with various strains of modernism, Chicagoan influences, and a love for ornate, evocative facades and really tall buildings. The style's century-long prominence simply couldn't end at Arkham's recent walls. Gargoyles are commonplace on massive buildings of brick, stone, and concrete, most roofs are flat, and their tall water tanks are characteristic of Arkham's silhouette, as is the basilica of the courthouse, several art deco skyscrapers, and the surviving bell towers and domes. Decaying factories and the

Dilapidated, dangerous streets dominate the vast urban prison

noir paintbrush of inadequate lighting have somehow allowed dereliction to aesthetically enhance the terrifying city, turning it into a stunningly atmospheric, deadly retro-futurist nightmare of collapsed bridges, flooded streets, rusting cranes, flaming chimneys, and barricaded apartments.

Blinking neon signs, the GCR Comms towers, highways claimed by water, vandalized statues, propaganda posters on once-pristine walls, debris, and an ominous Ferris wheel somehow tie in with the general ambience of crow-infested Arkham. This is no proper, functioning city. It is instead a perverse mockery of urbanism, offering a hellish and very brief existence to the vast majority of its inhabitants. Arkham isn't even a true prison, existing instead in a perpetual state of barely controlled anarchy and constant gang war. With hundreds of homicidal berserkers on the loose, political and misdemeanor prisoners have to band together and attempt to hide and defend themselves, often below the surface, in Arkham's putrid maze of old steel and ironwork. Aboveground, things are too lethal.

Access to guns is the only source of meaningful power, garbage has been piling up since the facility's opening, and loudspeakers remind inmates that failure to obey, conform, and comply are punishable by death. Everyone is constantly monitored but never kept safe, and even if Batman is said to maintain his own vigil over the project, it is Bruce Wayne who has been actively campaigning against it. And he's now got himself sent to Arkham City for it.

Mr. Wayne is far from the city's sole famous resident. Joker, the Penguin, Two-Face, Harley Quinn, and other super-villains have all been incarcerated here and are passionately trying to kill each other. Full-scale war is raging within Arkham's walls as extraordinary criminals draw new battle lines and shape space to fit their psychoses and rituals. Tiny empires and unique biomes are crafted using old Gotham as raw material. Villains are molding the city, claiming territories, and mobilizing massive gangs in pointless battles. Joker and Harley, being the first in Arkham, have grabbed the abandoned steel mill in its partly submerged southeast corner, fortified it, and converted it into a demented funhouse complete with roller coaster rides ending in industrial incinerators. Two-Face occupies the Solomon Wayne Courthouse and has half-scarred it. The Penguin commands his henchmen from the museum he drowned in water. Mr. Freeze enjoys the cold of the old police department's morgue.

What's more, dystopia is about to get even worse if the rumors surrounding the sinister-sounding Protocol 10 carry any trace of truth.

DESIGN INSIGHTS

Arkham City, the maximum-security penal town for Gotham's eponymous gangsters and criminal masterminds, would never have worked from an urban-planning standpoint. It is a monumentally awful, nonsensical idea, but also one that led to a fantastic, dark fantasy urban playground for Batman and his colorful enemies. This is an impossible place that's only vaguely similar to our cities, and yet one that masterfully balances the odd with the familiar, showing what can happen when key urban functions are taken away. This setting allows for a cleverly gated, closed-off open world to be filled with a large ensemble of characters from Batman's history without upsetting the wider DC Comics universe. Arkham City is arguably a blueprint in building a coherent video game setting without sacrificing decades of lore. A fine example in crafting a critically and commercially successful game with a city as its main character.

Familiar locations such as the GCPD building, Crime Alley, and Ace Chemicals, with their distinct and color-coded neon signs, make for excellent navigational landmarks and architectural fan service. Players can brood on gargoyles overlooking the city, climb gothic bell towers, and enjoy traversing a built environment created for Batman's unique version of parkour. Gliding through the skies is easy and satisfying, while the grappling hook makes reaching high points to scout or fly off from a joy. The urban environment allows players to swoop in on bad guys, stalk them from the ground, ambush them in shadows, and wrestle out of danger as they see fit in a wonderfully dense city that simultaneously feels large and claustrophobic. Batman actually being the greatest civic danger is still novel, and the inmate population's dynamic reactions to player actions were definitely innovative upon release.

Clever details like the parallax faked windows, and the fact that most buildings cannot be entered (and this never feels odd) are also worth mentioning. As are the impressively detailed, coherent, and architecturally wondrous interiors of the buildings that can actually be visited.

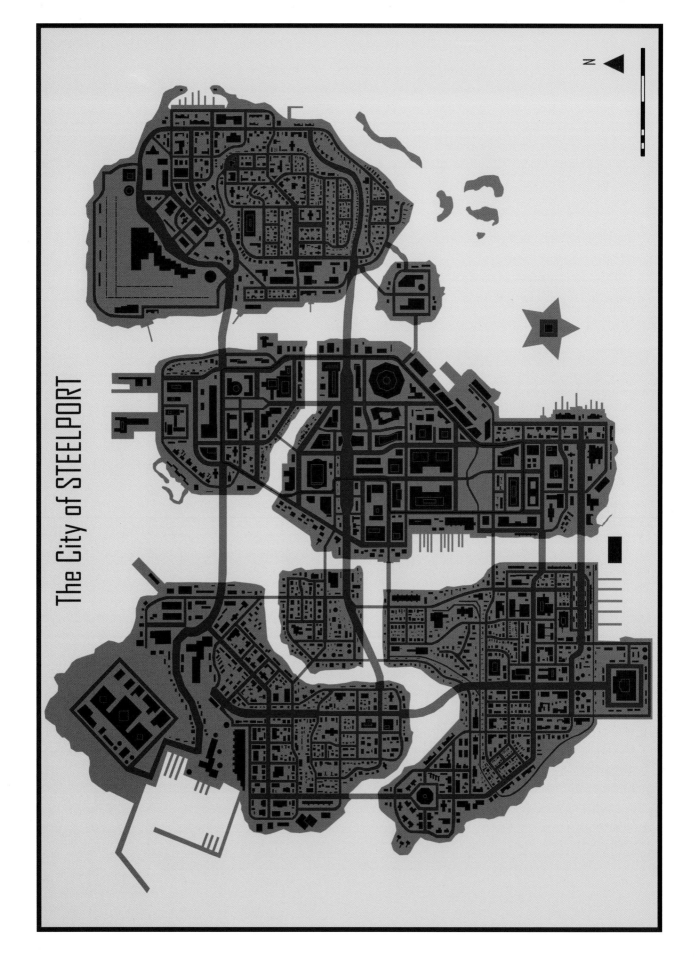

The City of STEELPORT

26

STEELPORT
Saints Row: The Third

GENERAL INFORMATION ////////////////////

City: Steelport

Game: *Saints Row: The Third*

Developer: Volition

Publisher: THQ

Release Date: 2011

Genre: Action-adventure, Open World

Platforms: Linux, Nintendo Switch, PlayStation 3, Windows, Xbox 360

Only Steelport, a generic yet outlandishly weird metropolis spanning seven islands, stuffed with warped versions of famous architectural landmarks, could have chosen Burt Reynolds for its mayor. Then again, this is where *Gangstas in Space* was filmed; the less sensible sister city of Stilwater—a place famous for its annual hosting of the Murderbrawl at the Steelport Arena and the city-wide festival of the Genkibowl, held for the mega-popular TV show *Professor Genki's Super Ethical Reality Climax.*

Steelport, the home of Steelport Airlines and commonly described as Detroit-meets-New-York-meets-Chicago, was founded back in 1827 by blue-collar industrialists, and flourished throughout the turbulent 1800s. Its many Romanesque and Gothic churches, all dated to the nineteenth century, are the venerable witnesses of the city's rise and subsequent fall from grace, as it succumbed to economic crisis and societal collapse.

Today, the tangled network of invariably run-down, cracked, sloppily patched roads and highways, the rusting elevated train tracks, and the elaborate bridges, tie in—in an almost cinematic way—with the profoundly industrial cityscape of the metropolis. Chimneys, water tanks, and mobile-phone towers dot a skyline dominated by unusually tall skyscrapers and far too many languishing factories. The enormous statue of a worker pouring molten steel, the city's symbol on the star-shaped Magarac Island, desperately apes the Statue of Liberty, and keeps reminding of the old glory days, when daily production quotas were an honest way of living—that's now dying alongside mass transit, diners, and mom-and-pop grocery stores. Casinos are bringing in the profits these days, and they keep opening them among the still-smoking chimneys, making sure they are accompanied by sex shops, bars, brothels, and flashy neon clubs. Drug dealers and pimps do business under oversized tacky billboards, and good taste is suffering an undignified death during nights that become increasingly spectacular and deadly.

Suburban Steelport occasionally offers the illusion of normalcy

Steelport has fallen into the hands of the multinational criminal enterprise, the Syndicate. The strict corporate structure of this loose alliance of gangs looms over everything, comprising Morningstar's slick sex traders, Luchadores, and the cyber-goth Deckers. Syndicate Tower, the tallest, most visible building in town, marks the epicenter of their territory and exhibits the power of the city's gangster overlords. Buildings and districts glow with their gang colors, and crime wantonly redecorates urban space to fit its unsubtle tastes. Only international crime superstars, the 3rd Street Saints, can hope to challenge the Syndicate's dominance. Having merged with the Ultor Corporation to become an unstoppable media and consumer empire, they have earned the energy drink sponsorships, shiny headquarters, movie deals, and chain of Planet Saints superstores to take on anyone. Their bloody clash with the Syndicate—an out-of-proportion turf war—has already terrified and fascinated the locals, panicked the police, and drawn the attention of the heavily armed Special Tactical Anti-Gang (STAG) unit.

STAG, infamous for staging terrorist attacks and employing fighter jets, is bound to bring even more chaos to Steelport's hedonistic battlefield. Daily shootouts, unmanned drones, and airstrikes already wreak havoc throughout the bullet-ridden, intoxicated city. Gangs fight with

pistols, machine guns, and rocket launchers, but, as conflicts escalate, so does surrealism. Quickly outgrowing tanks or attack choppers, war is nowadays waged via exploding pimps, gigantic purple dildos, and guns that shoot mind-controlling octopuses. And while the toll of leveled buildings, civilian deaths, and incinerated factories keeps on rising, crime bosses party on roof gardens protected by armies of purple ninjas, venerable industrialists fortify their estates, and far too many people frantically drive around town with tigers in their cars. Adding to the overall weirdness are kitschy, unsuccessfully sexy streetlights, human cannonballs, speeding pink cement mixers, naked people enjoying their walks, furry bunnies riding in golf carts, and citizens eager to cheer any and all attempts at reckless driving. As for the prevailing fashion, it is determined by the Let's Pretend store's eclectic offerings, ranging from spaceman suits to BDSM outfits.

Shockingly, an otherwise drab city of muted browns and faded reds is lurking behind the enormous flashing screens and neon signs. With the exception of Downtown, with its obscenely tall postmodern skyscrapers, most of Steelport is poor and industrial, its manufacturing identity still barely clinging to existence, as old mansions and mills alike are converted into massive brothels and casino clubs. But then, any modification can be accommodated by the city's non-

existent plan. For decades, factories, bungalows and residential towers have been mixing freely, the complete lack of zoning regulations allowing apartment buildings to be constructed next to chemical plants. Skyscrapers still sit comfortably next to steel mills as every inch of the city is gradually being transformed into a wild, spreading red light district—the political economy of crime embedding itself across metropolitan islands, districts, and neighborhoods.

From the central business district of villainy in Steelport's Downtown, past high-rises, skyscrapers, massive hospital complexes, wharfs, and historical mills, gangster money has infected everything. Stanfield's predominantly single-family house neighborhoods are overflowing with gangsters, the nuclear power plant of Burns Hill is about to be sold to the Saints, parks are turning into no-go zones, and cribs are sprouting all over the place. The Luchadores govern the poor of the Carver Island District, whereas Steelport Arena, New Baranec, Port Pryor, the Grove, and the Wesley Cutter International Airport are constantly

Above: Dressing up as a one-eyed, armed tiger feels banal on these wild streets
Below: Even the tallest skyscraper isn't safe from parachute attacks

fought over in an unending turf war. Even Camano Place, Rosen Oaks, and the insignificant Espina are caught in the madness, but it is from the restricted southeast district—the so-called Armory where the National Guard and STAG are based—that all hell is bound to break loose. Rumor has it that even a zombie apocalypse is in the cards.

DESIGN INSIGHTS

Steelport was obviously designed more as a ridiculous open-world theme park for adults than a believable city. It revels in being unreasonable, and thoroughly embraces the absurdity of a setting that tries to hide its cynicism with goofiness. Lowbrow environmental gags, daftly named locales, joke vehicles, and exaggeratedly unrealistic spaces fusing factories with casinos quickly kill off any expectation of realism. Successive over-the-top moments, throwaway jokes, and a constant emphasis on oddness reveal the (silly) narrative premise of postmodern gangsters running the world, around which the construction of the game city was organized. Steelport always had to allow for violent, absurd play.

The city was also designed so that players can easily orient themselves and quickly find their bearings. Downtown's super-tall towers are constantly visible, gangs and their distinct colors are tied to specific districts, large straight highways connect major islands and landmarks, and an abundance of road signs make navigating easier. Buildings such as the Syndicate Tower, the Steelport Arena, or the Downtown hospital, which distinctly stand out, are always central to the game's progression, while the planning of the city—supported by its industrial nature—facilitates exaggerated combat in its large open spaces, yards, and warehouses. Too-wide streets that and spacious intersections enable racing through town and the comfortable maneuvering of beastly vehicles such as tanks. Furthermore, the physical appearance of Steelport is dynamic, and can be significantly altered over the course of the game. Players can, for example, decide whether to blow up the top section of Syndicate Tower, and whether to transform the nuclear power plant into a skyscraper.

Although Steelport is completely fictional, it crucially remains recognizable as a city by broadly referencing general conceptions of urbanism. Downtown, for instance, is archetypically dense, and its skyline features numerous buildings resembling familiar skyscrapers such as the Empire State Building. The steelworker statue, another reference to New York and its famous landmark, further adds a sense of history to the place and implies a more believable, less outrageous past. Not overly constrained by realistic proportions, Steelport is reminiscent of exaggerated places such as Batman's Gotham or Superman's Metropolis, albeit one not sculpted by ink on paper but by an advanced proprietary editor that Volition developed. Said tool was—among other clever features— evidently capable of automatically texturing freshly extended roads or raised buildings and implementing substantial changes on the fly.

27

KAMUROCHO
Yakuza 0

GENERAL INFORMATION ////////////////////////

City: Kamurocho

Game: *Yakuza 0*

Developer: Ryu Ga Gotoku Studio

Publisher: Sega

Release Date: 2015

Genre: Action-Adventure, Open World

Platforms: PlayStation 3, PlayStation 4, Windows, Xbox One

It is 1988 and Tokyo, one of the greatest metropolitan centers in the world, has been enjoying the most prosperous decade of its history. The seat of the Emperor of Japan, leveled during the Great Kantō earthquake of 1923 and firebombed to cinders during World War II, is beaming proudly once again. Brand-new skyscrapers, ambitious architecture, the imposing Tokyo Tower, and large beautiful parks define its reconstructed landscape. Futuristic monorails, efficient new subway trains, and wide boulevards move millions around this vast, booming real estate market, powering an economy that can do no wrong. Japan's industry is redefining the cutting edge. It is leading a digital revolution, manufacturing the most popular cars and electronics, and ensuring the yen keeps on exploding in value. Money flows like water. Unemployment rates barely register, and newfound riches simply have to be spent.

This bubble economy is what is fueling the increasingly over-the-top excesses of the decade: an orgy of materialism, where money is everything and nothing. Millions of yen are effortlessly earned and spent, and people seem to be reveling in the glamor and unbridled decadence of the time. Getting rich is easy, and easier still when joining the Yakuza. They do, after all, seem to control all the action in Tokyo's red-light district of Kamurocho, and are eager to promise the most beautiful women, the fastest cars, and the most exclusive clubs to the young men willing to do their bidding. Over a thousand Yakuza run, extort, or control over a hundred enterprises in a Kamurocho that is overflowing with discotheques, luxury shops, and entertainment establishments. Eastern Japan's largest criminal organization, the Tojo Clan branch of the Yakuza, runs most of it, and is determined to not only hold on to its territory but to expand it. Kamurocho is profitable and thus desired—and dangerous. It is where the dreams of crime lords come true, and where salarymen come to blow off some steam. A seedy adult paradise, it is violent and debauched; a place that lures tourists and locals alike with its high-class restaurants, promising nightclubs, and gambling houses; a place where businessmen wave 10,000 yen bills to stop taxis.

The famous entrance to Kamurocho

神室町

The gray, and occasionally beige, buildings and the inconspicuous phone booths of Kamurocho's infamous Theater Avenue, Taihei Boulevard, Pink Street, and Nakamichi Alley do not look too different from most of Tokyo's. Modernist and brutalist architecture, a few hints of traditionalism, a tendency toward kitsch eclecticism, but also elegant shrines can be found along the spacious straight roads and narrower, quieter side streets. A few covered market roads, dull apartment buildings, countless vending machines, and Little Asia's claustrophobic maze of alleys do not feel particularly special. Yet one can't help but notice a few too many signs and bars. Entertainment and commerce here cannot be contained on the ground floor, and even under a midday sun, the adult-oriented focus of the local businesses becomes apparent. People furtively rush into love hotels, fashionable punks try their best to look tough, street performers are mostly sexy, street vendors sell everything, garbage is piling up, the signs of recent violence are commonly ignored, and the people living and working here seem trapped. Kamurocho is a rare place where homelessness is obvious, and starkly contrasts with shamelessly luxuriant coffee shops, gigantic movie theaters, and the vibe of an entertainment district that caters to all tastes.

Public telephones are extremely popular

Kamurocho alternates between two states, and when night falls the almost subdued daily routine gives way to a loud, glitzy nightlife of myriad blinding lights. Sizzling neon reaches all the way to the sky advertising massage parlors, sleazy drinking holes, and karaoke bars, while sign upon sign move endlessly into the distance. A million blinking lightbulbs, animated billboards, and manga signs create a kaleidoscopic labyrinth of indulgence, adults-only delights, sin, profit, and crime. Beyond the bustling squares and boulevards, behind the omnipresent neon signage, twisting mazes of one-room gambling joints and saloons lack the glowing facades but not the excitement of this confusing, glorious, triple-X world. At night, everything else fades away, and streets seem to only hold cabarets, hostess clubs, discos, and catcalling sex workers. The unsavory underworld has a bright, mesmerizing front and stylish overlords.

The Yakuza are the epitome of fashion, and they most definitely are not hiding. They openly run their empire of sex, gambling, drugs, and entertainment, and manage their casinos, cabarets, clubs, and restaurants with panache. Whether it be in places such as the Heroine Karaoke Bar, the stunning dance floors of the Maharaja, the high-stake games of mah-jongg, or around erotic video booths, the well-dressed Yakuza stand out. They are fighting subtle turf wars, collecting money, running businesses, organizing underground fight clubs, and, when required, violently maintaining the peace. Their sense of honor and business acumen keep Kamurocho from becoming too dangerous, although crossing them could easily prove fatal. Fights here are often brutal, shootouts not unheard of, and people have been murdered, even if the nouveau riche were too distracted to notice. High-class revelers ultimately only care for louder clubs, more extravagant casinos, and flashier cars, and would do anything for a password letting them into the fabled underground red-light district of the Purgatory. Leisure suits, excess, and neon go hand in hand, and Kamurocho's nightlife is a legendary stage of parties, shows, gang melodrama, and, above all, power, money, and real estate.

Developers, gangsters, and developer gangsters are devouring all space. Bones are broken, and people are dying for an empty Kamurocho lot that has become the centerpiece of an immense power struggle. This small patch of land is poised to dictate the future of a massive development project, and immeasurably wealthy individuals and organizations across Japan will do anything to own what, to the naked eye, looks useless. Unthinkable machinations and conspiracies have been weaved around a filthy empty parcel of land surrounded by the ventilation ducts of insignificant buildings. But the Yakuza and their enemies can look beyond deceiving

Signs upon signs and blinking lights construct the image of Kamurocho appearances and see potential profit; they can recognize the hidden wealth built in the invisible financial structure of unrealized urban space. They understand the significance of a bare patch of land, for it holds the promise of unending expansion; the hope that their power is everlasting—and that the bubble will never burst.

DESIGN INSIGHTS

Kamurocho is a fictionalized version of Kabukichō, closely following and masterfully abstracting the architecture, civic design, and life of Tokyo's red-light district. The attention to detail is incredible, and covers real-life brands, street layouts, buildings, 1980s fashion, era-appropriate behaviors, and even street furniture. Every aspect of *Yakuza 0* is representative of a very particular time and place in Japan, which refreshingly avoids playing up any aspect of exoticism. Kamurocho believably recreates the economic bubble's days in an imaginary slice of Tokyo modeled after the recognizable real-life locations that encapsulated the excesses of the eighties. This is a game city worth studying by anyone interested in building semi-fictional open worlds heavily inspired by recent reality, and in the construction of quality, small-but-dense urban settings.

Despite Kamurocho being tiny by contemporary gaming standards, it does a better job of recreating the feel of a real city than the sprawling maps of many other offerings. Nothing here feels repetitive or generic. Unique stories, environments, and characters are densely packed in a virtual space that makes up in artistry and detail what it lacks in scale. Players do not drive in *Yakuza 0*, and walking helps with taking in the sights, especially as the game never evokes that sense of constant urgency. Cleverly, the danger of the streets themselves tends to push toward the discovery of safer routes, and with them hidden activities and points of interest. Players are subtly urged to explore every fleshed-out nook and cranny of a meticulously crafted environment, offering dozens of gameplay hours and a hundred dramatic, funny, clever, and even touching sub-stories. Interactive restaurants and shops and new mini-games are found in every block, and add to the place's texture. Fully playable versions of classic Sega arcade games, baseball cages, pool tables, and more are all available to play, and often come with their own stories and well-designed game systems.

Yakuza 0 takes an already vibrant setting and further enriches it with the melodramatic charm of crime lords, kind-hearted gangsters, and real estate moguls battling for control of the district. Excellent writing, impressively directed cut scenes, and successful tonal shifts ranging from playful weirdness to unexpected kindness add pathos and joy to Kamurocho's exploration. A sense of place permeates the narrative, which revolves around a tiny empty piece of local land, influencing the mechanics and ambience of the neighborhood. Kamurocho is full of clubs that switch ownership, and shops that grow as players decide to invest in them. Furthermore, local history and dynamism extend beyond *Yakuza 0* and into the wider *Yakuza* series. It is a history that spans the whole series, as Kamurocho evolves and its residents mature. *Yakuza 0*'s empty lot, for example, eventually grew to become *Yakuza 1*'s Millennium Tower.

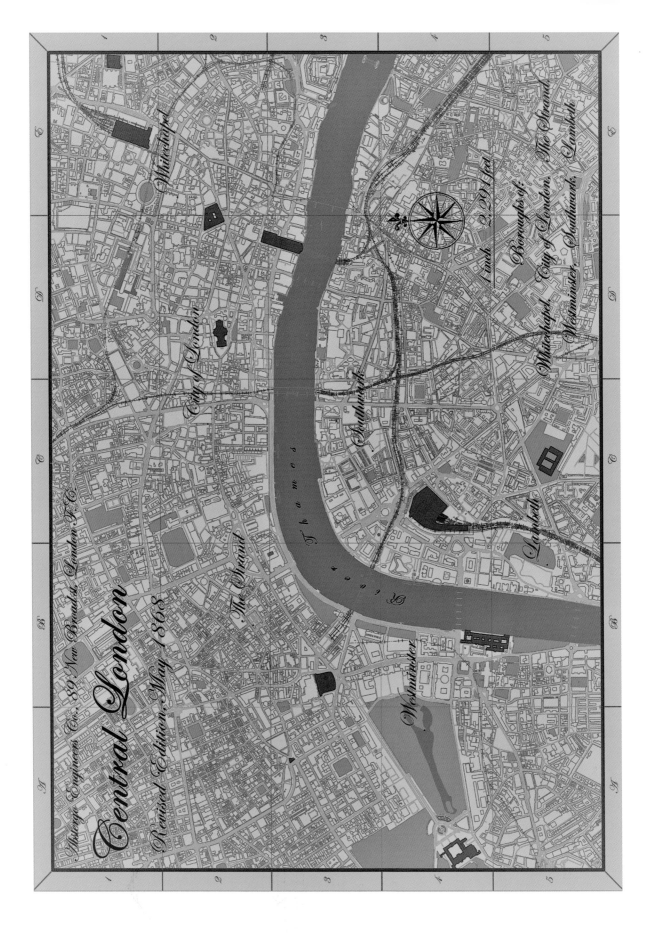

Waterga Engineers Co., 89 New Broad St, London E.C.

Central London

Revised Edition, May 1868

Whitechapel

City of London

The Strand

Westminster

Southwark

Lambeth

T h a m e s

R i v e r

1 inch = 0,20 tyd

Boroughs of:

Whitechapel, City of London, The Strand
Westminster, Southwark, Lambeth

28

LONDON
Assassin's Creed: Syndicate

GENERAL INFORMATION ////////////////////

City: London

Game: *Assassin's Creed: Syndicate*

Developer: Ubisoft Quebec

Publisher: Ubisoft

Release Date: 2015

Genre: Action-adventure, Open World, Stealth

Platforms: PlayStation 4, Xbox One, Windows

London, the capital of the most powerful empire in the world, and home to Queen Victoria, is the epicenter of the Industrial Revolution and the richest of cities. It is the first metropolis; the biggest aggregation of human life, and, as Henry James argues, the most complete compendium of the world. It encapsulates a rising new age with all its hopes and horrors. London is neither pleasant nor cheerful, but is most definitely magnificent. Despite the fog, the diseases, the dirt, the smoke and fire of industry, the black rain, the inhuman pace of life, and the cruelty, it is still awe-inspiring. Fascinating and often beautiful too, with its parks, architectural wonders, countless train tracks, and tons of exotic goods flowing in from the Thames. The sheer spectacle of its scale and the impossible vibrancy of its streets hint at what humanity can achieve. This is the urban expression of Britain at its peak, dominating colonies and whole industries, and giving birth to financial capitalism as the world revolves around the pound sterling.

Fueled by money and production, the metropolis constantly expands, always transforming itself in a perpetual process of building, demolishing, and rebuilding. Its population, barely a million in 1801, has exploded in less than seventy years to almost 4 million, and keeps on growing as thousands of black smoke pillars rise from new factories and houses. Steam power and the burning of coal bring gas lighting to streets and residences, and drive the endless expansion of textile and steel manufacturing, breathing life into massive factories, the cathedrals of industry, and progress. Trains and steamboats unload products and people alike into the capital, and, on certain days, crossing the Thames can be as easy as jumping from boat to boat. The Industrial Revolution is in full swing. It is an era of unprecedented wealth, impossible invention, productivity, and growth, of unprecedented centralization, where everything seems connected to the central steam machine; a golden age of affluence and extreme, moralized profit, albeit one paying a heavy price in pollution, exploitation, and far too frequent deaths.

London, the modern mecca of trade and technology, encompasses the empire itself, and with it, its citizens. People from Africa, Asia, Australia, and Europe have given birth to a truly multicultural

Gloomy, gaslit Victorian streets

city, the best and the brightest from around the world making their home in the great international center of imperialism. Diverse goods and groundbreaking ideas circulate in an environment where lascar sailors hold festivals and mixed-race families are almost accepted. Cosmopolitanism, and occasionally internationalism, flourish as fallen maharajahs, overthrown aristocrats, Irish survivors of the Great Famine, and luminaries such as Charles Dickens, Karl Marx, Florence Nightingale, and Charles Darwin are all brought together. Everyone is accepted here, and cutting-edge science can effortlessly co-exist with cheap penny dreadfuls, spiritualism, and the rising fashion of window shopping. Horse-drawn buses, brightly colored shops, illegal opiates, enticing advertisements, theaters, pubs, and thousands of carriages bring unceasing excitement to the city Queen Victoria rules from the splendor of Buckingham Palace.

Surrounded by great parks, the palace's majesty is contested by a large number of imposing landmarks. Westminster Abbey, the British Museum, St. Paul's Cathedral, Trafalgar Square, and the Tower of London all draw attention, but few have become as popular as the neo-Gothic clock tower housing Big Ben. Designed by Augustus Pugin, and completed less than a decade ago, this is the biggest and most accurate four-faced chiming clock in the world. After all, metropolitan life does require clocks, and the city's new emblem is not alone in combining beauty with functionality. The St. Pancras railway station, the imposing edifices of contemporary factories, and the glorious cast-iron and plate-glass structure of the Crystal Palace are all meant to facilitate the city's economy, and achieve beauty and scale apt for the achievements of industry.

Victorian architecture is not exclusively interested in housing machinery and gigantic cogs, though; it also houses the people operating them. Enamored with revival styles from the Neo-Grec to the neo-Gothic, glass and brick are so depended upon that their taxation has been abolished. Large apartment buildings of red brick and occasionally colored stucco are growing in popularity, and the houses of the middle classes now require accommodations for servants. Small gardens are widespread, even if they pale when compared to the private parks of the great houses owned by the elites. There are also important innovations that are less noticeable: sanitation regulations finally demand correct drainage and toilet facilities, access to tap water is increasingly common, and indoor gaslighting can be found in many houses.

The vast majority of the built environment has been constructed by successive housing booms, providing tens of thousands of profitable houses to an expanding, deprived population. Rows upon rows of small, stuffy, back-to-back houses have been built in extremely cramped conditions, and are only broken up by the factories among them. These squalid living conditions have inspired utopian thought, the ideal of the pastoral suburb, and, more important, the innovative notion of institutional planning, as it has already been expressed in the Public Health Act of 1848.

All the clever planning, however, cannot hide the deep poverty of the metropolis. The poor are dying in factories and slums, the average lifespan of workers is thirty years, and infant mortality rates are so high that many don't even bother naming their newborn children. Hellish workhouses and legislation targeting the homeless and unemployed reveal the cruelty the production of riches is based upon. Class war is one-sided, and the unorganized workers are spending their energy despairing, dreaming of imperial glories, or worse, joining vicious street gangs, even as, finally, trade unions seem to be rising. Unions have effectively pushed for child labor laws protecting children under the age of eight from factory work. Still, 95 percent of the population, including all women, have yet to earn the right to vote, and the revolutionary fires of unrest are growing in London's boiling cauldron of progress and poverty. It is the best of times, it is the worst of times, as Dickens claims, and while Darwin is publishing his theory of evolution and modern medicine is being born, an ancient order of assassins seems intent on reclaiming the technological wonders for all.

London's Palace of Westminster

DESIGN INSIGHTS

The London of *Assassin's Creed: Syndicate* is a truly ambitious virtual city. It is necessarily far from perfect, and obviously romanticized, but still a fascinating rendition of both the metropolis and the era it recreates. Closely following London's geography and shape, the game offers a believable, spacious, and entertaining open-world/theme-park version of Victorian city planning. It features real boroughs, brilliantly researched architecture, and the recognizable elbow bend of the Thames. Landmarks such as Westminster Abbey or Buckingham Palace and their immediate surroundings have been (almost) faithfully recreated and correctly placed in relation to each other, whereas the areas in between have been subtly shrunken and abstracted, while retaining their character-istics. The game's map follows the overall structure of the historical city as it has been captured in Victorian maps, designs, illustrations and photographs, thus retaining its architecturally and geographically distinct districts and the defining elements of its image.

On the whole, this feels very close to the Victorian London most would imagine, even if histori-cal authenticity had to be balanced with production logistics and level design needs. The map has been (for the most part) only slightly transformed, and certain textures and models are occa-sionally reused. Wider than would have been accurate, roads enable the driving of horse-drawn carriages, and make the typically tedious task of getting to far-off locations quicker, while the exaggerated traffic of the Thames conjures images of bustling trade as it lets players cross the river by playfully jumping from boat to boat. The layout of the train tracks has been subtly altered to form a loop, allowing the train-based player HQ to provide tours of the city's more than 200 fully modeled blocks, dozens of landmarks, and miles of lovingly recreated facades. Cleverly, each of said blocks features slightly fewer buildings than in reality, an abstraction that is never really noticeable.

A one-to-one recreation of the metropolis would have been impossible, and so *Assassin's Creed: Syndicate* mainly aimed to stay true to the age, managing to craft a convincingly beautiful visual representation of Victorian London while embracing the outrageousness of its plot to hide any discrepancies. When joyriding with Florence Nightingale on a black carriage to rescue Charles Darwin, people tend to be less inclined to notice repeating textures. On the other hand, the amount of detail and the meticulous attention to roof-scapes, chimney stacks, wet cobbled streets, and pub interiors are simply breathtaking. The developers also recreated the vibrancy of 1868 Lon-don, and attempted to capture its essence by incorporating a dynamic soundscape, birds, a very British climate, and, crucially, a system of life-like vignettes populating the streets with gang members, bystanders, policemen, urchins, professionals, families, and workers, whether they're shouting at each other, walking, playing cricket in parks, or browsing store windows. Further enhancing its believability is the fact that *Syndicate*'s London is one of those truly rare game cities that constantly feels under construction, as unpaved streets and unfinished buildings are being worked upon.

29

MILTON
The Long Dark

GENERAL INFORMATION ////////////////////

City: Milton

Game: *The Long Dark*

Developer: Hinterland Studio

Publisher: Hinterland Studio

Release Date: 2017

Genre: Survival

Platforms: Linux, Mac OS, PlayStation 4, Windows, Xbox One

A blind old lady holding a rifle sits next to a crackling fireplace. She has lost a child, her mind has been ravaged by pain, and her final days will be spent trapped in the deserted town of Milton. Her complete distrust of all outsiders is painted on her stern visage, a painful reminder of society's collapse, even if the dimly lit windows of the crumbling mansion she lives in are the sole sign of civilization in miles of untamed wilderness. Hers is the last chimney still smoking in Milton, for this lady, the Grey Mother, decided to stay here even after the very last of its residents, the poorest or the proudest, abandoned it. Electricity is out for good, and only the aurora borealis and the moon can occasionally penetrate the clouds to keep the total darkness of the long Canadian nights away.

Grey Mother's mansion

The post-disaster North's breathtaking wilderness, stripped of all traces of technology, frames a seemingly hopeless human struggle, a drama the Grey Mother and her native Milton share with the wider Pacific Northwest. All technology has stopped functioning, international communications are now impossible, and nature itself seems to have turned savage. The once lively, rich and productive Great Bear Island is now completely cut off, and its rustic communities, including Milton, stand largely abandoned. A frozen, hostile and admittedly stunning wilderness devoid of human activity surrounds isolated settlements. Uncaring forests and rivers and packs of predatory animals now rule where once-thriving industries exploited mines, dams, and logging camps. The remaining scattered pockets of humanity battle hunger, relentless cold, and bears on an almost primal landscape, often with nothing but primitive spears, and huddle in the caves that once drew adventurous travelers from around the world.

Nestled deep in the mountains of Great Bear Island and surrounded by deep ravines, loud waterfalls, howling beasts, and icy creeks, Milton was always secluded and maybe a bit eerie. Now, during the unending blizzard, the town is gradually being reclaimed by the very surroundings that once defined it. The river leading to the Milton basin is permanently frozen, and delineates

Milton's concrete Post Office still stands in defiance of the apocalyps

the northern and western borders of town. Bridges cross it to connect the settlement with the large farms to its west and the path toward Perseverance Mills to the north, a path passing by the abandoned but still scenic graveyard surrounding St. Christopher's austere wooden church. Steep mountains lie to Milton's east, where a surviving radio tower can easily be spotted from afar, as can the wooden water tower to its north. At the south road's junction lies Orca Gas Station, its sturdy walls occasionally providing shelter for nomads, showing the way toward the collapsed tunnel blocking the last way through—and past—the mountains.

Milton was always too small and private to appear on every map, but entering it today through its barely standing wooden gates, the difference between being a quiet town and an abandoned town becomes painfully obvious. The last of the old mountain towns feels discarded, empty, and sad. Dead, even. Snowstorm damage remains neglected, and wolves roam the snow-covered crossroad that essentially constitutes the town. Milton once lived along two intersecting streets, but now, it is lined with husks of abandoned cars, collapsed fences, knocked-over power lines, and boarded-up or burned-down houses. These days, the Grey Mother says, raiders and beasts alone walk the streets among the reishi mushrooms and the frozen dead bodies. Brutal reality, however, has neither completely erased the distinct character nor the beauty of the place. Under the crushing weight of snow, one can still discern lovely porches and simple but cozy houses. Most buildings here are traditional wooden constructions with a single story, brick and concrete being

Snow covered Milton is all but dead

used sparingly in places such as the modernist facade of the Milton Post Office and the equally deserted Milton Credit Union. The local school, recently serving as a welcoming refuge, has been reduced to ashes, and only its rusting bell and adjacent playground survive.

Stone fireplaces, encircled by the half-burnt beams that were once homes, have been standing at the same spots since the town was founded back in 1911 to shelter the miners of the then flourishing coal industry. Built along the supply route from the coast to the interior of Great Bear Island, Milton's location made it a convenient stopping point that thrived all the way through the 1980s, when the town's economy truly boomed and its population reached 1,000 people. It was the eventual construction of Highway 15 that bypassed Milton and ultimately led to a period of decline. In the 2000s, the population was little more than 100, and following the Collapse, it fell to a dozen—including the Grey Mother, the last resident of the ghost town.

But the Collapse was never just local. It reached far beyond the frigid Canadian wilderness, and past the Pacific Northwest. It affected everyone, everywhere. Millions perished, a thousand industries vanished, and countless highways were left to crumble as panicked humanity sought comfort in the density and warmth of the cities. Economic activity became increasingly centralized, farmlands were lost, and rural communities hollowed out, as people fled to metropolitan areas in search of greater stability and perceived safety. The crisis deepened, and brought along worldwide political instability. For places such as wider Great Bear Island and the already remote Milton, the Collapse was close to terminal, but it was the apocalyptic event dubbed "The First Flare" that finally killed them off. Tied to the reappearance of the aurora, this geomagnetic storm disrupted all electronic and electrical devices, destabilized weather patterns, awakened dormant tectonic forces, and deeply upset wildlife behavior. Predators that once avoided humans now attack on sight as civilization itself is on the verge of collapse. Food shortages have led to widespread looting and violence in urban centers, while starving bandits roam the wilds. Even if hope can never truly die, the Grey Mother has decided to mourn her long-dead Lilith, and brave the apocalypse on her own with a gun in her hands.

DESIGN INSIGHTS

"We made a decision very early on in the project, when we branched our Survival and Story experiences into two different paths, that we'd leave the world of Great Bear intentionally vague for Survival players. The idea was that when we launched *Wintermute*, our story mode, it would feel like even more of a grand unveiling—players would finally get a clear picture of the world we'd created for them. By the time we launched the first two episodes of *Wintermute*, back in August 2017, many of our players had already been enjoying 'the quiet apocalypse' for years. So we needed to make a strong statement with Milton.

"Most real places don't exist in only one time—they tell the stories of their past through the blend of their architectural styles, their signage, the layers of use, and habitation evident in each building, the artifacts left behind, the stories woven into their spaces, and the scars that human exploitation leaves behind on their landscapes. Great Bear Island, the fictional setting for *The Long Dark*, has a complex history, and the world the player passes through needs to passively reveal that tale.

"The story of *Wintermute* also exists in more than one time—there is the player's post-crash present, where Mackenzie and Astrid struggle to survive the aftermath of the geomagnetic disaster that brought their plane crashing into the northern wilderness; there's the story of their past together, and the mystery of Astrid's 'mission' and the contents of the precious hard case; and there's the story of what happened to Great Bear before they—or the player—arrived.

"We created Milton as a container to house all these stories and histories. An introductory setting that would—through its aesthetic and feel as a 'virtual space'—try to communicate the nuances of Great Bear's history, the post-crash present, and also some hint of what the player may encounter in the future. We used Milton to enrich the player's understanding of the history of the world many had already inhabited for years—the post-'big one' earthquakes that brought Great Bear's once-thriving resource economy to its knees; the economic and societal collapse that came in its wake; the growing resentment toward the wealth of the mainland, and its historical exploitation of the island's resources. And, eventually, the final quietening of the world and its burned-out technology, observed by the ambivalent—but beautiful—aurora flaring across the night sky.

"We see Milton as much more than a small grouping of aging houses high in the mountains. Its people stand as a testament to Great Bear's difficult past, its tragic present, and, potentially, a sign of its silent future."
—Raphael van Lierop, creative director of *The Long Dark*

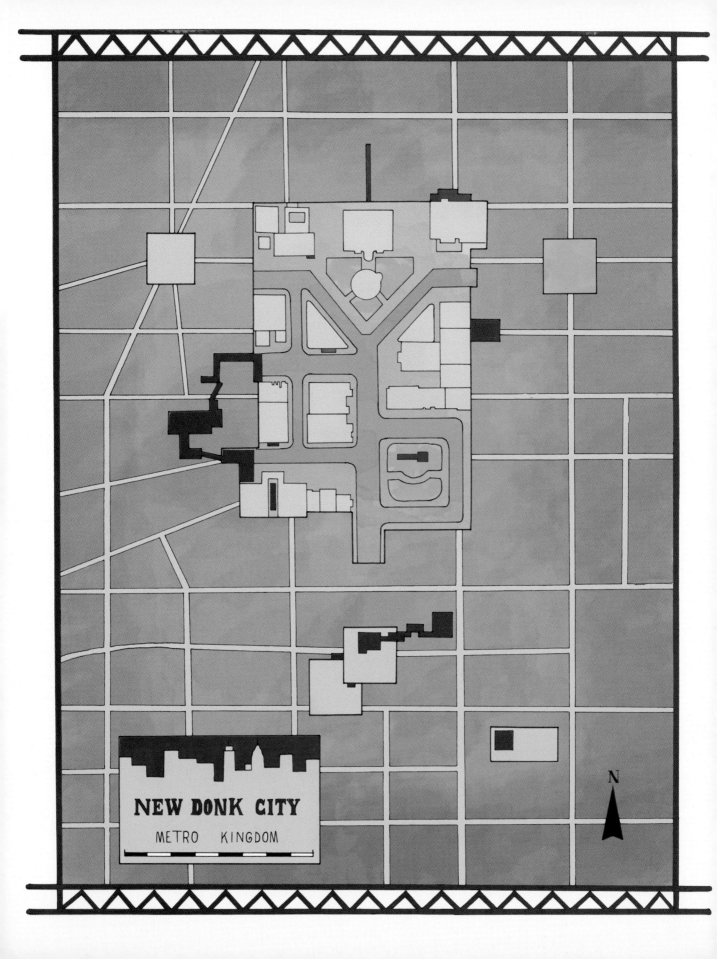

NEW DONK CITY

METRO KINGDOM

N

30

NEW DONK CITY
Super Mario Odyssey

GENERAL INFORMATION ////////////////////

City: New Donk City

Game: *Super Mario Odyssey*

Developer: Nintendo EPD

Publisher: Nintendo

Release Date: 2017

Genre: Platform, Action-adventure

Platforms: Nintendo Switch

Watering a tree on the roof of a glimmering skyscraper sitting atop another skyscraper could only happen in a city made of video games and surrealism. A town that couldn't possibly exist, and yet somehow lives; a city that never intended to function as one and instead prefers acting as an elaborate space for play. New Donk City, the Big Banana, or the City that Never Leaps is exactly this sort of town. It also happens to be the world's tallest city and the crown jewel of the sprawling Metro Kingdom, itself a constantly expanding metropolis; a truly contemporary kingdom consisting entirely of a continuous city, defined by the urban nature of its landscape. It is the world's premier commerce center and urban playground.

Being a city within a city, the core of New Donk is built on a towering mega-structure, surrounded by endless rows of vast skyscrapers that stretch all the way to the horizon. Its majestic high-rises rest on a cyclopean concrete tower hundreds of miles above the surface with storm drains raining floodwater into the mists below. Inside this structure, a complicated drainage and sewer system keeps the city livable, while a wondrous power plant turns moons into energy, fueling its growth and prosperity.

The glass, steel, and concrete skyscrapers of New Donk City define the metropolitan character of a center primarily comprising modernist blocks, narrow roads, a few plazas, and some parks. A place often mirroring signature New York architecture such as the Empire State and Flatiron Buildings, majestic art deco entrances add a touch of elegance to its densely packed environment. The verticality and upward momentum of the city is constantly evident, and its roofs are brimming with cafes, gardens, pools, and aging water tanks. Among imposing modernist creations and humble but beautiful brownstones with characteristic outdoor fire escapes, the New Donk City Hall, the tallest and most important landmark, is the symbol of this great city, and offers the finest views of the complex skyline and the grandiose bridges of the kingdom.

Countless colorful billboards and posters dot the streets as information and advertisement are the key local industries. New Donkers are keen to market anything: shows, foreign kingdoms, social

New Donk City, Metro Kingdom, in all its elevated glory

events, and occasionally villains, with the campaign for Bowser's wedding a notorious example of the latter. Tourism, music, and trade are also financially important, and it's no accident that the world-famous Crazy Cap flagship store is located right here in a converted theater.

New Donkers, these industrious city folk, live comfortable lives, and dress uniformly and exclusively in dashingly dull gray suits and hats, their 1950s-inspired homogenous style only offset by colorful visitors and artists. Homogeneity, though, does not mean New Donk City is all work and no play. This is a happy, joyous town that may lack children, but has embraced street games. RC Cars, jumping rope competitions, street performances, and the occasional doomsaying keep things lively, whereas the slot machine parlor offers more intense thrills. Thankfully, lovely parks, strategically placed benches, amazing views, and open-air cafes allow for deep relaxation in a welcoming place without crime and homes open to all.

Locales such as the Squawks Park, Dixie Theater, Tiny's Piroshkis, Expresso Espresso, and Banana Bagels are constantly bustling with life—all life from Stingbies and Goombas to Piranha Plants, tank-like Sherms, and tiny populations of Fuzzies and Bullet Bills. As for the rumors regarding hidden Ogres, they are as believable as those of a Cloud Kingdom in the skies above, even if everything is possible in a city where streets are named after the mythical figures of the Donkey

Kong saga and red construction gliders are commonly used to hop around. Being decidedly urban, New Donk appears to be in a perennial state of reconstruction, change, and expansion, and its cranes, girders, and pipes add interesting transportation options to those too bored to hail a taxi or too scared to jump on one. Then there is always the option to stylishly ride in a mini rocket or on one of the numerous, unexpectedly svelte scooters, which can be easily parked on any roof and can allegedly outrun a T-Rex.

New Donk City can be terribly exciting indeed. Its mayor, the larger-than-life Pauline, was once rescued during the construction of the city from a gigantic ape, and has since been a fearless leader, unafraid of even the weirdest mechanical monster and is always willing to embrace life to its fullest. It is she who brought the big bands to town and she who organizes its spectacular festivals. The city may have seen some rough times, but like its mayor, it endures, shines, and celebrates its history in public fetes that many have described as once-in-a-lifetime experiences.

DESIGN INSIGHTS

New Donk City is a playful, almost perfect example of the marriage between aesthetics, planning, architecture, and game mechanics. It is the quintessential *Super Mario Odyssey* level, and has utilized the very first realistically metropolitan setting in the series' history to provide it with some of its most over-the-top moments. Combining Mario's colorful world with realistically proportioned humans and buildings was a novel move for Nintendo—a move that gave players a scale they could measure against Mario's acrobatics, and that successfully juxtaposed the silly banality of New Donkers to the cartoon qualities of every other character.

Playing on the *Odyssey* formula, every kingdom is defined by its visual theme and consistent population. The city is inhabited by humans in suits just as the Cap Kingdom is populated by ghosts with hats. New Donkers are essentially one of the game's species, albeit a humanoid one that, by definition, wears gray. Aesthetically crucial residents aside, the city itself is very obviously based on New York, and is thus instantly recognizable as a modern metropolis despite its tiny size. The Mario-fication of NYC also provides a fantastic (day and night) skybox, and has obviously guided the level's flair for upward movement.

Odyssey really puts the metropolitan setting to work in a level simultaneously focused on platforming and celebrating Mario's lore. Densely packed buildings allow for wall jumps, ever-present taxis act as moving trampolines, traffic lights can be climbed, and spark pylons always take players up—up to where the stars and coins can be collected, strengthening a design that allows players to quickly transition from the ground to the top, and vice versa. Additionally, Metro Kingdom's rooftops provide vantage points that reveal alternate routes and hint at secrets and hidden treasures. The city usually conceals such things in its diverse interiors. One of the Flatiron-inspired buildings offers a T-Rex chase sequence, and close to the City Hall lies an old cinema, which lets players experience level one to one of the original *Super Mario Bros.* in front of a live, gray-attired audience.

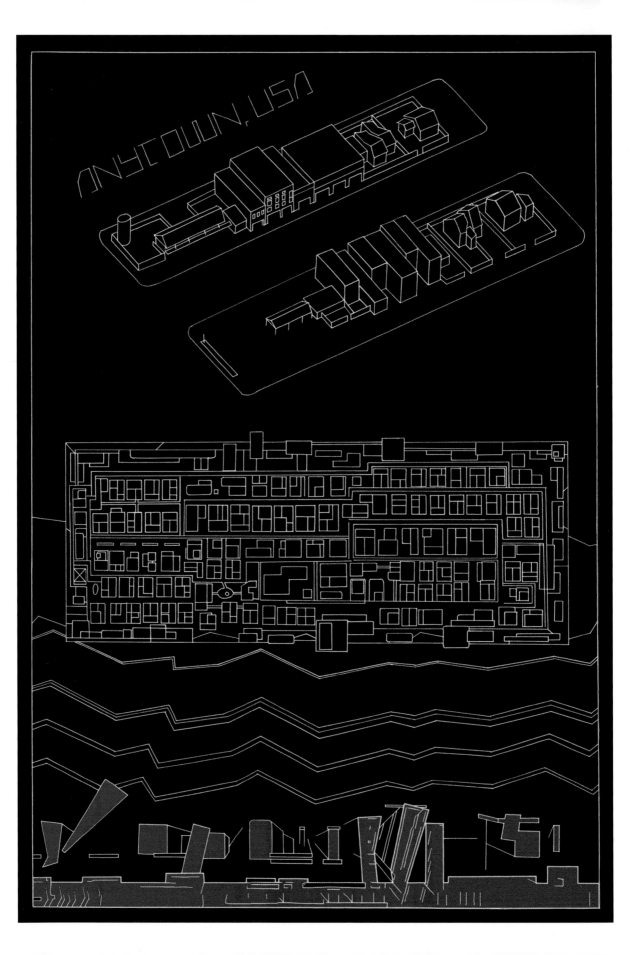

31

ANYTOWN, USA
0°N 0°W

GENERAL INFORMATION ///////////////////

City: Anytown, USA

Game: *0°N 0°W*

Developer: Colorfiction

Publisher: Colorfiction

Release Date: 2018

Genre: Exploration

Platforms: Mac OS, Linux, Windows

With a bit of luck, any truly ambitious road trip can evolve into an incomparable experience, although a touch of supernatural good fortune is required to travel past some very specific desert dunes—and a very particular gas station—to reach the glowing wireframe Main Street of Anytown, USA. From there on, your first steps away from physical reality and toward a surreal digital multiverse can be taken. Just cross the gates of Anytown's old-fashioned movie theater and you'll be whisked away into a wonderfully weird new world to embark on a fantastical, multidimensional journey through space and time. Expect a virtual vacation through a cosmic labyrinth, where floating doors and traversable manifestations of limbo lead to unexpected neon realities, unexplored worlds and undefinable cities, and where the delights of the unknown are rendered in pure color and sound.

As for Anytown itself, well, it could be anywhere. Its vernacular architectural style would feel at home throughout most of the western United States, and even if it looks eerily familiar, it most definitely is not a real city. We can never really know, but the town is either a container of or an entrance to another realm of existence. A city made up not of actual buildings and people, but a non-Euclidean entity comprised of cities, landscapes, and non-physical space; a dimension of curious joy, whose urbanism seems to reside in glitch space. This string of urban realities is to be experienced digitally, and never inhabited; a succession of totally unusable spaces and algorithmic creations meant to facilitate visually stunning utopian cityscapes and dreamy landscapes, but never to properly function.

These fully explorable odd geometries, each occupying its very own pocket reality, are arranged in a shifting cosmic maze, in a polymorphic network where no one ever gets lost. Despite their fluid topology and the apparent randomness of their elements, these are not procedural creations, nor have they been crafted by some sort of world-building poetic AI. A human designer's forethought and intent are always evident, and never tastelessly obvious, in these worlds inhabited by almost sentient, unrecognizable creatures—some of which actually look like traffic (although they could never run you over). Here, danger is never real, psychedelia is a given, and space is imaginatively and

Sometimes it is not about a place; it is about a feeling

architecturally organized. You may jump from and to impossible heights, and occasionally safely walk through intangible walls, always unsure about the physics guiding your existence, impressed at the deep abstraction of your surroundings, and wondering about life among the bizarre geometries.

Each of the sharp, angular, insanely colorful worlds you'll visit is a mash-up of visuals and sounds. Bright glows, unexpected pastel hues, monochromatic architectures, and kaleidoscopic landscapes distort around you, describing mysterious spaces. Obvious nods to the greats of modernism and cubism support the proposition many wanderers have put forth: that the cities, buildings, and vistas hiding in Anytown are akin to living in three-dimensional paintings with their own individual soundscapes, moods, and reactive platonic shapes; an avant-garde exhibition of paintings you can spatially immerse yourself in.

Cities of neon, noir metropolises, prismatic towns, ruins of forgotten urbanism, and deconstructed squares are waiting to be experienced. To get to them, you'll travel through oneiric maelstroms, imaginary shifting swamps, azure landscapes, and mnemonic oceans. And then you might get to decide what everything is, stands for, and is called. Naming dimensions and baptizing cities can be an integral part of such a journey of discovery, even if simply relishing in urban vignettes oscillating between peaceful and foreboding can be more than enough too. You may attempt to find meaning in your surroundings or wisely relax and savor them.

Some of the dreamlike environments feel as if they belong in a sci-fi movie; some let you imagine stories and histories while traveling between the twin cities of light and darkness; and others offer spectacular cyberpunk views from affluent penthouses, all aiming to please and raise intriguing questions. As for the 0°N 0°W coordinates, look them up and you'll find the geographical anecdote of Null Island. An island that doesn't exist, where the prime meridian and the equator cross in the Gulf of Guinea. Visit 0°N 0°W and you'll only encounter a rusting weather buoy floating in the ocean.

DESIGN INSIGHTS

"The aim of *0°N 0°W* was to transport players to an otherworldly dimension of the unexpected, a place full of surprises where one never knows what they'll encounter. To accomplish this, an interesting balance had to be struck between the familiar and the unknown. Hence why the adventure starts in "Anytown," the archetypal main-street–lined small town. While aesthetically parodic in the overall theme of the title, this town is grounded in reality: there's a gas station, a supermarket, a bar, a couple of houses—all the staples that form the identity of a small town and make it relatable. Most people have at some point in their lives visited such a town, so the adventure begins in a shared memory we can all identify with, which works in contrast to the absolute pandemonium of visual exploration that quickly unfolds.

"The concept behind *0°N 0°W*'s urban design investigated the hypnagogic qualities of urbanism. In particular, when one explores the repetition of forms, strange things happen to one's state of mind; one might identify an individual building's figurative qualities only for those traits to fade away, leaving only the shapes and interstitial spaces. Interestingly enough, even when entranced in such adventures, occasionally a structure or area pierces through the blurred mass that momentarily halts the urban explorer in a reverie of observation. This phenomenon guides the expression of all cities, hence why there are gigantic, relatively homogenous metropoles with focal points of detail scattered about for players to find. The cities also embody an oneiric evolution in terms of interpreting urban design; while there are grid-based layouts with mostly horizontal navigation, the other end of the spectrum presents cities that, for example, are not grounded on the physical limits of gravity and, instead, float ethereally in space. This gradient of expressions offers a completely different and constantly changing sandbox of exploration.

"A big influence on the formal qualities of the cities were the early twentieth-century art movements formed by artists such as Kandinsky, Braque, Duchamp, Doesburg, Torres, Calder, Miró, and others. Taking the amazing three-dimensional characters imbued in their paintings and turning them into a playground for the senses—a playground to explore, to get lost in, contemplate, and hopefully walk away from inspired and happy." —Max Arocena, creator of *0°N 0°W*

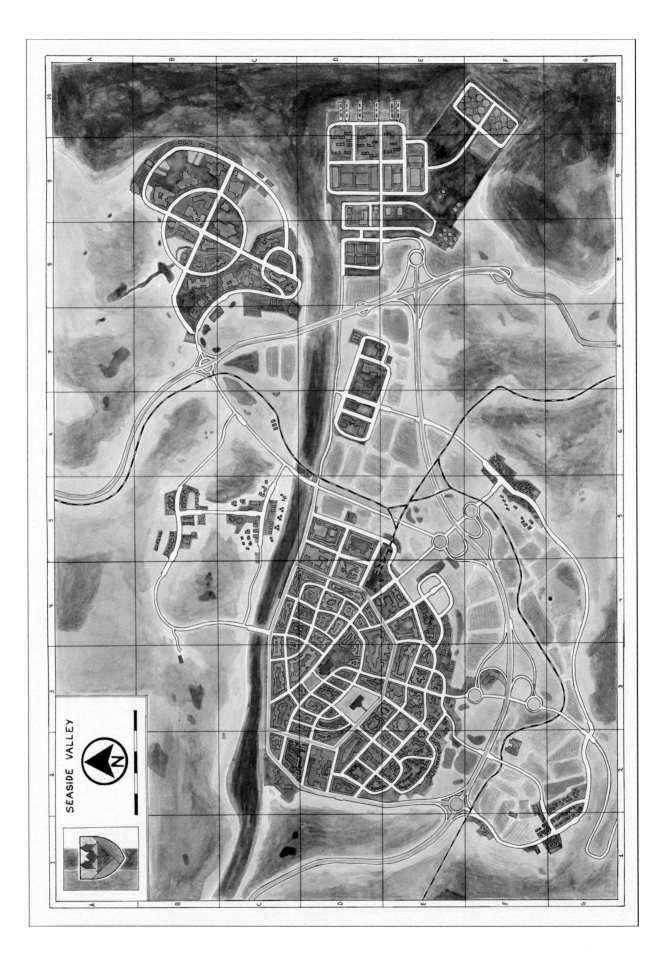

SEASIDE VALLEY

SEASIDE VALLEY

32

Bus Simulator 18

GENERAL INFORMATION //////////////////////

City: Seaside Valley

Game: *Bus Simulator 18*

Developer: stillalive studios

Publisher: Astragon Entertainment

Release Date: 2018

Genre: Driving, Simulation

Platforms: PlayStation 4, Windows, Xbox One

The quintessentially European city of Seaside Valley looks like a planning experiment gone unexpectedly right. It may not be a truly egalitarian municipality surpassing all restrictions of contemporary society just yet, but homelessness, heavy pollution, and extreme poverty are definitely absent, as are any signs of fabulous wealth. Seaside Valley lies on the fairer, quieter, more sensible and tranquil side of urbanism, where things seem to be flowing smoothly, natural and manmade elements are combined into a cohesive, functional whole, and everyone seems to be holding decent jobs. This is a good place to live in.

A successful city, and an embodiment of social-democratic utopia ideally located on the south bank of a scenic river flowing into the North Sea, Seaside Valley lies on a fertile valley surrounded by lush forests and picturesque hills. Its location, initially chosen to provide safety and access to fresh water during the medieval era, has allowed for a rich agricultural tradition, and has helped it evolve into a trade hub and major harbor. The combination of sea, forest, calm weather, pleasing topography, unique geology, and an interesting interplay of urban and rural areas have lately brought tourism to town too.

This nicely planned, rather densely populated city is a delight to explore. Getting lost in the clearly labelled, categorized roads is almost impossible; the Valley's districts are distinct and intriguing, its landmarks defining, and its spaces legible enough to make navigating from the old town all the way to the harbor effortless. The place's structure is reminiscent of the concentric zone model, but with a typically European center where the historic and modern downtowns are separated by a ring road—formerly the city walls. Farther out, the suburban ring includes fields and smaller, low-density, often agricultural communities, while the outermost zone contains the harbor, the industrial zone, and the new, tech-heavy AstraPark development.

At the city's medieval heart, in its centuries-old geometric center, the majestic cathedral and its lively square anchor the mixed-use downtown and sit in the middle of a web of narrow cobblestone roads lined with a wonderful variety of architectural styles. The old town's northern edge,

Seaside Valley's central bus station

Driving through the city's old core can be a surprisingly pleasant way of spending one's working hours

the river with its beautiful waterfront, is lovely to walk or drive by, but also a place to relax and enjoy the public sunbeds far from the noise of the modern downtown. From the massive new apartment blocks of Schobergrounds in the east to southwestern Maryville and working-class Scharfetter Field, the center's construction activity is usually heavy and often irritatingly loud.

The much quieter southern suburban zone encompasses the town of Steineck and the small community of Westfield, whereas north of the city core and the river lies picturesque Siegwalden, with its single-family river-homes and a few modest villas. To Siegwalden's west, beyond the abandoned dirt road, hides the old sawmill, whereas to its north is the farming exurbia of Oakville. Toward the sea lies the new high-tech district of AstraPark, with its postmodern twisting sky-scrapers, fancy sky-bridges, massive research center, and imposing skyline, while farmlands and cow fields fill most of the semi-rural space between the city's sub-centers. It is to the east of the city core where agriculture intensifies to industrial levels, and yellow fields give way to storage towers, warehouses, logistics companies, fleets of trucks, and factories, eventually leading to the commercial harbor of Port Amber. The latter's docks, gantry cranes, container terminals, and oil refineries are crucial to the local economy, and yet oddly not serviced by the rail network.

Rather unexpectedly, the town's train network bypasses the industrial district too, and seems exclusively focused on the transportation of passengers. The bulk of intra- and inter-urban traffic is handled by cars, buses, and trucks, with many residents choosing to walk or ride their bicycles in the wider center. As for the several challenges of vehicular traffic, these are admirably handled by a well-designed yet far from perfectly preserved road network that would relish the support of an equally well-designed mass transportation system. Admittedly, even if a tram network could be described as necessary, the bridges crossing the river are more than adequate, road visibilities are excellent throughout, and the town's brutalist roundabouts are stunning, safe, and efficient.

For now, it is up to the recently reintroduced bus service to support the bulk of commuting, battle the dominance of the private automobile, and lead, alongside the wind turbines, the fight against CO2 emissions. Its colorful high-tech buses, often decorated to celebrate worldwide events, cover most major routes, and are also spearheading the "Be a tourist in your own town" campaign, which could frankly be bolstered by more elaborate pedestrian zones. Not that the Valley's sidewalks aren't spacious or richly furnished. After all, such an economically diverse, booming place has to be attractive to prospective new residents, and putting up with a less than lively nightlife is always easier in an otherwise hip, bilingual, affluent city that loves its shows and events.

DESIGN INSIGHTS

"The design for the city of *Bus Simulator 18* (*BS18*) drew from our *BS16* experience, though for *BS18*, we wanted to create a bigger, better place that wouldn't feel cramped, and would allow for free space between the different districts. Several other constraints were taken into account: the city had to look distinctly Central European and sport a river, and as we aimed for a USK rating, we couldn't have any violence, drugs, rude graffiti, or liquor stores. We even had to remove schools, hospitals, and also police and fire stations, as implementing all the relevant vehicles and special human models would have been prohibitively time-consuming. These decisions led to a utopia-like city free of crime and injury, where graffiti is always artful.

"When we weren't satisfied with the *BS16* design workflow, I tried something new: after some research, I made a rough sketch and fired up *Cities: Skylines*. Using terrain.party, I imported the height map of Tulln, Austria, into the game and started working on the map. First, I edited the terrain to add the sea to the east and some mountains to the north; I then started with the large road connections and moved to the increasingly smaller ones until I was down to individual city blocks. I used the zoning tools to define where each type and style of building would be placed, directly planned for nice vistas using the first-person camera mod, and finally exported the street layout and terrain.

"This worked astonishingly well, but led to an exceedingly large city, the southern part of which had to be cut. During production, it was also decided a railroad was needed, and the map was thus slightly redesigned. Railroads are, after all, usually built before speedways, and extend deep into the city. Overall, though, the final design only required a few changes, including the ones made to the AstraPark. This was initially planned as an unlockable area, but we decided to turn it into our starting one. It looked lovely, offered a view of the areas players would eventually unlock, and provided wide, easy-to-navigate roads.

"As for road names, we tried using these to tell the history of the city, as often happens throughout Europe. There is a Ropewinders Road, a Shipwright's Alley, and an Amber Gate. Additionally, we also used the names of team members for places such as Stocker Square and Grois Alley, and even included a very special church on the hill close to Steineck based on a small church in South Tyrol where our CEO got married.

"Finally, we designed a flag and a crest for the city. The crest shows a town surrounded by hills and is close to the water; the flag's colors symbolize land, water, and sky."

—Alexander Grenus, game designer at stillalive games

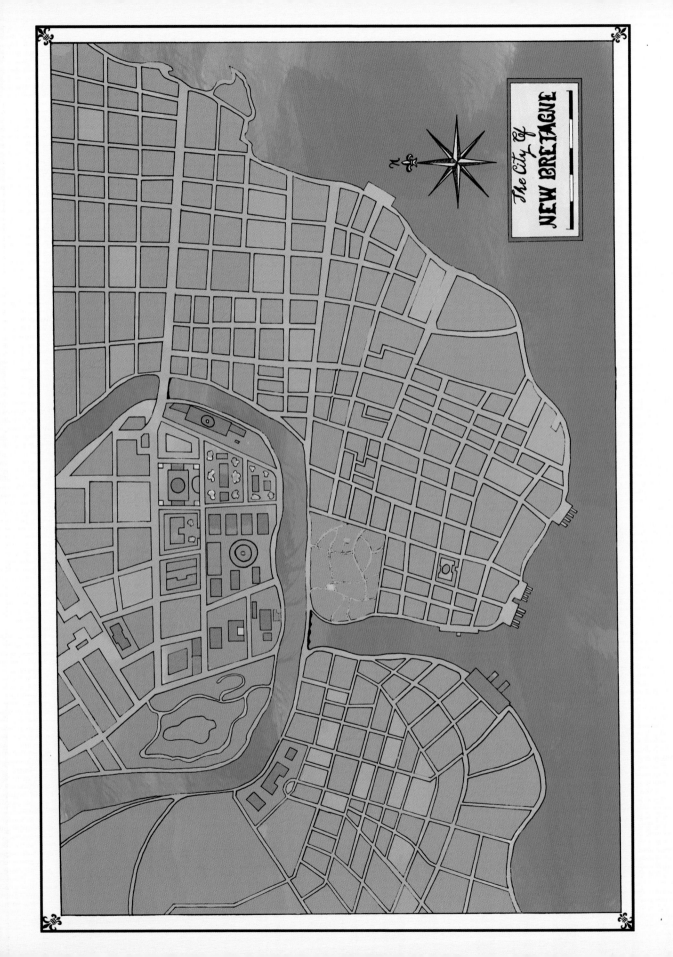

The City Of
NEW BRETAGNE

NEW BRETAGNE
Lamplight City

33

GENERAL INFORMATION //////////////////

City: New Bretagne

Game: *Lamplight City*

Developer: Grundislav Games

Publisher: Application Systems Heidelberg

Release Date: 2018

Genre: Adventure

Platforms: Mac OS, Linux, Windows

Streets and courts darting in all directions are losing themselves in the unwholesome vapors hanging over rooftops, rendering the dirty perspectives of New Bretagne uncertain. This metropolis is a kaleidoscope constantly shifting from majestic to dangerous, from filthy to magnificent, while effortlessly alternating between old and new, and exploding in size. New Bretagne, also known as Lamplight City and the Jewel of the Hodgeman, is the most important harbor of the Atlantic, and Her Majesty's pride in the commonwealth of Vespuccia, the most radiant of all of the Crown's colonies.

New Bretagne is ruled by the queen and an elected prime minister, who are making sure this thriving industrial center remains a beacon of technological progress and civilization in the New World. The city was modeled on London, influenced by New Orleans, and allowed to evolve its unique flair. With lush parks, impressive buildings, and exciting finance, New Bretagne effortlessly promises a shining future, even if it rests upon the shaky foundations of poverty and exploitation. Deepening class divisions go hand-in-hand with groundbreaking technological advancements, and the electoral choices between progressive and conservative candidates seem almost point-less when the river itself is employed to isolate the well-off from the pauperized masses.

But even when isolated and kept out of sight, destitution still breeds plague, and desperation always pushes toward a life of crime, providing the city's syndicates with an inexhaustible recruit-ment pool. And as quantity is bound to bring about qualitative changes, New Bretagne has become the global capital of weird crime. Death by spontaneous combustion, for instance, frequently pop-ulates the pages of the popular *Brentwell Magazine* in a town where men have been hanged for practicing black magic and slavery was abolished less than fifty years ago—and this only due to the invention of the automated cotton gin. Most servants in New Bretagne are former slaves working for their old masters, and often enduring their still-tolerated savagery.

In an environment of such stark inequalities, racism and sexism found the fertile ground they needed to flourish. Black people are cut off from higher education and many coffee houses do not

Protests still seem a bit unfocused, but New Bretagne's working class senses something is going wrong

Downtown New Bretagne as witnessed from the Chum

allow women. Instead of equality and openness, there is colonial cosmopolitanism with a touch of West Indies exoticism, meaning this revolutionary era of steam is progressive only on the surface. The majority of Lamplight City knows this, and openly voices its dissatisfaction. Political turmoil is palpable, strikes and demonstrations common, the sabotage of the Luddite-inspired Reddites a given and individual terrorism not unheard of. The organized workers' movement is slowly growing too as new, occasionally untested machines make exploitation more efficient and dangerous, and drive many to unemployment.

Looking up to the skies, on the other hand, reveals the hopeful side of modern technology. Airships are nowadays capable of connecting continents and bringing mankind together, while the increased industrial output should theoretically be able to soon feed and clothe everyone. The everyday applications of steam power are evident throughout the city, heating its houses, organizing its offices, powering its factories, and lighting its streets. Robotic boxing trainers, pneumatic mail, typewriters, ferro duplicators, analytical engines, and self-driving mechanical cabs are reshaping all facets of life, while the next revolution in tech is apparently just around the corner. Harnessing the still vaguely defined "aethericity" is said to be able to provide with unlimited power—possibly enough to revive necrotic tissue—and turn Vespuccia's largest urban center into the foremost technological hub of the world.

The cityscape is already prepared for change, and will easily adapt to any new requirements. For now though, most of the buildings are made of brick and wood, feature distinctive balconies, and, when mixed with the newer tall structures, create an impressive, varied skyline. The majestic architecture of public buildings and the striking clock towers offer New Bretagne its trademark landmarks, and add to the atmosphere of glowing gas lamps, smog, and the abundance of intriguing characters. The territory comes with myriad shadowy corners, twisty alleys, and complex geography that must be responsible for giving birth to New Bretagne's famous detective novels. The town's countlessly interesting spots have surely also played their part in influencing Bretagne's literature and penny dreadful—it would be impossible to ignore the menagerie of delightfully weird taxidermy shops, intriguing clubs, classy coffee houses, spiritualist societies, opium dens, and brothels—although, to truly understand New Bretagne, one has to get to know its four boroughs.

Lyon, the financial and governmental district, is home to the serving prime minister, the parliament, the university, and the stunning Foster Park. It is extravagantly affluent, distinctly Colonial Georgian in its style, and filled with expensive stores, social clubs, restaurants, and upscale theaters. Uniformed policemen are everywhere to be seen in order to make certain revelers feel safe.

Gascogne, the original nucleus of the city and the largest of the boroughs, is dominated by Spanish Colonial architecture and is rather reminiscent of New Orleans. The St. Denis Cathedral overlooking the large cemetery and the town's biggest open-air market are important sub-centers of this relatively peaceful, multicultural neighborhood. Old French families and English-speaking

The illuminated streets of Lyon look particularly elegant during the night

professionals mingle with the most affluent of the freed slaves who have somehow managed to make Voodoo sound mysteriously fashionable. After all, there is a widespread belief that many places in Gascogne are haunted, despite the loudness of its entertainment districts. And if the Grand Dames' Ball is a quiet affair, the port of New Bretagne has attracted taverns, bars, and all sorts of wild, shady establishments around the docks, to the constant irritation of commuters waiting for the ferry to Cholmondeley and to the constant enjoyment of drunken sailors.

Cholmondeley, the Chum, is the poorest, most dangerous part of town. Muggings and murders are a daily affair, and people simply know that what little police exist is not there to protect them. Besides, the appalling living conditions are the greatest of the local hazards. Families live in condemned buildings, breweries, tanneries, and slaughterhouses, which add nauseating smells to the black clouds belched into the air from the factories. That plus a lack of access to health care and decent food make life expectancy in the Chum pitifully low. Industrialists who embraced the emerging autom-aton technology have never tried curbing pollution. On the contrary, they employ children and burn the cheapest coal to cut costs, while the jobless, crushed, and the poorest of the poor rot in shel-ters, prisons, asylums, and hellish workhouses.

It's no wonder, then, that the workers' aristocracy and the middle classes prefer living in Worcester. It may not be fancy, but it is at least decent and modestly safe; the air is breathable and its characteristic brownstones are pleasing to the eye. The local majority are of English ori-gin, and live in perfect harmony with a large Jewish community, while enjoying a rich selection of smaller art galleries, theaters, and pubs. Several businesses and even a few factories are located in the district, although what really draws the eye is the bridge crossing Hodgeman River into Lyon. For years, this has been the sole bridge of the metropolis, metaphorically and physically.

DESIGN INSIGHTS

"Coming up with a completely fictional city was an interesting challenge. I had to think about who founded it, what countries settled there and influenced the architecture, the culture, the politics, etc. In the end, I decided to borrow bits of the histories of real American cities, specifically New York and New Orleans. The next thing was figuring out the layout of the city, thinking about things like where neighborhoods were going to be located, what the rich and poor areas were like, and where the major ports were. I looked at several nineteenth-century maps and started drawing New Bretagne. This served the dual purpose of allowing me to have a visual representation of the city for my own design purposes and as the in-game map.

"As for the design itself, I took my trusty notepad and just started writing. I came up with a short history of the city's settling and founding, subsequent power struggles, trade routes, archi-tecture, demographics, and climate. No detail was too trivial! Next, I made a list of the four bor-oughs, came up with names for them, and defined them in a single sentence. I then expanded on each, drawing a piece of concept art for them, as well as writing a more detailed description of who lived there, what the landmarks were, what kinds of businesses were generally in the area, and any fun miscellaneous characteristics. I also had a special section I called 'City Stories,' where I wrote a bit about things going on in day-to-day life, such as the competition between cab companies and how they were coping with new steam technology and self-driving cabs. I even went as far as writing a national anthem for the alternate USA, but sadly, it never found its way into the game.

"All in all, I had an extraordinarily fun time creating New Bretagne, and I honestly feel that one of Lamplight City's greatest strengths is its world-building. I think it's important for a writer to dedicate as much time and effort into detailing their settings as their characters."

— Francisco González, *Lamplight City* developer

34

ROCKVIL
A Mind Forever Voyaging

GENERAL INFORMATION ///////////////////////

City: Rockvil

Game: *A Mind Forever Voyaging*

Developer: Infocom

Publisher: Activision, Infocom

Release Date: 1985

Genre: Interactive Fiction

Platforms: Amiga, Apple II, MS-DOS, Atari ST, Commodore 128, Mac OS

For twenty years, Perry Simm lived the normal, modestly creative life of an aspiring writer in Rockvil, South Dakota, in a prosperous, dull, mid-size town calling itself the Jewel of the Quad State Area. Yet Perry Simm never existed in the physical world. In reality, he is PRISM, the first truly sentient AI, and his Rockvil is a groundbreaking computer simulation created exclusively for one digital being: him. The now-awakened Perelman-Randu Introductory Soliptic Machine (PRISM) has grown into maturity, and is, according to the April 2031 issue of *Dakota Online Magazine*, ready to dive deep into the extrapolated future of Rockvil in order to evaluate the Plan for Renewed National Purpose.

Said plan has been drafted to pull the economy of the United States of North America out of its slump, protect the souls of the young, and safeguard the nation against the threats of an intensifying Cold War. Even in a climate of financial crisis and extreme scaremongering, the plan seems a bit of an overreaction. It advocates for the complete deregulation of all sectors, mandatory military conscription, a strict "USNA First" trade policy, and the empowerment of the executive branch of government, as well as a return to traditionalist values and morals. The Plan for Renewed National Purpose aims to fix all, and PRISM is to enter a simulation of the typical Rockvil at ten-year intervals and record the projected realities.

In extrapolated 2041, Rockvil seems to be doing well. People are modestly content, and quietly proud of the 130-story Infotech Building, the sixth tallest in the world. The town, between the I-27 interstate to the west and Little Missouri River to the east, remains focused on its lively, denser, older city core, with its utilitarian grid, numerous parks, and the diagonal Centre Street. To its north lies the Rockvil Reservoir, the airport, and the new Border Security Force Base; to its south, the workers' districts. Although the simulation does not cover all of Rockvil's suburbia, the bustling downtown is modeled in its full detail, and includes the Halley Museum, the Huang Hall auditorium, the stock exchange, and, obviously, the City Hall. The wider center is also home to a lovely zoo, a

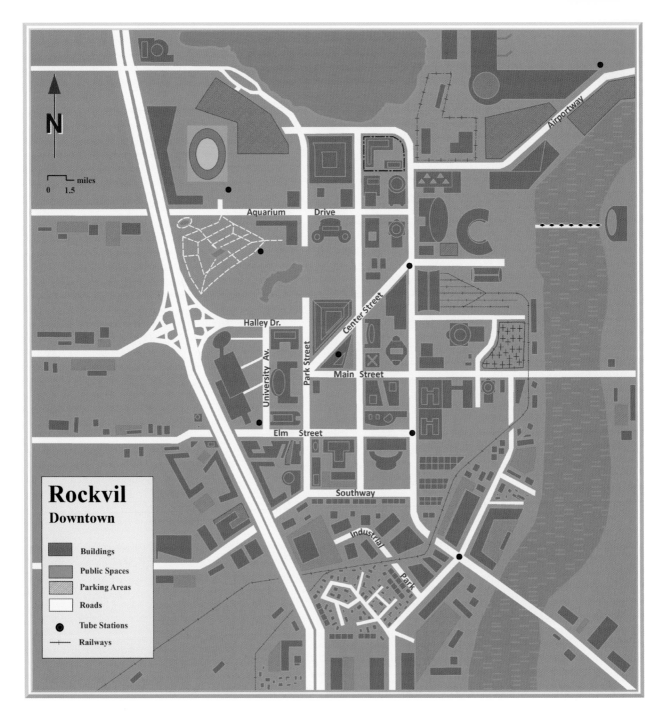

stadium, an aquarium, and several concert halls and theaters, as well as the famed North Central Station and Rockvil University. A shopping mall and a holographic multiplex couldn't go amiss.

Issues still exist, yes, and certain ominous signs too, but the overall optimism is palpable as the plan seems to have actually rejuvenated the economy. The recovery may not have crossed the southern rail lines into the poorer districts, and the prison may be getting overcrowded, but at least many of the inmates are drafted to fight for the motherland, and the police have gotten new flying cars. Besides, unemployment has hit record lows, the Tube and skybus services are fully operational, apartments feel safer than ever, and, as people are discussing mining the moon,

Rockvil: a simulated reconstruction for the year 2041

the exciting Heiman Village Two—a city within a city—is being constructed. So what if medicine is more expensive than ever, and that weird Church of God's Word cult is attracting a few followers?

It is in 2051's Rockvil that the cracks start showing. Pollution levels rise, technological progress has stagnated, and all traces of previous optimism have evaporated. The city is in obvious decline, clerks and workers are being laid off, and a police state is emerging. The Border Security Force conducts raids without warrants, capital punishment has been expanded, and an almost daily curfew is enforced to a background of blaring sirens. Crime is on the rise, and even more are seeking solace in the Church of God's Word. Its freshly completed black marble temple gathers thousands as skycopters announce prayer meetings.

After another decade of declining farm output and environmental degradation, hunger is real, the water effectively undrinkable, and the city's plunge horrifying. In 2061, televised public executions are organized in the stadium, and life sentences are routinely passed for violating the Uniform Morality Code. The brutalized society is getting brutal itself under the increasing influence of the Church of God's Word and the establishment of a racist, caste-like system. Public services are in complete disarray, parks are being turned into residential towers, and the Heiman Village Two fire killed hundreds in an ill-maintained city of weathered buildings. Rockvil U has been abandoned, public schools have shut down, skybus services have been terminated, and the Tube barely functions. And of course, the slums were hit the hardest.

And still the Church demands more violence—until all hope dies. By 2071, Rockvil has collapsed under the heel of theocracy. House arrests on charges of heresy and the reinstitution of slavery have brought terror to all but the richest of the ecclesiarchy. The vast majority of the slums now spanning the city survive on tiny rations of miserable food and live among deteriorating infrastructure. Ration fraud is punishable by death, most secular books have been banned, and torturing monkeys in the zoo or watching execution matches entertain the masses. Dissenters are considered "Beasts in Human Form" and sent to worship camps. By 2081, the devastation is complete. Savage cannibalistic gangs rule the collapsing streets, as feral dogs prey on humans, and the smoke of burning tires attempts to cover the stench of death. Rockvil is no more.

Thankfully, this is all still a simulation. An important warning delivered by the artificial intelligence of PRISM against the will of powerful senators. In reality, 2031 can be a new start instead.

DESIGN INSIGHTS

Rockvil is a major achievement—not just for its sheer size, but also for its dynamic nature and believability. It is laid out in a way that feels intuitively right. Steve Meretzky, coming from an engineering background, knew how cities work, grow, evolve, and look. He employed realistic zoning and density patterns to design an ever-changing but recognizably generic American city. Being completely imaginary, Rockvil enjoyed geographic freedom, while being text-only made it feasible in 1985.

It was bigger and more detailed than any graphic city of the era, and even the largest contiguous space to ever appear in an Infocom game. Still, it managed to fit in fewer than 256 kilobytes, as only the elements necessary to create its realistic environment and support the plot were included; the city had to be explorable over six different decades after all. A clever "You've reached the end of the simulation" defined its borders, and a successfully abstracted plan made navigation easier, despite an over-reliance on diagonal movement.

Over the course of the game, Rockvil's initial small-town atmosphere is gradually corrupted toward a hellish, post-apocalyptic version of itself. Landmarks and the image of the city change dramatically as civilization falls and dystopia emerges. The malleable, fundamentally dynamic nature of the city is impressive, especially as memory constraints often only allowed changing a single adjective in a location description to convey its new character.

The decision to make the player less of a participant and more of an observer really played into the key strength of interactive fiction: the construction of setting. Removing almost all puzzles further emphasized narrative and exploration, and allowed for deeper spatial immersion. Empathy was supported by experiencing the collapse of civilization, not as a wide-scale event but via the increasing decline of a specific small town, and a specific family (Perry Simm's).

35

TERRAPOLIS
B.A.T. (Bureau of Astral Troubleshooters)

GENERAL INFORMATION /////////////////////

City: Terrapolis

Game: B.A.T. (Bureau of Astral Troubleshooters)

Developer: Computer's Dream

Publisher: Ubi Soft

Release Date: 1989

Genre: Adventure, RPG

Platforms: Amiga, Amstrad CPC, Atari ST, Commodore 64, MS-DOS

Storms of red toxic sand rage across the dead surface of planet Selenia in the B15 system. Nothing lives on its harsh mountains, arid plains, and immense plateaus, and yet the massive, domed city of Terrapolis has been thriving on the Svorkoff highland since the very beginnings of the twenty-second century. Selenia's sole city, comfortable and cosmopolitan under the swirling reds and yellows of its domed sky, is a vast industrial complex focused on extracting and refining dytroxyne and licox—crucial resources for interplanetary travel—and offering scandalously low corporate taxes.

Birthed of the unbridled capitalism that allowed eccentric billionaires to own mega-cities and the temporal bridge technologies making almost-instantaneous space travel possible, Selenia was initially colonized by the obscenely rich Gordon Berghaz, who founded Terrapolis and claimed the planet. Following his death, his heirs appointed a governor general to rule in their stead, and invited the Confederation of Galaxies and its Bureau of Astral Troubleshooters to help safeguard the planet and its critical resources from potential terrorists and criminals. Once, even the complete devastation of the city by nucturobiogenic bombs was thwarted.

Such fears, however, are easily forgotten in this immense city of strange ambience. Claustrophobic, polluted, and humid, Terrapolis is also grandiose and invariably exciting, despite few of its tourist attractions surviving the 2150 great fire. Wide boulevards and high-speed highways bleed into promisingly dark alleys and vibrant streets filled with vendors and public videophones. The atmosphere is constantly tense as revelers mix with revolutionaries, and clerks and criminals alike are threatened by security robots and corrupt policemen. True locals know to quickly react to public shootouts and actually relish living in a somewhat dangerous extravagant patchwork of baroque entertainments, wild architectures, and unsubtle allusions to Haussmannian Paris.

Keeping with Terrapolis's nineteenth-century themes of cohesive neighborhoods, long roads, and enormous astroports, a horizon of skyscrapers glitters against the red maelstrom of the dome and

Selenia's habitable arches are an engineering marvel when one takes the planet's gravity into account

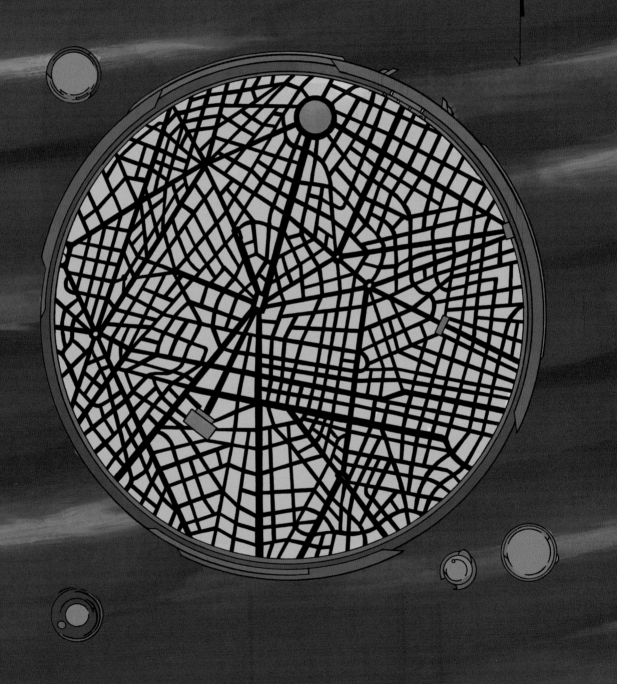

over a more conventional city of smaller buildings. The Terrapolis Central Junction, the city's geometric and functional center, radially connects its districts and always smells of fried femacs. To its north, residential areas teem with people, whereas to its south, the endless activity of the Astroport Square welcomes visitors with its bars, hotels, Krell exchange centers, autocabs, and the universally acknowledged junk-food cuisine of slimeburgers and chips. To the west of the Junction, by the medical district and the towering police headquarters, lies a concentration of monumental administrative buildings, fine hotels—including the mythical Grand Hotel—and luxuriant apartment towers. The industrial zones, as well as the old heart of the city, are to the Junction's east. There, among ruins of the 2150 catastrophe, hide the access points to the long-disused underground maintenance corridors of the city's engines, eerie evaporation chambers, and the Mobytrack's network.

Above ground, the Northeastern Airlock is the only way out to the open desert, provided one is daring enough to pilot a DRAG, and somehow no longer interested in the wondrous sphere of the city's famed Artificial Park. The latter, a favorite among locals and off-worlders alike, offers a rare sense of serenity with its wonderfully recreated alien landscapes, soothing gardens, and vast variety of unique but nonthreatening animals; the park's museum also includes a massive baby Krotospaiis skeleton. From the park, the A-312 trunk road leads to the less wholesome and more intriguing parts of town—colloquially known as the Hot Quarter—and thus to a menagerie of bars, arcades, clubs, and adult cinemas employing state-of-the-art sensoscope systems capable of neurally stimulating all five senses.

The Artificial Park of Terrapolis

Architecturally, the Post-Rythjuian rhythm provides the tone to Terrapolis's industrial look, with its emphasis on aestheticism, functionality, and mobility, combining modernism with obvious Gothic inspirations. Classical buildings aping the architectures of Earth, such as the governor's palace and the Museum of Natural History, add to a built environment of steel, glass, and exposed concrete. Pyramids, half-pyramids, domes, and monolithic skyscrapers intermingle with revival architecture, historical utilitarianism, and the debris of past urban sprawl, as sky bridges connect retrofitted buildings and arch-shaped apartment complexes span over busy highways. The visual layering of architectural typologies gives the city its theatricality and the penthouses of the super-rich terrans (and their resident cherubs) with its glorious views.

Humans of all classes are eccentric and irritatingly fashionable, yet far from alone. Robotic and organic species bring variety to this crossroad of civilizations, where three common tongues are used to allow a mosaic of different communities to coexist. The proud and svelte Glokmups, the monastic lizard-like Sabbelians, the too-perfect Stickrobs, the almost invincible metallic Hulktronics in their bioplastic skins, and the information-hungry SAARs create a moving kaleidoscope of danger and style. Mineral of the cloth, hand-weaved dresses, self-cleaning, self-deodorizing suits, and thermodynamic shirts combine with elegant personal force fields, anti-radiation glasses, implanted Bio-directional Organic Bioputers, and retinal optomemorizers. In particular, the outrageously expensive and very exclusive Xifo club is a perpetual fashion show—a meeting point of the elites, and easily the least deadly of all the town's joints, as even pen-sized Voktrasof guns are impossible to smuggle past its bouncers.

DESIGN INSIGHTS

"It was back in 1987. Having published a fantasy RPG (*Iron & Fire*) and a fantasy adventure (*The Ring of Zengara*) on the Amstrad CPC for Ubisoft, and being passionate about artificial intelligence, I wanted to create a new RPG, but this time, in a futuristic, high-tech universe inspired by Philip K. Dick, William Gibson, Marco Patrito, Enki Bilal, and movies like *Metropolis* or *Blade Runner*. Impressed by the visuals of *Defender of the Crown* (Cinemaware), I began the creation of a much richer world with 16-bit graphics, and the Dynorama (an interactive sequence of cartoon-style images) was born, on the popular in France Atari ST.

"At that time, I was studying electronics in Paris and met other students passionate about video games, like Olivier Cordoléani (Cordo) and Olivier Robin. Cordo was particularly interested in graphics, and Olivier was a musician. Together, the two of them, me and my friend Philippe Derambure, who helped with the screenplay and programming, formed a team of four creators; Ubisoft provided the machines. I was responsible for the basic design, but everyone brought in ideas, reinforcing the multicolored character of the game.

"In the world of *B.A.T. (Bureau of Astral Troubleshooters)*, capitalist expansionism forces wealthy billionaires—owners of megacities—to extricate themselves from the Earth, build blackhole-powered space exploration machines, and take fortuitous possession of whole planets to satisfy their follies. Being inhospitable, the planet Selenia led to the protective dome of Terrapolis, a megacity deeply inspired by classical Earthen architecture.

"Wanting to write a non-linear script with multiple solutions and different types of gameplay, the rich universe of a city was ideal. This was populated by many types of creatures, allowing for a profusion of possibilities. Finally, and considering that mixing urban simulation and storytelling was the essence of the game, it was important to create different neighborhoods and a richness of interactions (mini-games, 3D simulators) in order to introduce a sensation of immersion, and thus reinforce the idea that a complete world had been recreated. The notion of a dynamic world was fundamental here, and the city itself an important actor of the game. The regularly regenerated non-player characters, for example, policemen, merchants, and thieves were proportioned according to the player's aggressive actions or negotiating prowess. The city was therefore a lung embracing a heart (screenplay), and that is why we can continue playing even when the story is over."

—Hervé Lange, *B.A.T.* designer and programmer

36

UNION CITY
Beneath a Steel Sky

GENERAL INFORMATION ////////////////////////

City: Union City

Game: *Beneath a Steel Sky*

Developer: Revolution Software

Publisher: Virgin Interactive Entertainment

Release Date: 1994

Genre: Adventure

Platforms: Amiga, Amiga CD32, iOS, Linux, MS-DOS, Linux, Windows

The smoking spires of Union City

The bleak future we were warned of has arrived. Pollution and war finally brought about the ecological collapse of the planet, and glorious Union City is one of the last places on Earth where the air remains effortlessly breathable. Under the ominous, unhealthy orange clouds, the jumbled silhouette of our huge metropolis rests beneath a steel sky. Air is being filtered, scrubbed of toxins, and recycled within the protective dome encasing the city, as every day, production outputs rise and its enemies despair. Union City is sprawling, powerful, proudly corporatist, and it deservedly thrives upon the ruins of old Sydney. Admittedly, it may have started to rust a bit, and the odd production hiccup may have drained some of its color, but its walls and massive gates keep the terrors of the Australian wasteland at bay, and progress and prosperity safely enclosed.

Outside, the undeveloped zone, referred to as "The Gap," the wasteland separating the antagonistic urban centers—where the majority of the population now lives—is home to dangerous fugitives, monsters, and mutants. Tribes of possibly socialist scavengers and hunter-gatherers have formed primitive, mutant, and deeply unethical communities. They shelter outcasts, migrants, and terrorists, regard cities as demonic, and, led by unscrupulous leaders, routinely steal Union City's air-dropped trash. Neither the toxic air nor the Gap Plague has eradicated them yet, although preemptive strikes against random villages seem to have thinned their population and reduced those economically catastrophic scavenging raids. Security in the Gap remains a top priority, even if Union City's main enemies are always the other five city-states; in particular, the one run by the evil Hobart Corporation openly promotes labor rights and whose communist spy saboteurs are undermining Union City's economy. They managed to sour the acquisition of Asio-City and keep on publicly attacking the neo-democratic principles of no labor representation and freedom from social benefits. These villains are waging an economic and ideological cold war, and even dare to fuel discontent within Union City itself.

Thankfully, our government is run by effective bureaucrats, and the proletariat is constantly

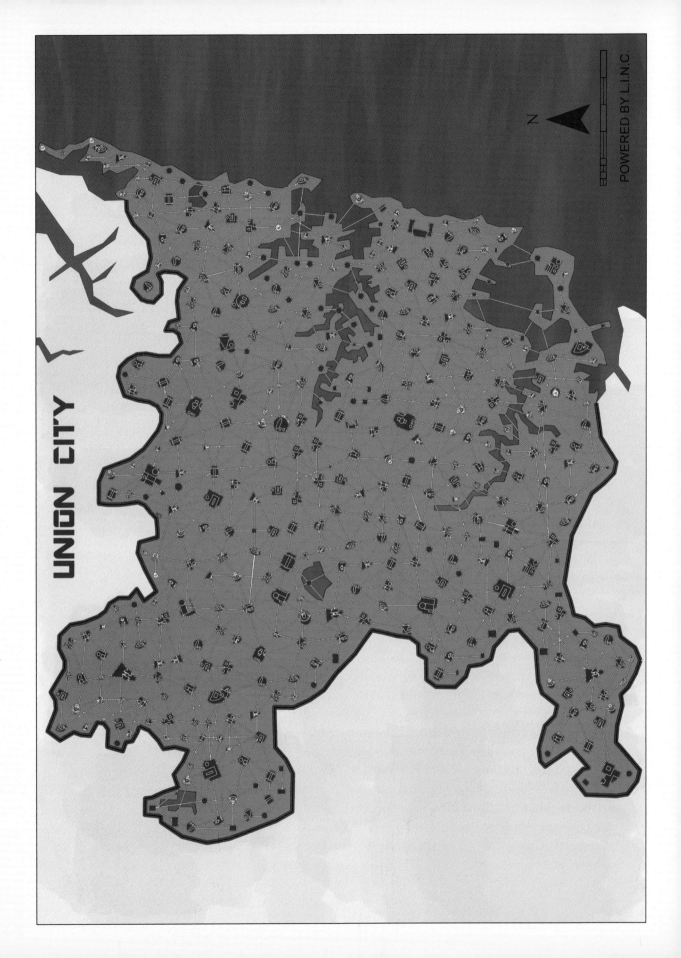

kept in line by the fully armed security forces. Some
may call this a police state, but day-to-day surveillance allows for exponentially improved management,
which in turn empowers expansion and production. The
fight against subversion is a fight for progress. Surveillance technology, after all, also enforces crucial
language laws, deters public air pollution offenses, and
safeguards the good neighbor code. Instigating riots is
now wisely punishable by either death or downgrad-
ing perpetrators to D-LINC status, the latter of which
withdraws all their civil liberties. When threatened by
Hobart infiltrators, carelessness is inexcusable and
pity for the D-LINCs is sickening. Deviation is unac-

ceptable, when a perfect digital entity such as our LINC (Logical Inter-Neural Connection) is

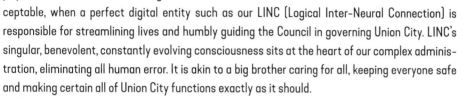

L.I.N.C. watches all space; even
mundane space

responsible for streamlining lives and humbly guiding the Council in governing Union City. LINC's
singular, benevolent, constantly evolving consciousness sits at the heart of our complex administration, eliminating all human error. It is akin to a big brother caring for all, keeping everyone safe
and making certain all of Union City functions exactly as it should.

LINC's eyes are everywhere, and can instantly punish terrorists. Citizens are reminded to stay
vigilant and alert at all times, even when life feels absurd and dull, or the underclasses' lack of
enthusiasm contagious. Rebels, hackers, and D-LINCs preaching decay on society's fringes should
be avoided, and apathy in the workplace reported. Knowing what one's work is all about is of course
not mandatory, and moral flexibility a virtue to be embraced for the sake of production quotas.
Any sign of paranoia or psychosis should be reported to a doctor, and presumably cured with some
fashionable plastic surgery improvements. Any holographic secretary can help with advice on
covering the costs; possibly by donating organs to be exclusively harvested postmortem. Avoiding
any of the banned religions such as the Church of Inward Contemplation should simply be a ratio-
nal choice, as any spiritual vacuum can be tended to at one of our countless jazz clubs, emporiums,
beauty salons, erotica outlets, wine bars, and world-renowned eateries: the Celestial Sandwich
Sushi Bar at the Otomo Junction, and Ultar's tavern, are the only places where eating like a barbar-
ian is famously encouraged.

Metropolitan space is organized in the semi-autonomous, towering megastructures we call
blocks. These soaring concrete spires of different shapes and sizes are connected to each other
via a dense network of safe sky bridges, elevated highways, and wide walkways. Astoria, Eyrie,
Granville Heights, Northbridge, Otomo Junction, Terminus Terrace, The Walkways, and many more
modularly designed blocks function as the city's cells. Huge pipes run along these magnificent
edifices that are always topped with fiery chimneys—symbols of Union City's industry. Social
and functional stratification are paramount in maintaining efficiency. All heavy industry is thus
located on the higher levels of blocks, middle-class residential areas are situated beneath them,
and the city's benefactors live humbly on the ground level. Vertical movement, supported by elevators (some exclusively reserved for robots), is meticulously monitored via biometric checks and
retinal scans in order to restrict the mobility of people suspiciously lacking in status and preserve
society's healthy segregation.

Blue-collar workers practically live in the factories at the top levels. They are occasionally forced to endure a relatively polluted atmosphere, but they have been blessed with excellent views and short commutes. Industry on the manufacturing levels manifests via nuclear reactors, gigantic gears and pistons, heavy-duty green-screen monitors, and wondrous heating and recycling systems, and is kept safe behind heavy metal doors and bulkheads designed to contain any failure. The architecture here is pleasingly functional, and at its best in the local hospitals and security headquarters. As for the mid-levels, they have been aptly designed to foster the creativity of the middle classes and offer comfortable living spaces, pale-colored squares, and rustic bridges connecting the many businesses of the commercial and service sectors. Managers, government officials, and industrialists—sensitive humans that all have to be shielded from all pollution—live on the lowest and ground levels. Paved stone streets, lakes, trees, flowers, neo-classical public art, and fine residences ensure the true heroes of society are allowed to operate at peak efficiency and avoid any corrupting temptations. Spacious mansions, exclusive clubs, and a selection of faux-Gothic cathedrals help alleviate the burden they carry.

The only restriction our leaders are forced to endure is that even they are not allowed to bypass the locked doors guarding the ancient underground subway tunnels and stations—for their own safety, of course.

DESIGN INSIGHTS

The world of *Beneath a Steel Sky* is a bleak, refreshingly neon-free Orwellian take on cyberpunk, with a few too many comedic touches and obvious *Mad Max*, *Blade Runner*, and *Paranoia* RPG inspirations. Its apt, eclectic influences helped Revolution Software craft a novel setting, which also referenced Terry Gilliam's *Brazil* and Fritz Lang's *Metropolis*, albeit with an inverted, vertical-class geography where the poor live at the top and the rich at the bottom of vast towers. Union City is essentially futuristic Sydney rendered in spires, with a few London references such as King's Cross station thrown in to playfully disguise it.

The game utilizes over seventy gorgeous backgrounds to showcase its obviously well-thought-out metropolis. Not only do these images present players with the architecture and feel of the place, but they make sure to elaborate on the vast city's connections and on the spatial logic of a unique but sensible world brilliantly designed to look coherent from all angles. Large openings allow the towering cityscape to be observed from evocative interiors, and many sweeping views are provided. Simultaneously, *Beneath a Steel Sky* grabs every chance to further flesh out its city. Much of Union City's odd culture, history, and function is brought to life via telling, archetypal inhabitants ready to show off their indifference, malice, expertise, or paranoia. Kids playing video games on benches and simple vignettes of people purposefully moving around add extra believability to the proceedings.

The latter is the result of the Virtual Theatre engine (originally appearing in *Lure of the Temptress*), which allowed for characters to follow scripted daily routines and helped construct the sense of a lived-in world many adventure games of the era lacked.

37

MIDGAR
Final Fantasy VII

GENERAL INFORMATION ///////////////////////

City: Midgar

Game: *Final Fantasy VII*

Developer: Square

Publisher: Sony Computer Entertainment, Eidos Interactive

Release Date: 1997

Genre: JRPG

Platforms: Android, iOS, Nintendo Switch, PlayStation, PlayStation 4, Windows, Xbox One

Their names may have been forgotten, but we do know that back in the days before Shinra Inc. built its metropolis literally on top of it, Midgar was eight individual towns. Less than a century ago, locals lived peaceful rural lives that served no empire, until Shinra constructed its imperial capital on a massive plate directly above them. This floating superstructure overshadowing the rustic towns and fertile lands of yore was meant as the physical manifestation of the corporation's power over people and nature both. New Midgar buried the past in perpetual gloom, and focused on building a ruthlessly efficient new world of profit, ambition, technology, and magical research.

Aptly, the megalopolis quickly rose to become the most advanced city on the planet Gaia, and a resource-hungry embodiment of greed, raw power, and environmental disaster. A place where the new coldly replaces the old, and where the wealth of a tiny elite displaces the lives of the many. A god-sized factory at the center of world economy, culture, and politics, its gargantuan energy demands could only be satisfied by eight Mako Reactors. Draining the planet's life force on such a scale quickly and visibly burdened the city's surroundings, and now Midgar lies in the center of a scorched wasteland of its own making near the coast of Gaia's Western Ocean.

But Gaia, a vast and varied planet, hasn't been fully drained yet. From the freezing arctic to the still lush forests and ancient deserts of the Western Continent, many haven't even sensed the rising danger, and only a few are skeptical of Shinra's practices. This is still seen as an exciting age of magic and technology for all, and only Midgar-based rebel groups such as AVALANCHE are actively fighting against the devastation.

Then again, Midgar's own identity is contradictory. The place simultaneously runs on electricity, steam, and magic, employs the latest technical solutions, and yet is falling apart, while technologies once meant to liberate are now exclusively used for surveillance. Mechanized monsters,

Legible urban design at its best and most ominous

MIDGAR

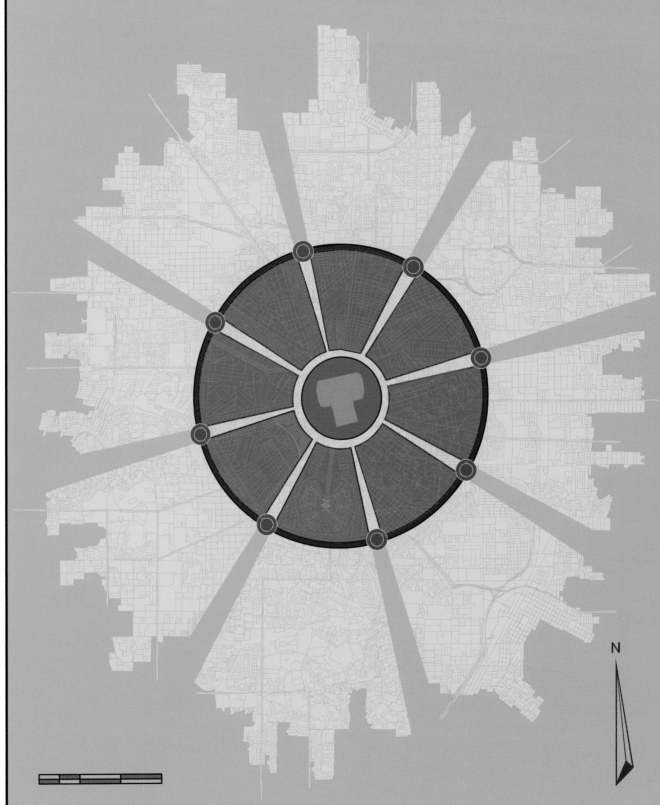

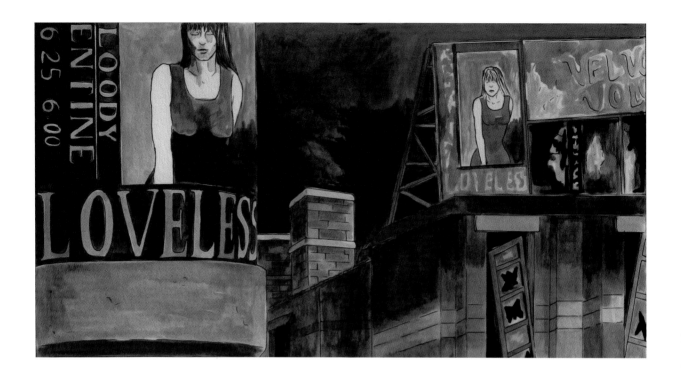

dazzling experimental animals, and body enhancements harmoniously coexist with whimsical chocobos and rumors of the Knights of the Round appearing to protect the poor. Most of Gaia's races can be found in the metropolis, including the Cetra, the legendary Ancients who can speak to the planet itself as effortlessly as Shinra's police force extracts data from dead bodies.

No expense is spared and no moral barrier is safe when it comes to safeguarding Midgar's police state for the benefit of its rulers. Security forces are everywhere, and all city affairs are run from the emblematic, heavily fortified Shinra headquarters at the metropolitan heart. A towering building dominating the cityscape and radiating political power, President Shinra, the mayor, and each of the company's departments are housed there, tellingly along the barracks of its private army. It is from this very building that Shinra imposes its will, directs Midgar's development, and ensures the city doesn't literally fall apart.

New Midgar, the upper city on the plate, is, after all, hovering 164 feet above the roofs of the old one, its immense weight supported by a massive central pillar and eight gigantic columns on the plate's periphery. This upper city is divided into eight sectors organized around Sector 0, the central, circular sector devoted to Shinra's HQ. Sectors 1 to 8 run around the dish, starting with number 1 in the north and going clockwise in a city that looks spectacularly similar to a pizza, the slices of which are vast residential sectors separated by concrete walls and fueled by Mako Reactors. Bureaucracy dictates that subdivisions also apply to the lower part of the metropolis, with each sector essentially comprising slum and plate sections.

The rich live above the poor in a grim physical expression of a deeply divided society, where the oppressed always linger in the literal shadow of their oppressors. The gigantic plate blocks all natural light from reaching the working masses, while those living on it are enjoying an affluent world of cobbled streets, fine architecture, stylish offices, and trips to the fashionable port town

Shinra's neglect is often too obvious

Lower Midgar hides many architectural treasures, and this particular cathedral hides a small garden

of Costa del Sol. Not surprisingly, the plate is thoroughly policed, and even a robotic air force makes sure the occasionally riotous slums never really disturb its routine. The shanty towns below are connected to the plate via the city's vigorously monitored train system, although the authorities are more concerned about the numerous, difficult-to-control hidden passages connecting the two tiers. The Midgar Highway is generally considered safe.

Cut off from the sky by the shiny city above, and the outside world by energy walls, the slums are further divided by walls between sectors. They are home to bitter poverty and harsh lives. The least fortunate may never live to see any sky but the iron one above them, whereas the luckier homeless often find shelter in concrete pipes. Identity and hope are easily lost under the pressure of a fierce one-sided class war, forcing people to live among discarded junk, surrounded by ruins and desperation. Petty crime flourishes, but it is the crime lords with close ties to the elite, such as Don Corneo of the red light district who make life a living hell. And yet, amidst derelict mobile homes, leaking roofs of corrugated metal, starving scavengers, and withering cottages, true hope refuses to die. Lower Midgar is filled with heartwarming pockets of humanity defiant against all cynicism, and plucky citizens keen to fight for a better future, or at least make the best of a bad deal.

Besides, life is never dull down there. Daily struggles, small miracles, countless little stories, and a myriad of unique locales keep things lively, and occasionally wonderful. There's Tifa's bar, serving warm, home-cooked meals hiding in the thick of the 7th Sector's outrageous menagerie of small shops, and there's the small church in Sector 5 where a rogue ray of sunlight somehow found a way through the metal ceiling and made flowers bloom. Unusually fluffy monsters can be seen roaming in the abandoned areas between sectors, and there's always the maze of rusted metal that is the Train Graveyard, serving both as a showcase of Shinra's neglect and as a very intriguing playground. Even more intriguing, however, are the passages leading through Midgar's extensive sewer system to the secret subterranean settlement of Deepground, although few will openly discuss them.

As for the future, it seems to be holding great disasters and great triumphs, capable not only of dooming or liberating the metropolis but the planet itself. Not unlike Rome, Midgar is more than a capital. Its presence looms over Gaia, and the specter of the Promised Land haunts the dreams of leaders and revolutionaries alike.

DESIGN INSIGHTS

Midgar, possibly the most iconic location in the Final Fantasy universe, was the result of a successfully implemented imaginative design, and probably one of the major reasons why *Final Fantasy 7* is as revered as it is. Moving away from the original decision to set the game in New York proved a masterstroke that provided it with a spectacular opening setting built around the simple idea of extreme class division. A huge, intimidating but beautiful and instantly readable city is introduced via a breathtaking cut scene showing off the imposing Shinra Tower at the center of the tiered, pizza-like city.

After this opening sequence, there is a brief scene in which players escape via train, allowing non-player characters to explain Midgar's layout and the camera to pull back and establish scale, as the train is shown like a little speck along an elevated track above the gargantuan city. As the story advances, more of the place's intricacies and idiosyncrasies are revealed, and the plot even masterfully draws tension out of Midgar's tiered design, playing with its obvious structural flaws: the danger of the plate crushing those below it.

The details of the metropolis are revealed bit by bit, in a process actually helped by hardware limitations that forced the use of pre-rendered backgrounds. Its carefully selected, elaborate shots give players a curated tour of Midgar. Shots pan down from rooftop to street-level; the camera zooms out to reveal immense buildings, or in to focus on dramatic interactions; and scenes are always perfectly framed. Everyday life is what brings vibrancy and warmth to the setting. Seeing how the poor of Midgar scrape by—and having supporting characters voice their frustrations—provides the city with a sense of life. Interestingly, the game's designers realized that, in reality, we tend to only know neighborhoods really well, and so they tried to mostly focus on this level.

What's perhaps the most ingenious aspect of Midgar's design is that, when players are in it, it feels as if the city is the entire world, as even its name is reminiscent of the Norse name for Earth (Midgard). Only leaving the city reveals this elaborate setting to be a tiny black spot on the planet's face, and a monument to a strong rural–urban divide powered by Shinra's greed.

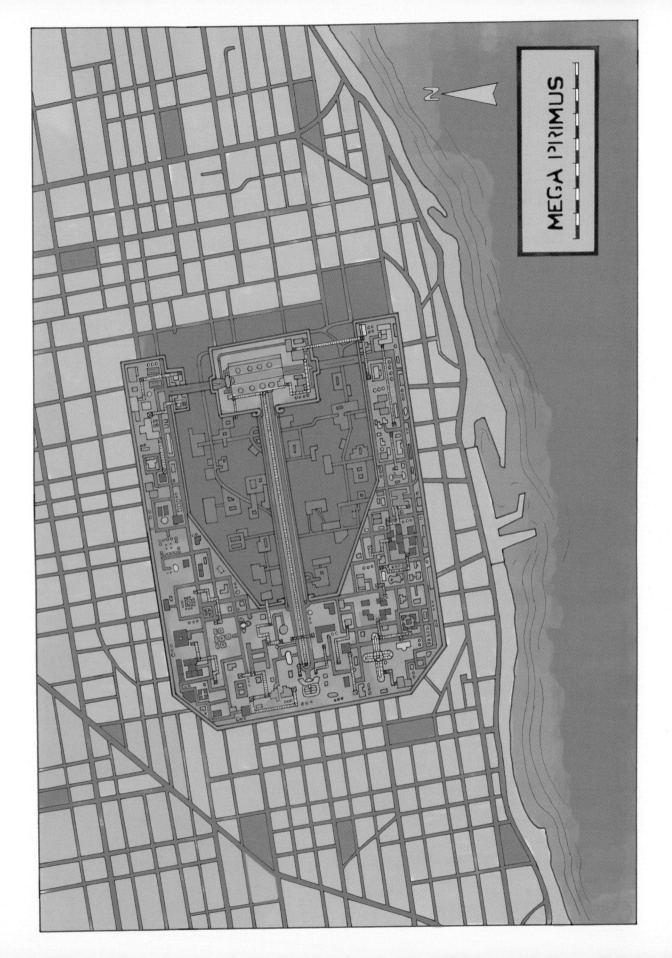

MEGA PRIMUS

38

MEGA-PRIMUS
X-COM: Apocalypse

GENERAL INFORMATION ///////////////////

City: Mega-Primus

Game: *X-COM: Apocalypse*

Developer: Mythos Games

Publisher: MicroProse

Release Date: 1997

Genre: Real-time Strategy, Turn-based Strategy

Platforms: MS-DOS, Windows

Half a century has passed since the battle of T'leth and the second alien war, but the deep scars on Earth's biosphere have yet to heal. Severe atmospheric and climatic changes forced millions to leave for off-world colonies, and led to the construction of self-contained, self-sustainable megacities to house the remaining population. Commissioned in 2080, Mega-Primus was the very first settlement constructed under the Megapolis Plan. Built over the ruins of Toronto, Canada, this beacon of hope has already become an important historical achievement. Under the constant threat of invasion, and surrounded by a toxic, hazardous atmosphere, the meticulously planned vast city has been thriving. Featuring the most advanced technology throughout the Sol System, it blends the finest human and Sectoid achievements to provide comfort and safety to a population growing healthy, genetically engineered babies in procreation parks and educated, disciplined citizens in psionic schools.

Interceptors and Valkyries patrol the skies above the gleaming walled city, while the densely populated, impoverished slums surrounding it are reminiscent of spatial distinctions from the Middle Ages, only reimagined on an unprecedented scale. Ravaged by war and environmental collapse, the slums, these remnants of the old world, are like little Victorian walled cities themselves. Within the actual walls of the metropolitan core, the geometric center is occupied by the senate building, surrounded by the most affluent of citizens and most spacious of parks. Organized in sectors, and following the logic of the proposed garden cities of the nineteenth century, Mega-Primus is not a claustrophobic city. It brims with vegetation, and is capable of growing its own food on its hydro-farms, purifying its water and manufacturing its goods. The metropolis is organized in specialized zones of residences, offices, leisure activities, and, of course, production, and comprises a wealthy, energetic, heavily protected C-shaped area connected to a suburban but equally well-protected, equally walled spaceport.

The future of humanity will, after all, be determined in Mega-Primus. If it falls, Earth falls, but even the metropolis's alert defenses never anticipated UFO attackers swarming through

The X-COM way to urban warfare

The modern metropolis had to be idyllic!

dimensional, tetrahedron-shaped gateways. The city is under siege, and its government has had to quickly re-establish X-COM to combat the threat posed by a ruthless race that has already enslaved the Sectoid civilization. As popular concerns rise, X-COM crafts patrol the streets, and covert bases are being built inside inconspicuous office blocks or warehouses. The young utopia is in danger and civil unrest is threatened, while authorities ramp up defense efforts. Water purifiers and crucial manufacturing facilities are under constant guard, and resident corporations have been asked to contribute to the maintenance and repairs of the urban tissue and its infrastructure.

The senate is the heart of the city-state. Housed in a marble edifice dominating the central sector, it acts as a hub of legislation, justice, governance, and democracy, where the thirteen elected senators hold council. From the senate chamber derives much power, but not all. Important city services, including policing, have been subcontracted to various competing corporations that have subtly undermined democracy, although they have handily provided fortified police stations, which act as the first line of defense against invaders. A police run by Megapol, a manufacturer of weapons with a stake in prison services, has unsurprisingly led to further tensions, especially with the poor and the non-human minorities. Corporate intervention and a rising alien threat are continuously stressing society, fueling physical and cyberspace violence, family breakdowns, crime, and even fanatic cults. As the quality of life deteriorates and profits shrink, the Cult of Sirius builds temples to worship the alien master race, and the invaders attempt to infiltrate or befriend key corporate stakeholders (and it does seem as though many of the intercepted and downed UFOs land on the buildings of competing enterprises). The threat is insidious, and will try to capitalize on petty differences and instigate ethnic hatred, often against the easy targets of androids and the Mutant Alliance, who represent Sectoid-human hybrids.

With the exception of a few injuries, the cityscape itself remains mostly unaffected and proudly glowing in its honest optimism. Futuristic shapes, bold art deco curves, symmetry, unexpected angles, and elegant lines combined with splashes of bold, often primary colors define the architecture of Mega-Primus. A coherent but varied style, typical of all planned communities, it influences everything from exclusive apartment buildings, vast housing complexes, and attractive office buildings, to corporate headquarters, utilitarian factories, and shopping malls inspired by the original Crystal Palace. An ideal ratio of open space and built-up areas reflects the cheerfulness of the mid-twentieth century, and hints at suburban aesthetics that tie in perfectly with the retro-futuristic style of all flying or land-based vehicles. Despite an ideological over-reliance on private transportation, however, it is the massive spaceport that handles passengers and goods to and from off-world colonies and the efficient, clean People Tube network of anti-gravity pathways that cover mass transit needs. Its owner, Transtellar, prides itself in connecting people and businesses.

Not unlike transportation, the city's fiercely guarded self-sufficiency has to be attributed to the efforts of the people working at Synthemesh's factories, Energen's power plants, and Evonet's recyclotoriums. Corporate activity defines a great part of everyday life. The miracles of Nano-tech allow people to live longer and healthier than any human before, while the large hospitals of Mega-Primus offer life-extension services to the richest, and limb replacements to the gravely injured. Synthemesh employs the finest apparel designers, and Sensovision's broadcasts bring virtual-reality experiences to all homes, as well as GravBall matches to those who cannot afford to spectate from expensive seats at Astrodome stadiums. What remains to be seen is whether these powerful corporations are convinced that their profit lies in serving humanity's needs.

DESIGN INSIGHTS

Unlike the first two X-COM games, *Apocalypse* takes place in a single city: Mega-Primus. Each of the game's difficulty settings provides a different civic layout, although no iteration is big enough to evoke the feeling of a megacity. What makes this virtual metropolis stand out is neither its believability nor its size; it is the complexity and ingenuity of its systems, its dynamic nature tying directly into the needs of the tactical gameplay. Mega-Primus has been crafted as a reactive, convincingly functional urban world complete with a pleasing night–day cycle. Its detail makes the game feel like an indirect city-sim of interlocking systems, networks, and destructible elements. As a result of combat, districts may be leveled, and aerial battles can potentially damage buildings, upsetting the owning companies. Another way these organizations can turn hostile (or at least decrease funding) is when heavily armed X-COM squads cause havoc or harm civilians and conduct unwarranted raids.

Uniquely, the funding of player-run X-COM doesn't depend exclusively on fighting aliens but on minimizing collateral damage, preventing alien corporate takeovers, and nurturing patrons. Organizations can demand compensation, openly attack X-COM forces, or withdraw their support, with substantial effects on how the city can be used. Should Megapol, responsible for the police, be kept safe, the police will maintain a strong presence and engage aliens. Similarly, keeping the mutant population happy will open up more recruitment options but make certain political alliances unattainable. The interactions between X-COM, political entities, and corporations are complex and demand diplomacy, as non-player character groups will fight covert battles against each other or even buy and sell property as their financial situation changes.

Every aspect of the city's infrastructure has been assigned to a corporation, which also controls certain neighborhoods. Mega-Primus is thus a dynamic urban-political battlefield with key objectives influencing the strategic functions of space. Controlling transport, propaganda, the People Tubes, and other amenities can be crucial. Enemies can deny services, infrastructure like roads can be destroyed, reinforcements may be blocked, and not having access to the spaceport can prevent the arrival of newly recruited scientists. The degree of alien infiltration and influence is not merely a statistic either; it has a spatial aspect expressed in a particular building or region. Additionally, specific building types provide different strategic bonuses and tactical challenges or opportunities for players and adversaries, depending on their location, function, and architecture.

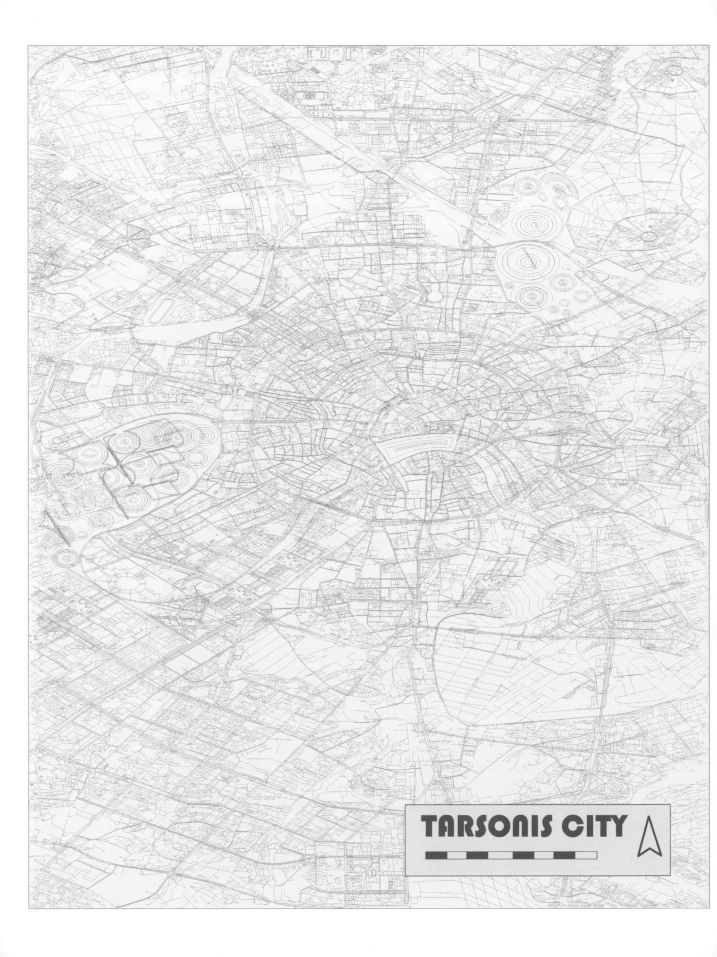

TARSONIS CITY

39

TARSONIS CITY
StarCraft Series

GENERAL INFORMATION / / / / / / / / / / / / / / / / / / /

City: Tarsonis City

Game: *StarCraft Series*

Developer: Blizzard Entertainment

Publisher: Blizzard Entertainment

Release Date: 1998, 2017

Genre: Real-time Strategy

Platforms: Mac OS, Nintendo 64, Windows

Tarsonis City is no more. The bustling metropolis of planet Tarsonis, Koprulu sector's capital and founding place of the Terran Confederacy, has fallen. Its four moons now only shine upon ruins, and human life barely survives in tiny embattled pockets as brutal civil war and the invasion of the Zerg Swarm have all but incinerated the cradle of the sector's civilization. Tarsonis, the planet where colony ship *Nagglfar* once proudly made landfall leading the four carriers that brought terrans to the sector, and powerful home of the ATLAS supercomputer, is no longer the colonizing force that inspired awe to its enemies. Its megalopolis has died.

Tragically, there had been decades of warnings, and a constant rise in desperate dissatisfaction that the Confederacy's increasingly tyrannical and corrupt rule chose to ignore, although, frankly, no one expected an alien invasion. Arcturus Mengsk, of course, the charismatic leader of the Sons of Korhal rebel group, was quick to use such an invasion and bring full-scale civil war to the planet. Rebel and Confederate forces battled in city streets, whole precincts were eradicated and burned, but in the end, it was the zerg that devastated Tarsonis City. Whether deliberately lured to the planet, the aliens attacked in their billions. The rapidly evolving insectoid masses of the Swarm, driven by pure devouring instinct, overwhelmed everything—not even nuclear weapons could stop them. It was this loss of the planet and the utter devastation of Tarsonis City that dealt the Confederacy's deathblow and allowed Mengsk to declare the Terran Dominion and kickstart his empire.

Over two billion people were killed and even more were forced to evacuate the planet, seeking refuge in other human colonies, as the Zerg Swarm, led by Kerrigan, the Queen of Blades, overran all defenses, built its hives upon mountains of corpses, and, finally and unexpectedly, abandoned the planet for reasons unknown.

Now feral zerg, smugglers, and terrorists infest the dead husk of the city, as all attempts to salvage it have failed. The planet has been turned into a ghost world and its capital into a deserted wasteland. Winds scream through abandoned tunnels and barely standing hallways, while shattered skyscrapers vaguely resemble the old skyline of the bombed-out, devastated city. The ruins

Dead empty shells comprise the skyline of Tarsonis City

The flags of the Terran Confederacy
once flew here

of Tarsonis City are all that are left of the once-glorious metropolis at the center of the Terran Confederacy. A capital so vast its suburbs had greater populations than whole planets, Tarsonis City was a megalopolis stretching all the way to the horizon, a shining beacon of human civilization, and the keeper of the memories of an Earth lost to history. It ruled the Confederacy in every meaningful way: the heavily defended epicenter of a heavily defended planet.

The once wondrous, sprawling cityscape was punctured by the spires of its tallest, most emblematic buildings. The Terra Skyscraper, the Kusinis Tower, the Universe News Network building, and the black marble of the Ghost Academy dominated high-rises, opulent mansions, slab-like apartment complexes, extravagant universities, and the wildly asymmetrical, often temporary architecture of the slums. It was a shining city of opulent gardens, veranda parties, and immaculately dressed butlers managing mythical penthouses, casting deep shadows over extreme poverty, and hiding cruel oppression. The slums, in reality, ran throughout its tissue, destitution being palpable even around the senate building.

The barely surviving poor kept the vast megalopolis functioning, and provided recruiters with an inexhaustible pool of soldiers. A complex if corrupt governance system centered around the monumental city council managed the vast population, maintained an intricate mass transit system, protected its political patrons, and ran an ill-reputed police force that in turn tried to control the wild traffic of hover cars, land-based vehicles, and armored convoys of the rich. Working the Traffic Control Department was a notoriously tough job, only marginally helped by the omnipresent high-tech surveillance systems. As for the overbearing sense of oppression, this was partly offset by Tarsonis City being a hub for the arts, famed for its musical traditions and varied nightlife.

More chaotic than the network of clubs, pubs, bars, gambling dens, and concert halls, however, was the plan for Tarsonis—if, of course, there ever was one. A central business and governmental district, the core of the New Gettysburg area and the city's suburban outskirts could be discerned with relative ease, whereas distinct patches of farmland as well as a now-destroyed lake brought subtle variation to the chaotic, weirdly uniform, endless urban sprawl. The southern and southwestern part of Tarsonis City consisted of the Gutter: a monstrously massive, crime-ridden slum infested with pawnshops and petty criminals, itself subdivided into countless smaller districts and suburbs.

But now, poverty and class have been equally eradicated. The Gutter, New Gettysburg, Sookdar's Point, the Hacker's Flat, and even the gated Kristios community have all been wiped off the face of Tarsonis. And although the war seems to have paused, and self-appointed Emperor Mengsk has vowed that Tarsonis City shall be restored, even in times of peace and prosperity, such an endeavor would require centuries of reconstruction.

DESIGN INSIGHTS

StarCraft's Tarsonis City is barely glimpsed outside of cut scenes or a few interesting tile sets and lines of dialogue, and yet still has a fascinating story to tell. It is a story of politics, societies facing war, and an epic space opera. Narrating events of such import via a city is always a good idea. Only a city is a character that can encapsulate and embody history in easy-to-summarize ways. Sadly, however, too little of Tarsonis is actually shown, and even less is allowed to influence the gaming experience itself. Its maps do not really feel different to any other tile set, and Tarsonis City is too fractured in its presentation to allow players to conjure a complete, more immersive image, and thus add gravitas to its eventual ruination.

NEW YORK

0   0.5   1   2   Miles

40

NEW YORK CITY
Deus Ex

GENERAL INFORMATION /////////////////////

City: New York City

Game: *Deus Ex*

Developer: Ion Storm

Publisher: Eidos Interactive

Release Date: 2000

Genre: Action RPG, Immersive Sim

Platforms: Mac OS, PlayStation 2, Windows

The head of the Statue of Liberty

The widespread optimism of the late twentieth century was evidently unfounded. In 2052, the world is a brutal, chaotic place, its rulers hidden behind veils of lies, secrets, and conspiracies. Disease, political violence, cheap drugs, and environmental degradation kill millions every year as the global economy is on the verge of collapse, and the gap between the insanely wealthy and the desperately poor has reached its historical apex. The world is spiraling into complete disorder, privacy is proving fragile, and the media scapegoat and spread hatred in an attempt to draw attention away from the real culprits. And yet dystopia is far from complete. Cybernetics have improved or replaced human body parts, and are moving on toward augmenting the human species on the nano level, promising superhuman abilities and better health—but not for all. Many bodies still reject such augmentations, and even worse, a lethal viral pandemic known as the Gray Death ravages the population without the predisposition for nanoaugmentation. Ambrosia, a vaccine by VersaLife that nullifies the effects of the virus, is in critically short supply, and thus only finds its way to high-ranking government officials, the super-rich, and a booming black market.

With common people losing all hope, mass riots are a worldwide phenomenon, as is the rise of organizations deemed terrorists. From the National Secessionist Forces (NSF) in the USA to the French Silhouette, there is an abundance of militant groups claiming to fight for the downtrodden against the supposedly democratically controlled United Nations Anti-Terrorist Coalition (UNATCO). The latter is headquartered in New York City in a bunker beneath Liberty Island following the extravagant insurrectionist bombing of the Statue of Liberty. The now-headless statue and its forgotten welcome to the tired, poor, and huddled masses of the world stands witness to an undeclared urban war between terrorists, states, cartels, and agents of mostly unknown powers. The situation in the symbolic center of the United States is incredibly tense. Battery Park, for example, once home to the town's antique artillery batteries, has been closed to all citizens due to undefined terrorist actions, and has had its shanty town evacuated, throwing a desperate

The headless Statue of Liberty

mix of junkies, Gray Death victims, and homeless back to the streets to spread odd rumors regarding Castle Clinton and hidden underground settlements.

Generally, however, New York hasn't changed much. There is absolutely no need whatsoever to start calling it anything like New New York or Neo New York. The grid defining Manhattan's form for over two hundred years remains unchanged, with Broadway running diagonally through it and all the way through the Bronx, one of the five unchanged boroughs of the city alongside Brooklyn, Manhattan, Queens, and Staten Island. Vast, wonderful Central Park and its lakes have survived another century, as have world-famous architectural landmarks such as the Flatiron Building, the Empire State Building, and Frank Lloyd Wright's Guggenheim Museum. Imposing skyscrapers still define the skyline, and the monotony of the high-rise canyons is broken up by lovely old brownstones, massive apartment buildings, and a few surviving Tudor Revival mansions in the suburbs. Even the large metal dustbins lining the streets are distinctly old-fashioned, and gentrification seems to have gone nowhere. In fact, the city's slums are growing around the persistent glow of the ever-luxuriant Fifth Avenue, and geographers have actually argued that the metropolis, despite its multitude of subtle changes and a growing reliance on choppers and speedboats, closely resembles its 1970s version.

On the other hand, New York never looked this gray, oppressive, or blocky. Tiny sections of the urban fabric have already collapsed into a wasteland for the desperate and sickly poor. Violence on the streets is commonplace, water rationing is a harsh reality, and countless outcasts, homeless, and drifters have found shelter in abandoned sewage and subway tunnels. The Ambrosia black-market thrives, yet those immune to the Gray Death seem more interested in stylish ties, cosmetic body modifications, flashy implants, and catching up with the latest retro-futuristic trends in leather jackets and sunglasses. Neon signs have also made a return, and co-exist with bipedal defense robot patrols, area-wide EMP fields, automated street cleaners, and the public computer terminals of the subway stations.

Sections of LaGuardia Airport have been sold to private companies or secretive billionaires to help relieve the city's debts, and the Brooklyn Naval Shipyards are now owned and run by the Submarine Warfare Division of the United States Navy. As for Hell's Kitchen, it has, unsurprisingly, reverted to its old destitute self. Once a bastion of working-class Irish Americans who were eventually displaced by wealthy Wall Street financiers, the neighborhood has once again succumbed to dereliction and red-lining. The 'Ton Hotel, formerly a Hilton with a malfunctioning sign, symbolizes the decline of an area where naming bars the "Underworld Tavern" sounds just fine. When simply striving to survive in Hell's Kitchen does not provide enough excitement, there are always the local warehouses brimming with NSF activity, the suspiciously out-of-bounds old water-treatment facility, and the infamous arms-dealing Smuggler's Den to liven things up.

It is of little wonder that in such times, conspiracy theories are so popular. In a world where hope seems all but dead and human clones are technically feasible, stories of black helicopters, Area 51, gray aliens, millionaire anarchists, and benevolent god-like AIs thrive, and respected outlets of the mainstream press seem overly keen to report on the Majestic 12, the Illuminati, or the ever-popular Knights Templar.

DESIGN INSIGHTS

Being an important evolutionary link in the chain forged by *Ultima Underworld*, *System Shock*, and *Thief: The Dark Project*, *Deus Ex* is an immersive simulation with RPG, adventure, and shooter elements—a game that provides enough options and cohesive visuals to spatially immerse players in a universe somewhere between the *X-Files* and *The Da Vinci Code*. It presents players with open-ended problems—not specific puzzles—and lets them use its versatile, moody environments to achieve their goals. Stealth, sniping, subterfuge, and hacking are just some of the options in a virtual city where verticality serves both gameplay and atmosphere. The choice of an alternate future New York is appropriate, as a realistic version of it would have been too restrictive, but a place grounded in recognizable reality is always compelling and easier to both design and introduce. Thus, every identifiable building shown in-game is close to its real-life counterpart, at least on the outside.

Deus Ex offers large, open, meticulously designed levels that have been masterfully selected, gated in a New York City that comes packed with a widely known history, prominent famous skyline, and architectural typologies that could be decently replicated by the boxy technologies of its era. Abstraction is abundant but successful, even if all civic elements seem to exist at a somewhat symbolic level: shantytowns composed of three shacks, a single model of a rat standing in for a whole health hazard, and four people around a lit barrel representing homelessness. The game's massive levels couldn't be filled with all the details required; only the most iconic ones could be picked, and atmospheric empty spaces had to be employed. In *Deus Ex*, a simple office hallway can often feel like a cavernous, almost alien cathedral from a 1990s version of the future.

Muddy textures and scant polygons also serve the distinctive fashion sense of future New Yorkers well, while further amplifying the sense of desolation. Finally, the dynamic sections of town are worth mentioning, as *Deus Ex* does go out of its way to showcase how New York changes every time the player returns to it. The Osgood and Sons warehouse, for example, is eventually torched and demolished, whereas the nearby free clinic periodically opens and closes. Making sure players would see and notice these changes in a game of many options and approaches was of course guaranteed by an unashamedly linear plot.

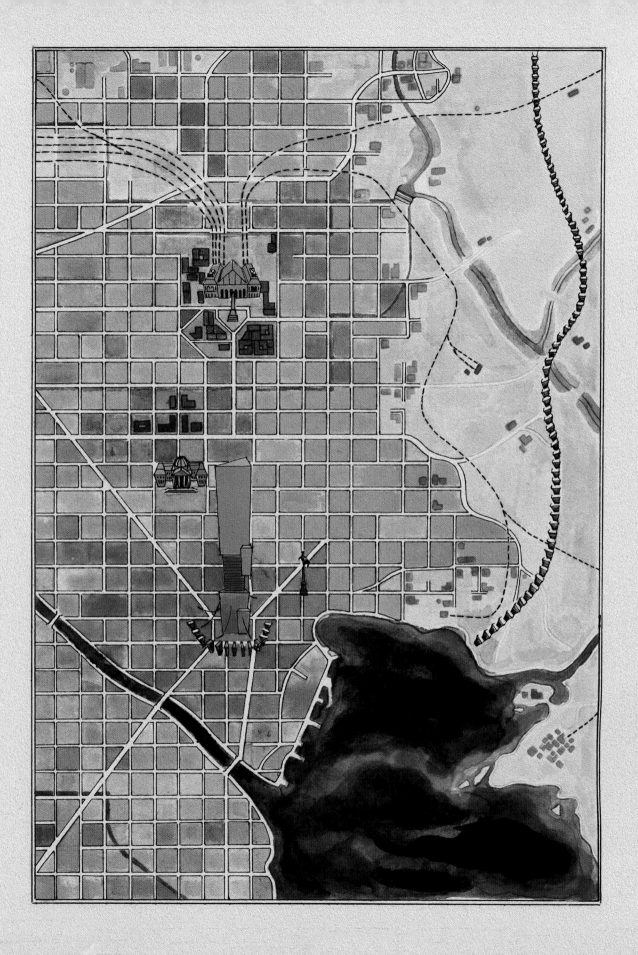

41

CITY 17
Half-Life 2

City: City 17

Game: *Half-Life 2*

Developer: Valve Corporation

Publisher: Valve Corporation

Release Date: 2004

Genre: First-person-shooter

Platforms: Android, Linux, Mac OS, PlayStation 3, Windows, Xbox, Xbox 360

There aren't any children in City 17. The dilapidated playgrounds are devoid of life, and will remain so for as long as the all-encompassing Suppression Field keeps on preventing human procreation. And it's not just the playgrounds that stand abandoned either. Many of the city's buildings are crumbling, and even more have been empty husks for years. Despite the soft daylight and long, almost romantic shadows, City 17 is neither a happy nor a vibrant place.

City 17's characteristic yards

Even pinpointing its exact location is tricky. The direction of the sunlight and the widespread use of the Cyrillic alphabet suggest Eastern Europe, most probably Bulgaria, yet one can also find a few signs and graffiti in Greek or even Scandinavian languages. With its exact location remaining a mystery, not much can be known of the place's early history, besides the fact it wasn't always called City 17. The architecture that still stands, itself a monument of better days, allows a simple reconstruction of the city's evolution from the neoclassicism of the nineteenth century, to early modernism, to the Soviet functionalism that followed World War II, to postmodern styles, to a truly alien, cold, and monolithic version of brutalism.

Following the Seven Hour War, along with the rest of Earth, City 17 is no longer under humanity's control. The unconditional surrender of the unified human government has turned the devastatingly powerful extraterrestrial forces of the Combine into the planet's new absolute rulers. It is they who constructed imposing citadels in major cities. It is they who chose to erect the greatest of the citadels in City 17, turning it into their de facto global capital, where Wallace Breen, former head of Black Mesa and Earth's current appointed Administrator, has his headquarters.

The gargantuan Citadel utterly dominates the urban landscape and sits at the new epicenter of City 17. This Combine tower is roughly four times the height of the Empire State Building, known to house the current government's most delicate functions and rumored to be hiding a portal of pure dark energy. It is of course neither the only alien construct in town nor the sole center tasked with controlling civic life. The heavily fortified Overwatch Nexus, probably an old

A police state always makes its presence felt—even at a central train station

A police state always makes its presence felt—even at a central train station

museum or government building, now protects the Suppression Device, and is the most evident hub of Combine military and police activity.

When it comes to spatial organization, City 17 adheres to the historically popular and versatile gridiron plan, which is broken up by a select few diagonal avenues, and is currently in the process of rearranging itself around the Citadel. The bulk of the built environment consists of wall-to-wall buildings organized around courtyards, mid-rise housing units, a relatively rich network of squares, and several specialized districts with the industrial one being the most prominent. Under Combine rule, most residential buildings have retained their use, even if the standard of living has plummeted and the population massively shrunk.

Before the occupation, the city must have been able to provide for a decent, even pleasing life and, among other land uses, sported hospitals, cafes, hotels, restaurants, shops, a once-vibrant harbor, and a service sector fossilized in the now-abandoned office buildings. Its industrial outskirts are still linked via rail with the urban core, but are considered off-limits to citizens. Unsurprisingly, accessing the surviving branches of the city's complex canal system is also looked upon with suspicion.

Not only has most of the town's infrastructure been left to crumble, but massive walls now cut through roads and buildings, disrupting the urban fabric for purposes either unknown or defensive. Whole districts have been broken up, and most of the economic and productive activities of the city have been eliminated. At least the power plants are still operational, and, unlike the tramways, most parts of the railroad network did survive, and are connecting the city to the rest of the occupied world. Sections of the road and highways network have also remained functional.

Cities are more than the sum of their buildings, plans, and infrastructure, and are actually defined by the civic life they nurture. Looked at this way, City 17 is seemingly all but dead.

Desperation looms over its silent squares and roads, and only the words of Administrator Breen are echoed through crumbling alleys. There are no fairs or demonstrating unions here—no drinking holes, no learning hubs, no culture or leisure.

The vast majority of the few remaining residents have been relocated here, often against their will. Smiles are rare and furtive looks common. Citizens clad in standard-issue uniforms do not remember much, and have to rely on rations of tasteless food handed out by machines to survive. Most keep their distance, speak little, and do not make friends, while the seemingly random abductions by the city's security forces keep everyone suspicious.

The Combine Civil Protection units—the everyday face of oppression—consist of human collaborators wearing riot police masks, enforcing curfews, and manning the countless checkpoints and roadblocks that make traversing the city a dangerous chore. They are aided by an elaborate network of static cameras, flying City Scanners, and menacing Strider Synths. As is apt in any system resembling a fascist dictatorship, glimpses of police brutality are a common element of the scenery.

The Citadel is imposing and it dwarfs all other edifices in City 17

Of course, humanity can never be completely subdued, and, despite the overwhelming strength of the oppressor, hope in City 17 refuses to die. It has organized itself, and is utilizing the urban environment to its advantage instead. The Resistance is running its "Underground Railroad," evacuating refugees via old tunnels and sewers, and hiding its labs and bases within plain sight. The constant sounds of a low-intensity war waged against the Combine will never cease until liberation is achieved.

DESIGN INSIGHTS

Half-Life 2 was a revolutionary game in many respects. It kicked off the era of downloadable games and forced the shooter genre out of its hallways and into rich, cohesive urban settings. City 17, an almost perfectly designed virtual place, has since inspired countless artists and designers by feeling huge, mysterious, lived-in, and intriguing, yet never being wasteful. Little is actually shown of the town, as most of it is traversed underground or through buildings and canals—but the illusion of a deteriorating metropolis is palpable. The visible elements are so rich in detail, so thoroughly researched and convincing that they effortlessly imply a believable city, and allude to a complex history.

City 17 is one of the most successful, coherent, economically designed, and memorable urban environments ever crafted. The imposing alien tower, the Citadel, instantly sets the tone, and acts as a major landmark that keeps players both oriented and focused on their goal. Combined with a network of minor landmarks consisting of elements such as the station square's obelisk or the horse statue, it makes the city easy to mentally map and thus legible to navigate.

The in-game use of actual urban configurations—along with the obvious existence of a concrete if rudimentary city plan—further help things make spatial sense and enhance immersion. Valve created the environments of *Half-Life 2* based on thousands of photos from Bulgaria, Russia, Romania, and Serbia, and successfully mixed elements from Sofia, Belgrade, and St. Petersburg, while wisely avoiding the Gothic elements that would have muddled its aesthetic clarity. The Overwatch Nexus in particular looks a lot like Serbia's House of the National Assembly, whereas the train station bears an uncanny resemblance to Budapest's Western Railway Station.

A living, breathing city also requires a sense of history, and urban history is almost always layered. City 17 has different tech levels coexisting, and buildings from several ages, regimes, and architectural styles standing next to each other. Crucially, everything placed in its space feels as if it is serving some personal or collective purpose—either for human residents past and present, or for the occupiers.

What's more, the urban layouts brilliantly serve the game's need for interesting battlegrounds. City 17's courtyards, canals, and streets provide ample tactical opportunities and varied arenas able to support entertaining encounters against a variety of enemies. As a final touch, the plot explains away the need for too many roaming citizens that would have burdened the game engine, and credibly restricts available routes, being itself part of a masterful design.

CITADEL
Mass Effect Trilogy

42

GENERAL INFORMATION //////////////////////

City: Citadel

Game: *Mass Effect Trilogy*

Developer: BioWare

Publisher: Electronic Arts, Microsoft Game Studios

Release Date: 2007, 2012

Genre: Action RPG

Platforms: Android , iOS, PlayStation 3, PlayStation 4, Wii U, Windows, Windows Phone, Xbox 360, Xbox One

The Citadel

Far into the Serpent Nebula, orbiting the star known as the Widow, lies the ancient, colossal, deep-space station of the Citadel. Located at the nexus of the galaxy-spanning Mass Relay network, connecting all species across known space, it is the single point functionally closest to everything else, and the foremost galactic hub for all space-faring civilizations. Its construction is often attributed to the now-lost civilization of the Protheans, although no archaeologist ever managed to confirm this. The still-cryptic technology powering the political, cultural, and financial center of the Milky Way could, in reality, be much older than even the earliest of the races.

The Citadel Council, the galactic community's supreme governing body, sits at the heart of the Citadel maintaining law and order through its diplomatic, intelligence, and military arms. The Council never governs directly, but passes judgment on laws regulating Citadel Space and the relations between civilizations. Only three species are represented in the Council, each holding a single seat—the asari, salarians, and turians—and it is the space controlled by these three that is unofficially referred to as Citadel Space. Most of the dozens of major races making up the population of the galaxy, including humans, are simply granted embassies on the Citadel, and are considered associate members. They are autonomous masters of their respective regions, but also entitled to bring issues to the Council for resolution.

The Citadel itself, a gargantuan construct aptly proportioned for its crucial role, has a gross mass of over seven billion metric tons. It is similar in shape to a pentagram, and consists of a central ring, the Presidium, from which five arms, called the Wards, protrude. The station's spaceports are located on the ring, which has a diameter of 4.5 miles and is 1,749 feet wide. Each of the Wards is 27 miles long and 1,083 feet wide, providing the Citadel with enough space to be the bustling metropolis it is, and gently rotating to simulate the required gravity for its varied inhabitants.

The Presidium is home to the Citadel Tower and the various governmental offices of the Council, as well as to embassies for all represented species. This tower rising parallel to the Wards is the

THE FIVE WARDS OF THE CITADEL

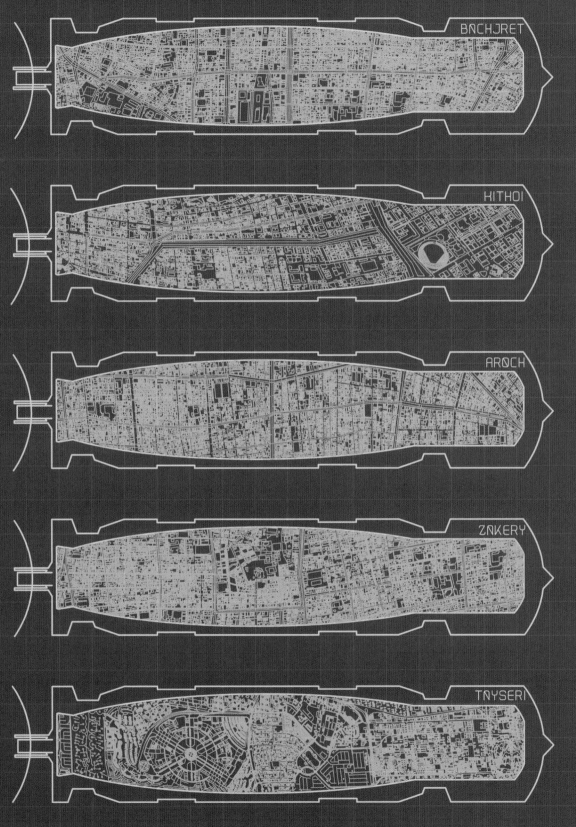

BACHJRET

KITHOI

AROCH

ZAKERY

TAYSERI

HILOMETERS

0   20   40

The idyllic Presidium

most distinctive landmark of the whole ring, and the place where the Council meets, decides and holds audience with ambassadors. Of course, commercial and recreational facilities are common throughout the Presidium, it being a place for the galactic elite. Exclusive stores, elegant restaurants, expensive apartments, and banks can be found in and around its financial and governmental districts, while the Presidium Commons is probably the most vibrant sub-center. As for its interior, it has been landscaped to resemble a lush parkland planet with buildings along the curving walls of the ring, blending in unobtrusively with their surroundings. No detail has been overlooked. Freshwater lakes, fields, trees, ponds, and fountains, as well as artificial sunlight and gentle breezes, make deep-space life actually pleasant. Additionally, the Presidium goes through a brief day–night cycle, allowing for six hours during which the holographic sky darkens.

The five Wards are the main residential and economic centers of the Citadel. Each is essentially a self-contained city home to millions, with a population density similar to late-twentieth-century Hong Kong. They are more utilitarian than the Presidium, looking more like traditional settlements with a stronger sense of verticality and an obvious lack of day–night cycles. The unending night admittedly allows for spectacular views of the Serpent Nebula and nonstop commercial activity, since most residents do not have to adhere to any common schedule, and so sleep and work according to personal need or preference. The traffic of flying cars and public elevators never ceases either, as businesses and markets simply do not pause, while metropolitan variety flourishes under glowing billboards and neon letters.

The need to house over 13 million people could only be satisfied by massive apartment buildings, and by turning all five Wards into dense forests of skyscrapers sealed against the vacuum. Breathable atmosphere only exists for approximately 23 feet above ground, allowing all races and classes to mingle without the need for special breathing apparatuses. In the Wards, slums, posh areas, middle-class districts, and specialized sub-centers, although generally separate, tend to bleed into each other in a sea of sushi restaurants, nightclubs, arcades, casinos, and concert halls.

Each of the five Wards has its unique traits, with Kithoi being home to the Council's Central Archives, the Taralos Amphitheater and Edroki Plaza, and Tayseri being proud of the Dilinaga Concert Hall and the Museum of Galactic History. The Zakera Ward is mostly known for its factory district and commercial zones, and Aroch (unofficially known as the Shalta Ward) is rumored to feature the self-proclaimed Finest Chocolate Shoppe in the Citadel. Even the supposedly unremarkable middle-class Bachjret Ward shines in its uniquely efficient, sensible, tidy city plan.

A view from the Kithoi Ward

What's more, the Wards form the core of the Citadel's defense. Being its heavily armored ballasts, they can close off the city, transforming it into a nigh-on impenetrable, heavily armored cylinder. Of paramount importance is defending the political heart of the galaxy from any cosmic threats. The Citadel is further protected by a powerful war fleet comprising mostly turian ships and countless surface-mounted turrets. Security on the station itself is covered by the 200,000 volunteer constables of C-Sec who provide pirate defenses, customs services, and enforcement, and handle all crime. With millions of residents, and additional millions of visitors, in a society that still hasn't evolved past poverty and ownership, crime sadly still exists, and is varied enough to include everything from petty thieves and Element Zero smugglers to disorganized pirates and the elusive Shadow Broker, the galaxy's most powerful trader of secrets.

Even mysterious criminal keepers of lore, however, do not seem to possess the forgotten knowledge regarding the bioengineered, insectoid, drone-like hybrids everyone refers to as the Keepers. These are a species native to the station who maintain and run most of its systems. As they completely self-destruct via extremely corrosive acids upon death, they have never been autopsied, and the laws against interfering with them are draconian. Besides, their silent race seems benevolent, and has been building and rebuilding the station for millennia and navigating its labyrinthine interior superstructure to keep it operational. The Keepers, however, are far from the Citadel's sole mystery. The place's history itself is essentially unknown, with scientists arguing it could have seen countless civilizations rise and fall, and that the Protheans, just like the Asari after them, simply discovered and never constructed it. Even the resilient material the Citadel is made of remains virtually unknown, and both the station's core and master control units have yet to be discovered.

DESIGN INSIGHTS

In *Mass Effect*'s epic saga of galactic proportions, a single location as a meaningful hub is a difficult problem that demands an elegant solution—and deciding upon the dynamic city of the Citadel was a masterstroke. The Citadel really managed to stand out, and became one of the most memorable locations throughout *Mass Effect*, evidently helped by the brilliance and originality of its concept but also by its well-selected influences such as the O'Neill cylinder, Babylon 5, Dubai, and Tokyo.

Coupled with the setting's excellent lore (where humanity isn't at the center of all), subtle hints of how ancient the station is, some wonderful art, and impressive establishing shots and cut scenes, the Citadel just worked. It held the trilogy together by offering a constant point that provided a miniature universe to explore under a single roof, and it evolved between return trips, was central to the overarching plot, and offered several quests and side-quests of its own. It progressed past a lifeless hub via tons of details, but mostly by letting players engage in conversations with all sorts of different people bearing their own unique stories.

Although as a city it never achieved perfection, and occasionally felt too small and cramped to fit its lore, the Citadel changed with the series. In *Mass Effect*, it was successfully massive but not particularly detailed, whereas in *Mass Effect 2*, it was confined in a few floors of the Zakera Ward and a handful of relatively dull locations. It did offer a decent glimpse of everyday life in the Wards, and of how corrupt any utopia can become, but it was out of scale, too small, and overly simplistic in its structure. Thankfully, *Mass Effect 3*, especially the Citadel DLC, brought the city closer to looking convincingly gigantic, and actually improved navigation, while at the same time making the place livelier. Monumental sizes were wisely showcased, and, intriguingly, the image of a metropolis in space reacting to all-out war was conveyed.

Also worth mentioning is the use of music, which helps to distinguish different sections of the urban tissue and suggests local ambience. The Presidium's smooth, lofty tunes in particular turned into the brooding, almost mysterious music of the Wards.

New Vegas, Nevada

Inner Wall

Outer Wall

New Vegas Strip

Freeside & Westside

Las Vegas Ruins

Mojave Wasteland

N

| 0 | 1.75 | 3.5 | | 7 | | 10.5 |
Miles

NEW VEGAS

43

Fallout: New Vegas

GENERAL INFORMATION /////////////////////

City: New Vegas

Game: *Fallout: New Vegas*

Developer: Obsidian Entertainment

Publisher: Bethesda Softworks

Release Date: 2010

Genre: RPG

Platforms: PlayStation 3, Windows, Xbox 360

Vegas never changes. Nuclear winter itself could not kill the town's hustle, and for as long as greed and passion can be sold, Vegas will endure. It will endure just as it has done since the very first casino opened back in 1941, when nothing was deemed too crazy to lure people to the middle of the Mojave Desert to gamble away. Casino owners quickly mastered the idea of reinvention. Over and over again, Las Vegas found the ways to stay fresh and transform without ever losing its outrageous self. It always promised everything and remained fashionable. Cowboy saloons welcomed tourists at the height of the Western craze, and bungalows with lawns celebrated suburbanization sweeping across the United States, only to be quickly replaced by the neon planets, huge signs, fake atomic bombs, and wild technological optimism of the Space Age. Futuristic Googie and aerodynamic Streamline Moderne architecture reshaped Vegas's silhouette, bringing in upswept roofs, boomerang shapes, exposed steel, and rounded edges. The very style that still defines New Vegas: the orgiastic, escapist pleasure zone enduring within the apocalypse.

The great nuclear war between the United States and China that devastated whole continents couldn't prevent the postmodernist heart of New Vegas from rising once again on the ruins of Las Vegas. Of the seventy-seven atomic warheads launched against wider Vegas, most were miraculously blown out of the sky, and only nine hit the surrounding desert. The city itself suffered substantial damage, but crucially avoided a direct hit. Much of it remained intact, and even retained some access to electricity, until, through the sheer will of Robert House, it got rebuilt. Roughly two hundred years after the fallout, the legendary Mr. House forcefully united the local tribes, transformed them into loyal casino-owning families, erected strong walls around the Strip, and once again lit it up.

With New Vegas at its core, and by having avoided heavy bombardment, the Mojave is an incubator for civilization, albeit one still partially engulfed in chaos and violence. Deathclaws, feral ghouls, rad scorpions, and vicious raiders still roam the lands, but the New California Republic, proudly on the verge of forging a new society, can provide mostly safe highways leading to where the real post-post-apocalyptic world is being born: the New Vegas Strip. Officially named the Free Economic Zone of New Vegas, the Strip, powered and watered by the nearby Hoover Dam, is what the old world must have looked and felt like. It is reminiscent of hope as its striking, colorful lights twinkle in the wilderness and its sparkling skyline advertises an absurd gambling oasis, promising safety and entertainment among the Nevada ruins. And Mr. House has made it abundantly clear that every outsider willing to spend their money is welcome to do so.

Following the ever-expanding reach and popularity of its casinos, the Strip has grown into a hub for merchants, caravans, opportunists, and everyday people wanting to hit it big. Downtown Vegas is packed with clubs and gambling opportunities, and the show goes ever on as money flows under the glimmering towers and massively illuminated signs. The skies here are bright blue during the day, and the streets stay illuminated throughout the night. Residents and visitors can experience life in freshly painted buildings, see the monorail, eat untainted food, and listen to those delicious rumors involving plans to colonize space. The last of the remaining ruins are being rebuilt, infrastructure is being vigorously maintained, and the few ancient cars still rotting by the roads only serve as rustic decorations.

A semblance of normality has taken hold of the Strip. A fragile yet cynical community is attempting to carve out a decent existence, only to quickly repackage and sell it to the hundreds of visitors. If you have the caps, living in the Strip is comfortable, and if you love those songs from the 1950s, you'll adore Mr. New Vegas playing them for the drunken soldiers, ruined gamblers, and prostitutes. As for the heavily armed, mono-wheel Securitron robots patrolling the streets—worry not. They are here to keep everyone safe and ensure handguns remain concealed in this adult playground of brilliant lights, phantasmagoric shows, and wild amusements.

In classic Vegas fashion, it is the great casinos that pump the heart of town. Fittingly, New Vegas's most prominent landmark is the pre-war Lucky 38 hotel and casino run by Mr. House

Freeside: still more civilized than the wasteland

himself. A towering mausoleum of the Atomic Age, the elegant establishment is an enduring monument to its owner's vision of luxury without decadence, and refinement without snobbery. A promise for a future reminiscent of a glorious past. The far less classy Gomorrah is managed by the Omerta family, and, gambling aside, it specializes in selling sex, cheap booze, and drugs. It is commendable as the only ghoul-friendly casino in the Strip, featuring semi-naked humans and ghouls dancing in cages and fires illuminating the kitschy faux-Persian décor. The Tops, controlled by the Chairmen, offers a more historically accurate Vegas experience with its Aces Theater, slots, tables, and fine selection of wines, although the best restaurant has to be the Gourmand at the Ultra-Luxe. This domed casino belonging to the secretive White Glove Society heavily pampers its elite clientele, and enforces a strict dress code of formal attire and white masks. The waiting list here is crazy, the bathhouse magical, and the Brahmin Wellington suspiciously divine. Roulette and blackjack are the only games offered, but the nearby Vault 21—an old Vault-Tec facility converted to a casino—seems to be offering more varied gambling options.

Outside the protected area of the Strip, thriving along the axis of the old South Las Vegas Boulevard, past the extravagant casinos, resorts, and residential high-rises lies Freeside, the slum surrounding New Vegas. It is modestly fortified and in much better shape than the ruins of the wider irradiated hinterland, but life here is evidently worse. Those who never got rich in the Strip, old tribes who didn't bow to Mr. House, new settlers, foreigners, beggars and less affluent merchants, and visitors live under the rather extortionist protection of the Kings and Van Graffs. Filth, danger, and ruined buildings abound, while the lack of luster in the old, smaller casinos is painfully obvious. Yet even here, under the Strip's glorious shadow, hope seems to have taken root. A young, complex society is slowly growing in its districts, becoming increasingly self-sufficient, offering opportunities and maintaining its protective, wrecked-vehicle roadblocks.

You see, all of New Vegas is important. It is a booming town of dreamers and desperadoes fiercely guarding its autonomy, and it is only sensible that the powerful factions vying for the control of the Mojave are interested in owning this oasis. The New California Republic, despite maintaining an embassy in the Strip, would relish an opportunity to control it, whereas the savage Legion, led by a man known only as Caesar, simply wants to assault, capture it, and probably crucify everyone who dares oppose them. Even the Super Mutants and the remnants of the Brotherhood of Steel would like to hold a stake in this epicenter of progress, and Mr. House seems to have realized that, once again, war might be inevitable.

DESIGN INSIGHTS

New Vegas starts off with the playable character getting shot in the head and left for dead in a shallow grave. In a single scene, it references pop culture Vegas stereotypes and captures Fallout's signature sense of violent irony, before introducing the New Vegas virtual city, a setting that finally puts the luck statistic of RPGs to good use, and immerses the player in a rich locale inspired by real-life Las Vegas (and its many tropes). A sniper perched in a dinosaur statue can join players, and a human brain in a jar is running the whole strip as Fallout and Vegas weirdness combine to give birth to the Elvis-impersonating Kings gang and the mob-like Omerta family. Additionally, the setting of Vegas allows for a splash of color to creep into the Fallout world and the inclusion of some fascinating, recognizable architecture.

The New Vegas Strip is the game's urban centerpiece, which avoided the nukes to preserve its neon majesty. It is a resettled town of flashy buildings inspired by historical reality. Obsidian based the Lucky 38 on the Space Needle-inspired Stratosphere Tower, the Ultra-Luxe was largely influenced by Caesar's Palace, and the Gomorrah by the former Dunes hotel and casino. Using the geography of an actual place and taking advantage of the liberty afforded by the post-apocalypse, the game imaginatively recreates a 1950s version of Las Vegas as a walled outpost of civilization. The retro-futuristic aesthetic of the Fallout series is perfectly served by the Googie and Streamline Moderne styles of the era, which, after all, are what most would expect from any version of Vegas. Late 1950s music and references further enhance the atmosphere, which was spiced up with a few 1940s country tunes and the odd early 1960s architectural element.

For added authenticity, several locations in and around Las Vegas—such as Lake Las Vegas and Searchlight—were faithfully recreated, alongside versions of the car Bonnie and Clyde died in and the famous "Welcome to Fabulous Las Vegas" sign from 1959. Surrounded by an equally authentic Mojave Desert, the detailed town feels convincing and exciting.

44

PROPAST, EUROPOLIS
Dreamfall Chapters

GENERAL INFORMATION //////////////////////////

City: Propast, Europolis

Game: *Dreamfall Chapters*

Developer: Blink Studios, Red Thread Games

Publisher: Deep Silver, Red Thread Games

Release Date: 2014

Genre: Adventure

Platforms: Linux, Mac OS, PlayStation 4, Windows, Xbox One

The twin worlds of Stark and Arcadia—science and magic—were separated by the impassable Divide twelve millennia ago, and, in the twenty-third century, the technologically advanced civilization of Stark finally reached beyond Earth, our solar system, and well beyond any notion of magic. Europolis, one of its greatest cities, sprawls across central Europe, encompassing Belgium, parts of France, the Netherlands, Germany, Poland, and the Czech Republic, with tendrils extending all the way to the former Baltic states. At the heart of the fading continent, the giant megalopolis is not a happy place. The sun has vanished in the unending rain, the economy has stalled, corruption reigns, pollution is deadly, and mega-corporations rule over towering districts of glass and light in a city-state with strict internal borders. Traveling from Vienna to Prague has never been this difficult.

It is in Propast, a sector of the Prague district, where Zoë Castillo, the only Dreamer of both worlds, resides; Zoë can dream herself in other realities, and once saved both Stark and Arcadia from enslavement. It is the thread of her story, weaving through the universe, that will unravel in the perpetual darkness of historic Propast. Poverty-stricken, ruled by crime and industrialized chaos, Propast is a cyberpunk dystopia of dark alleys, destitution, neon corporate signs, and wild nightclubs. Vehicles fly overhead, ad-bots harass, the failing EuroMetro provides mass transit, and quaint boats sail the toxic river. Life here is difficult for humans and impossible for plants. The poor are often forced to become live subjects for genetic testing or end up as junkies hooked up to dream machines, while the less desperate enjoy their lucid dreaming in TraumRaum, or 1001 Dreams, and savor the town's legendary street food. Propast is neither heaven nor hell. Its world of blue hues is defined by its contradictions, just as its architecture thrives on contrast and its political slogans compete with ads for attention.

Young Propast was built above old Prague. Impressive brutalist towers and glass skyscrapers cast their shadows on surviving stone arches, and Gothic, Renaissance, baroque, and modernist-era

Outside the Seraph Kavarna

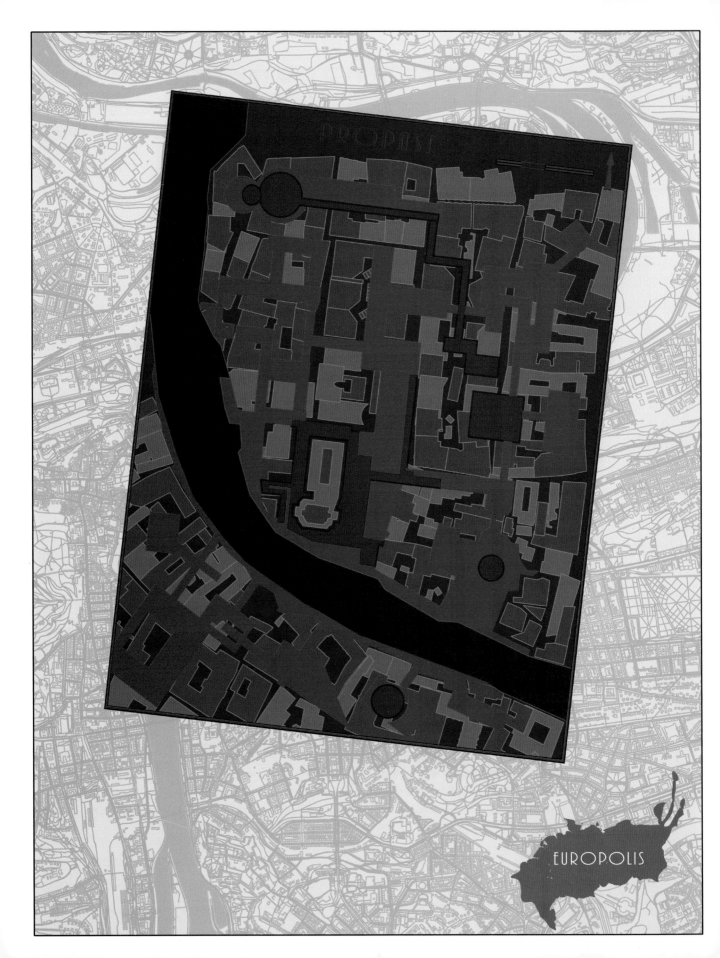

Crowboy-sponsored interactive maps help tourists and locals alike navigate Propast

architectural monuments. Expressionism, art nouveau, postmodernism, and Vienna Secession buildings have been retrofitted with new ventilation systems and connected to the sky-bridges network, or in rare cases demolished altogether. Steel and concrete towers have been erected directly on top of historical buildings, incorporating them as a foundation of sorts, and a new town has been constructed a tier above the old one. Propast's architectural layering is literal. The city exists on different levels, with the lowest one being the oldest, and with lively terraces functioning above old but still vibrant plazas—the spacious walkways connecting towers and tiers.

Nowadays, Crowboy-sponsored interactive maps guide visitors and residents through the city's varied, distinct areas. By the river, for instance, the Chinatown of the Bricks is lit with red lanterns, packed with shops, and ornamented with delicate statues of lions. Boathouses and floating restaurants lead the way to Pristaviste, the old riverside docks, and the square of the Collapse memorial. Nearby, the ironically named Sonnenschein Plaza is the only place in Propast

The most politically active food stall in Propast

with (admittedly artificial) sunlight, provided by an Original Consumer Goods sun suspended over a holosculpture by Emma de Vrijer. Staring directly at it may cause blindness and/or tumors that even the remixed beers of the adjacent Seraph Kavarnameta brewery could never hope to heal. This public terrace offers a stunning view combining the river, Chinatown, and a melange of old and contemporary architecture in a truly representative snapshot of the city. Below, the Shuk, or Souk, is a harmonious, beautiful maze of mostly Arabic and Jewish retailers of technology, hand-woven carpets, and masterfully bioengineered goats. Farther away, purple-lit alleys offer sexier delights, and even farther lies Kaprova, with its infamous dream dens and Madame Nyx's House of Dreams.

Even seedier nightclubs, sex joints, and illegal dream emporiums abound in Kaprova, hidden among the town's robot workshops, street performers, vendors, stalls, carts, and myriad shops. Sculptures, holosculptures, talking garbage bins, and those inexplicable "Mystery Towers" keep the streets interesting, and frame places such as the swanky Bitte nightclub—famous for its celebrity patrons and hallucinogenic drinks—or the Seshadri Tower. The latter, the tallest building in Propast, houses hundreds of posh offices and apartments and is considered prime real estate. And yet, right outside it, Nela Vlček's communist food stall sells its organic, non-engineered meals, reminding all of the stark political and class differences dividing the city.

Political tensions are rising throughout Propast and Europolis both. The financial crisis deepens, demonstrations are as regular as impromptu police checkpoints, and the population simply refuses to stop caring about the future. The political forces vying for control of the city-state's parliament are the conservative, corrupt Alliance of European Democrats for Freedom and Liberty, Konstantin Wolf's fascist European Dawn that is covertly being supported by corporations, and Lea Umińska's social democrats of the popular if suspiciously timid Unity Party. Marta Ribas, on the other hand, has united several Marxist groups to form the Manifesto coalition, spearheading a large number of demonstrations against inequality and the rising political power of corporations. With her exception, politics and corporations have been inextricably tied together for decades. The Syndicate, an institution parallel to the government and run by megacorps, has even managed to substitute the police with its own fully militarized EYE forces, operating both in the physical world and on the Wire. EYE monitors all communications and transmissions, and keeps tabs on independent journalistic outlets such as The Hand that Feeds, which dare to challenge mainstream views.

Thankfully, in a world where surveillance is all-pervasive, the people of Propast seem to still enjoy connecting outside of technology. There's a desire to meet face to face, and acoustic guitars still draw crowds here. And even if organized crime and a suffocating EYE presence can sometimes make Propast feel like a wasteland of decadence and crushed dreams, there's always community, excitement, and passion—hope, too, and Zoë Castillo, who seems to thrive among the multicultural mix of punks with holographic mohawks, traditionally dressed girls, and finely suited yuppies. If they can dream of better futures on the streets of a city founded on optimism, so can the Dreamer.

DESIGN INSIGHTS

Propast is but a small district within a vast city that players never get to see, and yet, with its density of detail and variety, manages to convince it is surrounded by a sci-fi megalopolis. Propast's Europe is a poverty-stricken, corrupted wasteland inverting the standard notion of an affluent West, which simultaneously mixes German, Polish, Czech, and French influences in its futuristic cityscape. Berlin and Prague, in particular, have been obvious sources of inspiration, along with the techno-noir brutalism of *Blade Runner* and Mega-City One.

Though a small open-world environment with distinct landmarks, concrete edges, and aesthetically apt public maps, Propast is confusing to navigate. On the other hand, it is densely packed, beautifully executed, and absolutely believable. Streets and alleys are bustling with non-player character (NPC) activity in a cyberpunk setting one can take seriously. A setting where actual people could lead different but convincingly real lives in spaces designed by planners and architects not as dystopian backdrops but for people to live in. Locals only suspect the dystopian nature of their universe, and refuse to give up hope for a better future. They care. They discuss and challenge reality and draw political parallels to our world. Conversations on the streets tend to be about police lockdowns, upcoming elections, or even racism, and really flesh out the setting from fresh perspectives. Few virtual cities have so pithily encapsulated civic life in so small an area, and even fewer have realized that a city is more than its buildings; a city is its society, its life.

Crucially, residents do not seem trapped in Propast. For all the junkies and poverty, almost happy, decent lives can be achieved. Zoë herself seems to revel in the sheer excitement of existing in a cyberpunk settlement, and she isn't the only one. Her bursts of genuine enthusiasm really do sell the place (and its food carts). Propast is an intriguing multicultural melting pot with its own slang, where citizens work in cafes, relax, fight for justice, and, occasionally, are nasty or downright xenophobic. NPCs bring vibrancy to streets filled with activity and the town's distinct districts. These can be told apart via local economic specialization, prevalent fashion, the occasional change of ambient color (e.g., red for Chinatown), or the recognizably different, diegetic music per area.

Finally, the layered structure of Propast does make sense as a futuristic wild evolution of European geography that preserves architectural traditions and monuments, while also serving the needs of corporate behemoths.

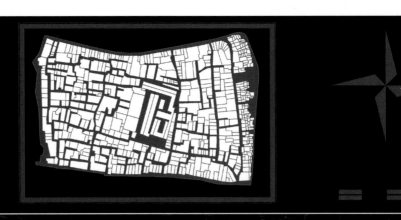

香港

九龍

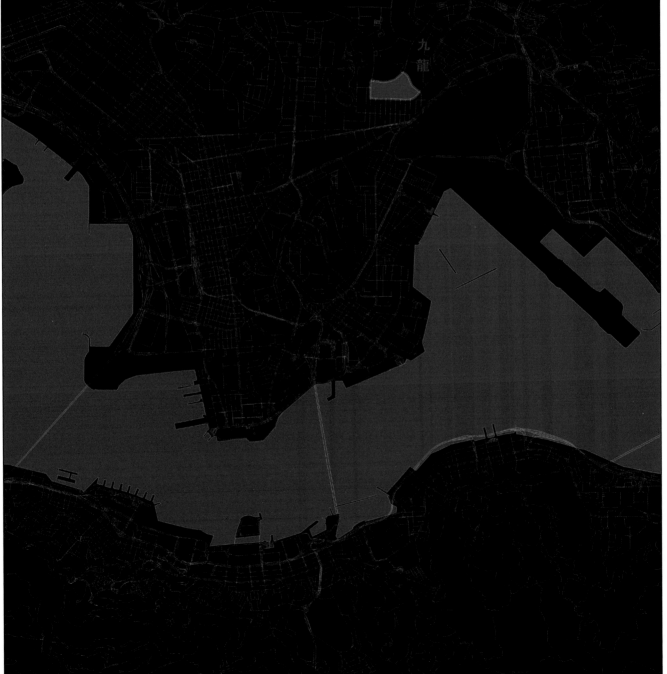

45

HONG KONG
Shadowrun: Hong Kong

GENERAL INFORMATION /////////////////////

City: Hong Kong

Game: *Shadowrun: Hong Kong*

Developer: Harebrained Schemes

Publisher: Harebrained Schemes

Release Date: 2015

Genre: RPG

Platforms: Linux, Mac OS, Windows

Few places have been as accepting of metahumans as Hong Kong, where megacorps are run by elves and trolls find themselves in control of crime syndicates. Things weren't initially rosy—here, too, parents used to abandon their orc or dwarf children—but Hong Kong's culture quickly embraced the evolution of humanity, as well as the rise of magic. Unlike the more conservative Japan and the Confederation of American States, in Hong Kong the cataclysmic changes brought about by the rise of the Sixth World were almost seamlessly integrated into society. The Awakened are now favored, the use of magic is widespread, and the respect and reverence for dragons is mandatory and somehow in balance with the ever-pervasive network of the Matrix and unchecked corporate power. Street samurai mercenaries may roam the streets, shamans openly clash with vampires, and elven deckers hack anyone for the right price—yet Hong Kong somehow remains a stable, prosperous harbor in the sea of chaos, warfare, and turmoil that is the twenty-first century. A vastly successful global center for business, here an orc can plausibly hope to become an accountant—provided, of course, she doesn't get accidentally murdered.

The Hong Kong Free Enterprise Zone, a land of stark contradictions, offers peace coupled with a lethal underworld. It is a city of bright lights, gleaming towers, and restless spirits, where life is cheap and everything is for sale; a city of turbulent history that once separated two empires. The city humbly began life as a loosely connected region of sparsely populated farming and fishing villages that were destined to become one of the world's most important commercial ports. For years, squeezed onto the peninsulas negotiated by British merchant houses, Hong Kong was forced to grow vertically, before abandoning the United Kingdom to join China. Following the return of magic, the city finally declared its independence in 2015.

The dominant ones such as Renraku, Ares Asia Holdings, Aztechnology, Eastern Tiger Corporation, and Wuxing rule the city, and surprisingly safeguard its identity. After all, some of these megacorps have local histories going back for generations, and sometimes tradition can be a

Even in the shadows of enormous corporate towers, the streets of Hong Kong remain vibrant and packed with all sorts of vendors

brilliant political tool when vying for control of the Executive Council, the single legislative and executive branch of Hong Kong's government.

In everyday life, reputation and respect are held above everything else as Hong Kong's culture is based on a traditional notion of influence and standing, combining honor and prestige, called guanxi. Neon signs adorn every shopfront, the aromas of food stalls are dense, discussions vibrant, the menagerie of drones irritating, and shadowrunners simply get ignored. Only when the Triad gangs go to war are the extroverted streets deserted. On the other hand, the rich enjoy the serenity afforded by walled gardens and floating restaurants, even when almost half the population seems to be barely surviving on the fringes of a society equally enamored of ancient tradition and bleeding-edge cybertech. In the shadows of the city's towers, an underworld of criminals, anarchists, hardened shadowrunners, battle mages, and corporate agents thrive, navigating layers of intrigue and conspiracy, and constantly fighting or collaborating with each other.

The practice of sorcery and ancient mystical beliefs are interwoven with daily life in this city of wild magic, intersecting ley-lines, ancestral demons, and visible astral space. Qi, the force of magic, good fortune, and prosperity, along with feng shui geomancy, molds actual geographies. The density of life and arcane energies peaks in the overcrowded Kowloon Walled City. This slum was built on the ruins of the old one, and around the enormous "Fortune Engine" qi machine meant to bring happiness to its residents. When the machine malfunctioned, the qi became catastrophically worse, and the Walled City rapidly devolved into a Triad-controlled hellhole plagued with excruciating nightmares. People claim to have even sensed Qian Ya, the Queen with a Thousand Teeth, moving among the squalor, chaos, and poverty of the 50,000 residents of Earth's most densely populated spot. Even the Gods of Death, the true royalty of Hong Kong, could hide in this maze of claustrophobic alleyways, under buildings rising beyond fifteen stories, and overshadowed by an extensive network of staircases and passageways formed on their upper levels. One can cross the entire Walled City without ever touching solid ground.

Club 88 in Heo

Beyond the Walled City, wider Kowloon, Hong Kong Island, and the New Territories comprise a metropolis of mountainous peninsulas and over 250 islands in the South China Sea. Broad avenues and glowing megastores contrast with the thousands of twisting passageways crammed with every kind of workshop imaginable. And as Hong Kong keeps on growing in its tight borders, the only way is upward. Out-of-scale corporate pyramids, skyscrapers, nineteenth-century Tin Hau temples, old remnants of fortified villages, fading colonial-era tong lau tenements, and Victorian and Edwardian constructions vie for space as Hong Kong grows ever denser. Signs upon signs, rebuilt pagodas, street vendors and cooks, holographic lions, lanterns, colors, and fully interwoven living and working quarters create a magical kaleidoscope of urbanism, albeit one dominated by more than six hundred skyscrapers.

And yet the island of Ap Lei Chau, with its impressively dense forest of corporate towers, effortlessly coexists with floating communities strung together out of barges and junks that are the offices, factories, and homes for those who have forever lived upon them. Everything shipped through or from the city-state will invariably pass through its harbor, in a tradition that goes back centuries to the era when Hong Kong was considered the sole gateway to China. It is no coincidence that the name Hong Kong itself literally means "fragrant harbor."

DESIGN INSIGHTS

Shadowrun's Hong Kong was mainly created to provide the dynamic background and evocative narrative foundation for a game primarily based on strong writing, rich text, and clever décor for its scene-setting. Hong Kong proved a truly successful and relatively unique choice for this. The city's *Blade Runner*-esque aesthetics, cinematic tradition, stunning, packed cityscape and rich folklore fit in excellently with the needs of the cyberpunk-and-magic RPG. Even if the game failed to showcase the city's glorious topography, it captured the recognizable dense neon essence of its image. *Shadowrun*'s retro-futuristic aesthetics blend perfectly with the style of the actual city, whereas over twenty years of *Shadowrun* world-building adds fascinating layers of storytelling to every character and locale. The in-game environments' visual style was based on the local British-Chinese mix of architecture, employed neon, and highly weathered materials, and was constructed using modular tiles, reusable props, and excellent level-design tools.

Yet Hong Kong didn't exclusively influence visual design. Its myth and history were mined for ideas and used to ground environments. Feng shui and qi, for example, were ingeniously employed to explain the hellishness of a new Kowloon Walled City and design missions where players infiltrate corporate strongholds and subtly disrupt the offices' feng shui by rearranging plants and furniture. Local mystical beliefs were meticulously researched to flesh out monsters, and Hong Kong's contrasts were emphatically brought forth. Unlike the loud, dangerous streets, the vast majority of the game's interiors were designed to be as serene and soothing as possible. Similarly, the rooftop sanctuaries of the super-wealthy, complete with elegant takes on ancient Chinese themes, contrast starkly to the garbage-covered alleyways of the poorer parts of town.

INDEX